WOMAN MADE

WO MADE MAN

GREAT WOMEN DESIGNERS

Jane Hall

7	Introduction
14	Aino Aalto
15	Rand Abdul Jabbar
16	Susi Aczel
17	Lindsey Adelman
18	Lani Adeoye
19	Ruth Adler Schnee
20	Anni Albers
21	Kawther Alsaffar
22	Jeannette Altherr
23	Karin Schou Andersen
24	Joyce Anderson
25	Carina Seth Andersson
26	Wendy Andreu
27	Antonia Astori
28	Jane Atfield
29	Gae Aulenti
30	Tomoko Azumi
31	Cleo Baldon
32	Lucia Bartolini
33	Stephanie Beamer, Crystal Ellis & Hillary Petrie
34	Dorothee Becker
35	Liisi Beckmann
36	Martine Bedin
37	Vivian Beer
38	Mercedes "Ched" Berenguer-Topacio
39	Otti Berger
40	Susi Berger
42	Laelie Berzon & Lisa Vincitorio
43	Nikita Bhate
44	Ilaria Bianchi
46	Ayse Birsel
47	Aída Boal
48	Lina Bo Bardi
50	Cini Boeri
51	Hedwig Bollhagen
52	Marianne Brandt
53	Bec Brittain
54	Gegia Bronzini
55	Barbara Brown
56	Maria Bruun
57	Rachel Bullock & Molly Purnell
58	Marie Burgos
59	Louise Campbell
60	Gloria Caranica
61	Etel Carmona
62	Maddalena Casadei
63	Anna Castelli Ferrieri
64	Carol Catalano
65	Jungyou Choi
66	Maria Chomentowska
67	Karen Clemmensen
68	Muriel Coleman
69	Kim Colin
70	Janete Costa
71	Matali Crasset
72	Ilse Crawford

74	Gabriella Crespi	136	Anna Karlin	197	Claudia Moreira Salles
75	Raffaella Crespi	137	Bodil Kjær	198	Maria Sanchez
76	Veronica Dagnert & Helena Jonasson	138	Florence Knoll	199	Cynthia Sargent
		139	Belle Kogan	200	Afra Scarpa
77	Lucienne Day	140	Lucie Koldová	201	Bertha Schaefer
78	Nada Debs	141	Ana Kraš	202	Zahara Schatz
79	Qiyun Deng	142	Teresa Kruszewska	203	Margarete Schütte-Lihotzky
80	Marie Dessuant	143	Agata Kulik-Pomorska	204	Emma Schweinberger
82	Freda Diamond	144	Sofia Lagerkvist & Anna Lindgren	205	Denise Scott Brown
84	Friedl Dicker-Brandeis			206	Kazuyo Sejima
85	Jane Dillon	145	Claude Lalanne	208	Inga Sempé
86	Aïssa Dione	146	Elizabeth Eyre de Lanux	209	Mia Senekal
87	Nanna Ditzel	148	Francesca Lanzavecchia	210	Mimi Shodeinde
88	Helen Dryden	149	Estelle Laverne	211	Alma Siedhoff-Buscher
89	Helen Hughes Dulany	150	Monling Lee	212	Jutta Sika
90	Nathalie Du Pasquier	151	Olga Lee	213	Trudi Sitterle
92	Ray Eames	152	Geke Lensink	214	Alison Smithson
94	Kiki van Eijk	153	Rosie Li	215	Sylvia Stave
95	Yeşim Eröktem	154	Francesca Lindh	216	Nanny Still
96	Lisa Ertel	155	Aljoud Lootah	217	Gunta Stölzl
98	Felicia Ferrone	156	Althea McNish	218	Marianne Straub
99	Andrea Flores & Lucía Soto	157	India Mahdavi	219	Marianne Strengell
100	Marisa Forlani	158	Rianne Makkink	220	Saša Štucin
101	Monica Förster	159	Cecilie Manz	221	Claudia Suarez Ahedo
102	Carol Gay	160	Sabine Marcelis	222	Hiroko Takeda
103	Marion Geller	162	Grethe Meyer	223	Reiko Tanabe
104	Ruth Hildegard Geyer-Raack	163	Hikaru Mori	224	Jacqueline Terpins
105	Emiliana Gonzalez & Jessie Young	164	Renate Müller	226	Faye Toogood
		165	Ignacia Murtagh	227	Helena Tynell
106	Anne Krohn Graham	166	Mira Nakashima	228	Patricia Urquiola
107	Johanna Grawunder	167	Paola Navone	229	Mpho Vackier
108	Eileen Gray	168	Greta von Nessen	230	Garance Vallée
110	Rachel Griffin	169	Stephanie Ng	231	Ionna Vautrin
111	Greta Grossman	170	Anna Maria Niemeyer	232	Lella Vignelli
112	Zaha Hadid	172	Libuše Niklová	233	Nanda Vigo
114	Virginia Hamill	173	Dina Nur Satti	234	Hisako Watanabe
115	Ineke Hans	174	Gunnel Nyman	235	Chen-Yen Wei
116	Eszter Haraszty	175	Moyo Ogunseinde	236	Donna Wilson
117	Trix Haussmann	176	Jay Sae Jung Oh	237	Esther Wood
118	Mette Hay	177	Ann Pamintuan	238	Sohyun Yun
119	Edith Heath	178	Luisa Parisi	239	Utharaa Zacharias
120	Franca Helg	179	Tamara Pérez	240	Eva Zeisel
121	Margarete Heymann-Löbenstein	180	Maria Pergay	241	Sandrine Ébène de Zorzi
		181	Charlotte Perriand		
122	Franziska Hosken	182	Clara Porset	244	Timeline
123	Rossana Hu	183	Andrée Putman	256	Endnotes
124	Marialaura Rossiello Irvine	184	Ingegerd Råman	258	Index
125	Shinobu Ito	185	Mary Ratcliffe		
126	Sophie Lou Jacobsen & Sarita Posada	186	Samira Rathod		
		187	Noémi Raymond		
127	Grete Jalk	188	Lilly Reich		
128	Nata Janberidze & Keti Toloraia	189	Margaretha Reichardt		
		190	Sylvia Reid		
129	Ania Jaworska	191	Coco Reynolds		
130	Hilda Jesser-Schmid	192	Lucie Rie		
131	Lisa Johansson-Pape	193	Estefanía de Ros		
132	Hella Jongerius	194	Pipsan Saarinen-Swanson		
134	Merve Kahraman	195	Latifa Saeed		
135	Ilonka Karasz	196	Mentalla Said & Jumana Taha		

Introduction

Few contemporary designers would cite children's book author Beatrix Potter as an obvious source of inspiration for interior design. For mid-century British architect Alison Smithson, however, Potter's fictional rendering of Peter Rabbit's home and his kitchen filled with pots, pans, and instruments of everyday use epitomized what she conceived of as a deeply personal form of design, with the kitchen utensils providing decoration revealing the honesty and authenticity innate to family home life.[1] Like many designers of her time, Smithson's approach was predicated on the notion that design should both do something and *look good doing it*. Her memory of Peter Rabbit's kitchen emphasizes the centrality of one's habitat to the concept of so-called Good Design, an idea popularized in the postwar period, communicating that how something is made, what it is made from, and the function it performs have integral value to the maintenance of everyday life.[2]

While Smithson invoked the folkloric in her writing, much of her own design, including the Trundling Turk I Armchair, or D38 (1953), was unwaveringly committed to modernity. And although this may at times have required rethinking gender roles, it did not always involve upending them. Another famous kitchen, the Frankfurt Kitchen (1926) designed by Margarete Schütte-Lihotzky three decades before Smithson's designs, shows modernity often did little to emancipate women from their socially ordained role as caregivers. Schütte-Lihotzky's fitted galley simply introduced greater efficiency to their domestic labor. The Frankfurt Kitchen tends to be treated as a piece of feminist design, though, because of a presumed link between Schütte-Lihotzky and her gender, and the associated stereotypes of the day. She, however, spent little time in kitchens, and even denied knowing how to cook, revealing that her knowledge of what makes life easier for the average woman came from simply listening to them: surveying their needs and workflow in order to inform her design, utilizing observation alongside scientific forms of measurement and data collection.[3]

Although they lived and worked in different times and places, what unites Smithson and Schütte-Lihotzky is their introduction of what could be described as a feminist design methodology, the former elevating the everyday, and the latter pioneering a user-led approach that was both qualitative and quantitative. In the early postwar period, Polish designers Maria Chomentowska and Teresa Kruszewska combined the two, each carrying out extensive research over decades, with much of their work focused on design for children.[4] With state funding, characteristic of European countries' reconstruction efforts, Chomentowska and Kruszewska's designs for schools and hospitals were mass-produced, reaching a wide audience for whom the cost of modern design was largely prohibitive.[5] Indeed, during the 1930s 10,000 units of the Frankfurt Kitchen were rolled out across ambitious public housing projects in Germany, demonstrating that women's inclusion in the nascent field of modern design did not just coincide with wider suffrage and access to education, but also brought an active engagement and centrality to the radical reorganization of society, and in turn, radical forms of financing through public spending.[6]

This book centers gender as a way of highlighting women's experiences of broader social and political emancipation, presenting furniture, lighting, products, and textiles, all designed by women, to assert the home as the location for much of that change.[7] It captures a wide range of women who, like Schütte-Lihotzky, were among the first generation of their gender to study design, many graduating with degrees in architecture, and who consequently viewed the design of furniture in particular as part of the politicization of interior space. Although a number of designers in this book were self-taught, such as the lacquer expert Elizabeth Eyre de Lanux and the weaver Gegia Bronzini, most of these short biographies reveal the parallel arrival of industrial and interior design as distinct disciplines within higher education, tracing their evolution right up to the present day. *Woman Made* therefore tells the story of design as a narrative of suffrage, education, and employment, but also speaks to the importance of technological innovation, global migration, and economic struggle. This book thus positions women as pioneers, while underscoring the obstacles they faced at a time when womanhood was still viewed as a professional disadvantage.

Such challenges are most evident in the canonical history of design by the conspicuous *omission* of women, rather than their presence. Even those partnered with famed men struggled for visibility. Franca Helg, Luisa Parisi, and Emma Schweinberger, for example, rarely stand out in their own right, despite having held significant roles in design firms working both with, and independently from, their male counterparts.[8] It is perhaps no coincidence that these examples are all from Italy, a country that in the 1950s began widely educating women in design subjects, but then failed to acknowledge their achievements within the workplace.[9] Both Helg and Parisi were trained at the Politecnico di Milano, a pedagogic hotbed for the design avant-garde that would produce some of the world's most extraordinary designers. Many of the designers in this book perhaps found greater success when they were *without* a male partner in tow (at the time the exception, not the rule) because it was more acceptable for women to combine interior design and contemporary art practice, seen as softer disciplines compared to architecture.[10]

This allowed designers like Cini Boeri, Gae Aulenti, and Gabriella Crespi to push the boundaries of architectural space, with Boeri's designs particularly challenging the function of the house as a prerequisite for the nuclear family unit; her proposal for independent sleeping arrangements supposedly caused many divorces.[11] These women were not necessarily designing objects and spaces specifically for women, nor were they defining the feminine; they were not interested in defending the singular (and often male) genius of design. It is unlikely that they would have recognized their own

work as feminist, in part because of how feminism was defined at the time; rather, their response to society's reorganization led to the emergence of approaches that were simply *women-led.*[12]

Again this meant not necessarily the production of the new, but refreshing critiques of the familiar. As British designer Jane Dillon, who spent time working with Ettore Sottsass at Olivetti in Italy in the late 1960s points out, the chair is one of the few household items that people regularly touch and physically occupy.[13] Her ergonomic design, the Moveable Chair (1968), upended the conventional relationship between object and occupant.[14] Adapting to movement, its ability to swivel countered the status of the chair as an immutable object and, as Dillon states, its ubiquity as a patriarchal symbol.[15] The Moveable Chair's bright pink coloring was a product of newly available dyes, a reminder that many of the most memorable aspects of design created by women are not necessarily a function of tired myths concerning gender preference, but the result of technological innovation.[16] Dillon's design worked not only as a satirical provocation exposing the political underpinning of design's gendered history and ideology, but also as a commercial proposition; put into production by Planula, it preempted the success of her later designs created in collaboration with Charles Dillon, which were manufactured internationally and at scale.[17]

The Bauhaus school in Germany is perhaps the most obvious precedent for the synthesis of material innovation, mass production, and commerciality with its woman-dominated weaving department—also its most profitable. The school's recent centenary legitimized a welcome focus on its women attendees, elevating the profiles of a celebratory few, although largely failed to investigate the impact of marriage, the holocaust, and Walter Gropius's favoritism on the majority, whose extraordinary works remain hidden from view.[18] Among the better-known Bauhaus alumnae included in this book are Anni Albers, Gunta Stölzl, and Marianne Brandt, but it also features ceramicist Margarete Heymann-Loebenstein, who owned her own pottery, manufacturing modern tableware that had a distinct graphic quality; children's furniture designer Friedl Dicker-Brandeis, who held art classes for Jewish children at the Czech hybrid ghetto-concentration camp Theresienstadt, and saved 5,000 of their drawings by smuggling them out to preserve their legacy; and textile artist Otti Berger, who, after an unfettered career working for herself as well as a number of British textile brands, like Dicker-Brandeis, perished at Auschwitz.[19]

While survival was certainly a prerequisite for success in the interwar and postwar period, another criterion was entrepreneurship, evinced by the many women of the Wiener Werkstätte and Bauhaus who ran their own businesses at a time when it was assumed commerce required the backing of a legitimizing institution or man. When Heymann-Loebenstein was forced to sell her successful factory under the threat of Nazi occupation, it was taken over by another woman designer, Hedwig Bollhagen, whose own iteration of the company evolved in parallel with Germany's political upheavals over the second half of the twentieth century and remains trading today.[20] Driven by commercial interest, design's close relationship with and reliance on industry has arguably not only been an agent in democratizing design, aiding in the production of inexpensive homeware, but also helped women succeed within business settings where design skill means both creative vision and production knowhow. Therefore, the steady rise in consumption after the war produced a market for domestic products, paving the way for design manufacturing giants like Driade, Kartell, Knoll, and Moroso, who in turn were vehicles for promoting the designs of their women cofounders, Antonia Astori, Anna Castelli Ferrieri, Florence Knoll, and Patrizia Moroso respectively.

For Ferrieri, who was married to the chemical engineer and Kartell co-founder Giulio Castelli, the company provided the infrastructure for innovation, pioneering

the use of ABS plastics to create products with bright and instantly recognizable colors and forms, such as Ferrieri's Componibili Modular Storage System (1967). Stating optimistically that the "future belongs to plastic," Czech toy designer Libuše Niklová predicted the widespread use of plastics with her joyful animal toys, all made possible by advances in the material's technology.[21] While she wouldn't know the material's future as an environmental threat, with three patents to her name, Niklová, like many women in design before her, was primarily an inventor, emphasizing modern design's foundation as a material science, guided by an aspiration to improve lives rather than profit from them.[22]

The globally popularized American concept of Good Design, resurrected from the 1930s by the Museum of Modern Art's (MoMA) director Edgar Kaufmann Jr. for a series of exhibitions and awards in the early 1950s, united technology and consumerism within the arena of the home.[23] With no domestic object left untouched by its mantra of affordability and functionality, the success of the award inadvertently disrupted modernism's male cultural hegemony by finally admitting women into the rarefied MoMA galleries, from which they had previously been excluded.[24] However, their entry remained conditional, evidenced by the absence of award recipient Ray Eames from the press release announcing the winners of the museum's 1949 International Competition for Low-Cost Furniture and corresponding exhibition. Eames's husband, Charles, was cited as the author of their entry, La Chaise (1948).[25]

Accordingly, while women slowly became recognized and celebrated for contributions to modern design, their success was partially reliant on their sales acumen under the assumption that women could best market to their peers, a growing middle class of housewives who influenced spending within the home.[26] Working for Libbey, an American glass company, designers Virginia Hamill and Freda Diamond became influential tastemakers with salaries to match. Diamond was even named by *Life* magazine the "Designer for Everybody" due to her ability to temper modernist designs with familiar, more conservative—and therefore more commercially viable—forms.[27]

In California, celebrities flocked to the Beverly Hills home-cum-showroom of Danish-born designer Greta Grossman, whose elegant, simple designs mirrored her own glamorous lifestyle.[28] Grossman almost single-handedly launched the understated modern design of the West Coast, a legacy illustrated in this book through designers such as Cleo Baldon and Muriel Coleman, and the more contemporary studio LAUN, led by duo Rachel Bullock and Molly Purnell in Los Angeles. Like Grossman, fellow Danish émigrée Greta von Nessen was also a celebrity of her day, often exhibiting new designs in hotly anticipated showings in her Manhattan apartment, chronicled in the *New York Times*.[29] Her Anywhere Lamp (1951) is considered a design of national importance, selected as one of twelve great American industrial designs to be featured on a 2011 postage stamp, the only one designed by a woman.[30] Yet given how little is actually known of von Nessen's life, it is surprising that her company, which she alone resurrected after her husband's death in 1943 and is still in operation today, features on its website his biography, but not hers.[31]

So while women gained some notoriety as designers through the packaging of their identities alongside the advertisement of their products, their invisibility in the wider history of design remains a familiar tale of exclusion. Despite the documentation of this absence in monographs dedicated to gender that date back to the 1980s, its reiteration here is an opportunity to highlight how the very concept of Good Design in the modern era has come to be identified with aesthetics developed in the West.[32] This historicization doubles down by marginalizing pre-industrial and craft traditions, many of which have traditionally been the work of women. One way this has happened is by the promotion of "design" as an activity separate from the actual process of

production, with alternative types of knowledge not recognized under the Western concept.[33] Another is how design has come to be associated with expressions of national culture, something alien to those who have no identification with modern nation states.[34]

This is not, however, to ignore entirely the interconnected story of women, as both designers and users, and modern design in non-Western parts of the world. Popular culture and craft traditions were championed in the mid-twentieth century by designers such as Italian-born Lina Bo Bardi in Brazil and Cuban-born Clara Porset in Mexico, who viewed such practices through a Western framework of industrialization.[35] In the Philippines, designer Mercedes "Ched" Berengeur-Topacio, who studied architecture because the queue to enroll for the women-dominated fine arts department was too long, went on to found the country's first professional organization for interior designers.[36] She trained in both the Philippines and the United States, and paved the way for contemporary design groups such as Movement 8, of which Ann Pamintuan was one of several female members, and whose sculptural wire-frame Cocoon Lounge Chair (2003) rethought the artisanal for a generation negotiating their identity within a globalized world.[37]

Historical examples such as these demonstrate the transnationalism of modern design, and the asymmetrical complexity of gender, education, class, and colonialism in the agency of designers to restructure indigenous materials and motifs. This dynamic can be seen most strikingly in the case of affluent French-born, American designer Noémi Raymond, who studied in both Paris and New York before working as an employee of Frank Lloyd Wright in Japan in the 1930s, where she was credited with pioneering a distinctly regional modernism that elevated the local vernacular.[38] As part of this work she hired a Japanese-American-born architect-craftsperson, George Nakashima, who then returned to America, setting up a wood workshop that resulted in a renewed focus on high-end timber furniture in the country. Based on traditional Japanese woodworking techniques, Nakashima's work has been continued by his daughter, Mira Nakashima. Raymond collaborated with her better-known partner, Antonin Raymond, and completed more than three hundred projects in the country, yet is probably one of the most overlooked designers of the modern movement, not least because of her gender, but also because her practice was based in Asia rather than the Americas.[39]

Women today find themselves at the forefront of agendas buoyed by regionally focused design festivals, biennials, and online platforms that seek to establish consumer markets in countries with rich local cultures, but nascent international economies, of design.[40] For example, in the UAE design remains a gendered discipline, with women leading its emerging contemporary design scene, and young generations chasing an elusive connection between craft-based skill, cultural heritage, and modern industry.[41] This can be seen in the work of Dubai-based designer Rand Abdul Jabbar, whose sculptural Forma furniture series takes inspiration from the forms of traditional dhows (sailing vessels), and is fabricated in collaboration with local boatbuilders in a gesture of cultural preservation by way of modern interpretation.[42] By embracing increasingly marginalized and regional practices, Jabbar's work expresses the duality of furniture's potential as both a functional object and means of social and cultural commentary, in which gender plays an essential part.

Designer Aïssa Dione, based in Senegal, addresses this issue by producing her fabrics using cotton grown in West Africa, to establish a local industry for design that makes use of, rather than exports, native produce. While the intersection of design, gender, and sustainability is reflected in various ways in the work of other designers in the book, it could—and should—fill the pages of an entire volume all of its own. For many contemporary designers, the residual legacy of modernism is largely

aesthetic.[43] The slowness and skill of the craftsperson represents a return to a way of making that rejects the speed, ease, and mobility of the free-market globalization that modernity gave rise to, and which we now recognize to be both environmentally and socially harmful to the planet. An introductory and revisionist history of design with women at its center, however, brings such issues into starker contrast with the status quo. If design can be thought of as an evolving vocabulary, *Woman Made* seeks to position women as key orators. A feminist approach, then, predicated on elevating what have been traditionally viewed as minor or marginal concerns, is a method for disrupting patriarchal ways of producing the world, and will invariably be of benefit to everyone.

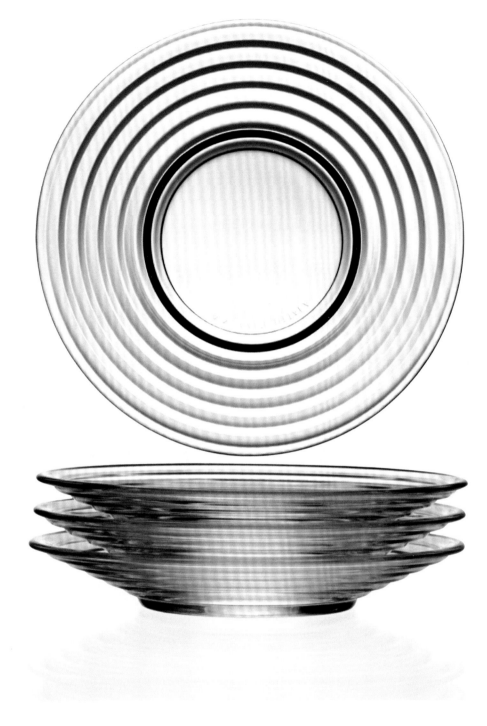

Finland was one of the few countries to allow women to enter the architectural profession before the end of the nineteenth century, so when Aino Aalto graduated in 1920 from Helsinki University, women were already a fixture of the industry. She quickly found work, eventually moving to the office of Alvar Aalto, whom she had met at university and who would become her husband and life-long collaborator. Aino had graduated before her partner, but was unable to start her own practice due to financial and social restrictions; this perhaps contributed to her initial impression of Alvar as arrogant and snobbish. Nevertheless the two became a couple, and went on to found architecture and interior design firm Artek in 1935, with Aino becoming managing director between 1941 and the end of her life. While Aino worked jointly on projects with her husband, they also had a habit of competing against one another in competitions. In 1932 Aino placed second in a competition held by manufacturing firm Karhula—which later merged with Iittala—for her Bölgeblick line of affordable utility glassware. Decorative and functional, the simple ribbed exterior of each piece—inspired by the effect of a stone hitting water—allows the Pressed Glass 4644 (above) to be mass produced from molds in a mechanized pressing process. The piece is still manufactured today.

| Aino Aalto | B. 1894, Helsinki. D. 1949, Helsinki. | Pressed Glass 4644 | 1932 |

In Dubai, the reshaping of the port through large-scale development risks erasing not only a key part of the city, but also its cultural heritage. During trips to the port, designer Rand Abdul Jabbar discovered that dhows, traditional Arabian sailing boats, were predominantly built through oral exchanges of knowledge. This disappearing craft, once central to the area's economy, inspired Abdul Jabbar to design the Forma series of sculptural furniture. Working with local boatbuilders to create a set of drawings of the traditional dhows, Abdul Jabbar reimagined them, translating their curved lines into contemporary forms that still honored their material logic and craft technique. The sculptural pieces in the Forma collection include a chair, stool (left), bench, and table, and collectively reflect a dynamic approach to design—one that embraces traditional regional motifs and references—that is emerging in Dubai. Abdul Jabbar is at the forefront of a group of young architects in the city who are using design to chart the Emirates' changing landscape through works that examine the contemporary through a historical lens. Formally trained as an architect at Columbia University in New York, Abdul Jabbar's practice moves fluidly across the fine arts, furniture design, and architecture.

| 2015 | Forma II Stool | B. 1990, Baghdad. | Rand Abdul Jabbar |

Suzi Aczel was born in Vienna, but fled to Argentina at the beginning of World War II, when the Nazis invaded the city. Settling in Buenos Aires, Aczel wanted to study interior and industrial design, but neither course of study existed there in the early 1950s. She instead trained in technical design and art history at the Manero Academy, discovering through friends that the designer Martin Eisler was willing to teach people who could then work with him. Aczel became an associate of Eisler's company Forma in 1952, where together they designed lamps, furniture, and interiors. Aczel made many of their works' technical drawings at a 1:1 scale in order to most accurately supervise the fabrication of their

designs with craft specialists. In 1959, along with Eisler and Arnold Hakel, Aczel created the studio Interieur Forma, which carried out designs for private residences. In 1961 they became the official distributor for Knoll in South America, bringing the work of major international design figures to the continent, including pieces by Eero Saarinen and Harry Bertoia. Aczel was the only woman to be appointed in 1976 to the board of the Center for the Investigation of Industrial Design (CIDI)—a government organization—a position she held for a decade. The children of Interieur Forma founders—Alberto Eisler, Gabriel Hakel, and Alejandra Aczel—now lead the company.

| Susi Aczel | B. 1931, Vienna. | Round Coffee Table | 1955 |

Following studies in literature at Kenyon College, Ohio, Lindsey Adelman took a job as an editorial assistant producing catalog texts for the Smithsonian museums. Observing the production and installation of artworks in the National Museum of American History inspired her interest in industrial design, leading her to pursue further study at the Rhode Island School of Design. Adelman went on to work for American lighting designer David Weeks before setting up her own eponymous design practice in 2006. Her hands-on and experimental approach helped her ride out a relative dearth of commissions due to the financial crash of 2008; Adelman still tests designs using full-scale models in her workshop, and has established long-term collaborations with other artisans, including glassblowers and blacksmiths. Adelman states that she is drawn to the immaterial quality of light and its ability to affect the mood of a space, which she augments using a textured material palette, often combining glass with materials like metal and rope. Her focus is on large-scale, sculptural works like the oil-rubbed bronze and white glass Branching Bubble Chandelier (right), which is available in various other configurations and materials such as brass and nickel as well as multiple glass colors. The light's organic form provides an interesting contrast to its industrial materials, a signature of Adelman's work. Her pieces have been shown at the Cooper Hewitt, Smithsonian Design Museum in New York and Nilufar Gallery in Milan.

| 2006 | Branching Bubble Chandelier | B. 1968, New York. | Lindsey Adelman |

Lani Adeoye has lived in Lagos, Toronto, Montreal, and New York, gathering inspiration for her designs from all over the world. At first self-taught, Adeoye started out designing furniture and interiors for friends and family, conducting her own research and taking in shows. She went on to attend Parsons School of Design in New York, where she studied interior architecture and was able to hone her focus and interests in the school's highly conceptual, process-driven environment. Her self-guided, experimental approach results in organically shaped sculptural lighting and furniture. Adeoye's design practice, Studio-Lani, draws on her Nigerian heritage, and is inspired by memories of celebratory communal events and music, including the talking drum, an iconic West African musical instrument. The drum has a sculptural hourglass interior and external strings, and is often made from leather, and Adeoye has translated its formal qualities into a unique collection of tables and stools. The Bata Stool (above) is also inspired by Yoruba culture—*bata* means "shoes"—and the chair, while woven using traditional methods in collaboration with local artisans, has a strikingly modern shape.

| Lani Adeoye | B. 1989, London. | Bata Stool | 2019 |

Still active into her nineties, Ruth Adler Schnee has enjoyed a career spanning more than seven decades, creating lively and refined screen-printed fabrics that defined mid-century modernism. Construction (left) is one such example, notable for its architectural composition and dynamic use of line. Originally from Frankfurt, Adler Schnee was forced to flee with her family to the U.S. after the Nazi pogrom of 1938. She spent World War II studying at the Rhode Island School of Design before settling in Detroit where Adler Schnee first studied costume illustration before switching to interior architecture at the Cranbrook Academy of Art, which she described as an "enchanted place." There she was influenced by the experimental pedagogy of Eliel and Loja Saarinen, with whom she had a personal relationship, and started a design showroom with her husband, Edward Schnee, in Harmonie Park, Detroit, with the aim of transporting the concept of Good Design into local residents' homes. In 1947 she participated in the *Chicago Tribune*'s "Better Rooms for Better Living" interior design competition. Her entry's textiles caught the attention of Chicago architecture firm Shaw Ness and Murphy, who helped launch her career as a fabric designer by commissioning her to make fabrics for their car showrooms. She went on to design textiles for some of the world's best-known architects and projects, including Buckminster Fuller's Ford Rotunda (1934) and Minoru Yamasaki's World Trade Center (1971).

| c. 1950 | Construction Furnishing Fabric | B. 1923, Frankfurt. | Ruth Adler Schnee |

Textile artist, printmaker, and teacher Anni Albers studied painting from a young age, flouting expectations that she would eventually settle into a life of domesticity. Instead, in 1922 she joined the Bauhaus, where she created abstract designs that introduced new materials, such as metallic thread and horsehair, previously unseen in weaving. She married fellow Bauhauser Josef Albers in 1925, and succeeded Gunta Stölzl (see p. 217) as head of the weaving workshop in 1931. Following the closure of the school by the Nazis, the couple left for the U.S. in 1933 at the invitation of American architect Philip Johnson, soon settling at Black Mountain College, an experimental art school in North Carolina, where Albers taught for over fifteen years. A 1949 exhibition of Albers's work, organized by Johnson at the Museum of Modern Art in New York, presented room dividers (left) displaying her highly inventive structures and thread combinations—it was the first solo show at the museum dedicated to a textile artist. From 1935, the Alberses made regular trips to Mexico, where Albers was enormously inspired by pre-Columbian textiles. Albers was also a prolific writer, and her seminal book, *On Weaving* (1965), is still in print. Her two-decades-long relationship with Knoll, for whom her Eclat pattern (1975–76) found the most commercial success, is testament to her exceptional ability to successfully span the worlds of design and fine art.

Anni Albers

B. 1899, Berlin.
D. 1994, Orange, CT, USA.

Free-Hanging Room Divider

c. 1949

Kuwaiti-born Kawther Alsaffar grew up in the Persian Gulf before moving to the U.S. to study industrial design at the Rhode Island School of Design. She went on to complete her education at the Royal College of Art in London, where she studied product design. Alsaffar returned to Kuwait in 2016 to establish her own design studio, Saffar, which produces contemporary, handcrafted furniture, homewares, and sculptural works. Collaborating with migrant craftspeople, Alsaffar explores the country's cultural heritage through her contemporary design vocabulary, which she describes as distinctly Kuwaiti for its blending of traditional and modern fabrication methods. The delicate but industrial-feeling Bungee Chair (left), for example, is crafted from a precisely welded steel-rod frame and woven bungee cord; its decorative patterning is an homage to her mother, who is an accomplished tapestry weaver. Her family name, Alsaffar, comes from the copper and metalsmithing trade, which is fitting as she often works with metal, as in her roughly textured yet gleaming Dual Bowls, which were created with the Alwafi Foundry in the Shuwaikh Industrial Area of Kuwait City, and combine two types of metal. They are made through a variation of the traditional process of sand-casting—an ancient casting technique using sand sourced from the banks of the Nile river to create molds. Alsaffar cites products like this as central to her practice for their elevation of local craftspeople and their design process.

| 2011 | Bungee Chair | B. 1990, Kuwait. | |

Kawther Alsaffar

Jeannette Altherr founded Barcelona-based studio Lievore Altherr (previously Lievore Altherr Molina) in 1991. The studio has been lauded for its humanist design approach, specializing in product design and art direction. Altherr believes design should be a dialogue between function and a specific interior site, a philosophy she applies to her role as creative director of Italian furniture company Arper. Having studied industrial design in Darmstadt and Barcelona, the German-born designer believes that a well-designed object takes a form that's seemingly inevitable. Many of her designs explore the changing shape and parameters of the workplace, where technology has allowed the "office" to occupy

numerous other spaces, including cafés and the home, inspiring Altherr to reinvent how a modern workplace should look. Altherr models this quality in her SAYA Chair (above)—made in collaboration with Alberto Lievore and fabricated for Arper—whose bold silhouette originated from playing with paper models. SAYA Chair is rendered predominantly in oak and finished with a natural stain in a number of colors. Altherr describes the chair as an ode to wood, whose organic nature is amplified through an exuberant form, with the chair's graphic seat back suggestive of a hug. Altherr formed a new studio, Lievore + Altherr Désile Park, in 2019.

Jeannette Altherr

| B. 1965, Heidelberg, Germany. | SAYA Chair | 2011 |

Danish designer Karin Schou Andersen has run her own studio, KSA Design, which now specializes in objects and furniture for outdoor use, since 1993. As a student at the Aarhus School of Architecture in Denmark, she was inspired to begin designing for inclusivity, specifically for people with physical impairments. A key idea behind the eight-piece Flatware set (below) was that each piece should have the same design profile, meaning single units of cutlery could be variously combined to support the widest range of individual impairments, including sports injuries, arthritis, or multiple sclerosis. Working before the advent of computer-aided design, Andersen produced a series of almost seventy-five handmade wooden models not only to visualize the design of the cutlery, but also to test it with real end users. The knife, for example, with its elegantly angled blade, is designed to provide a better grip to allow for cutting power while protecting the wrist. The cutlery attracted significant support from physical therapists, and was put into production by Amefa Apeldoornse Messenfabriek in 1981. It is currently in the permanent collections of numerous museums worldwide, including the Designmuseum Denmark, Copenhagen; the Centre Pompidou, Paris; the Museum of Modern Art, New York; and the Israel Museum, Jerusalem.

1979	Flatware	B. 1953, Denmark.

Karin Schou Andersen

After studying economics at New York University, Joyce Anderson moved from Brooklyn to Chicago following World War II with her husband Edgar Anderson. The couple lived in Frank Lloyd Wright's Robie House (1909) in Chicago—being fans of the architect—and while Anderson initially found work in economic research, she left the job after experiencing gender discrimination. Assisting her husband in his early furniture business, she began to produce her own designs, influenced in part by the Arts and Crafts movement emerging in the postwar period in the American Midwest. Anderson's ability soon paralleled that of Edgar, with particular expertise in finishing. She used challenges as sources of technical innovation; upon encountering spray guns too heavy for her use, she contacted the manufacturer, who adapted their equipment to provide lighter alternatives. Moving to New Jersey in 1950, the Andersons helped to found the New Jersey Designer Craftsmen organization, intending to render their modern designs in solid wood, as opposed to the plywood and plastics popular at the time. A 1956 *New York Times* article described Anderson as "the only woman in the world to carry sandpaper and linseed oil in her pocket." Anderson's distinct aesthetic incorporated curves influenced by the rhythms she felt when using machinery, a feeling she likened to a dance.

| Joyce Anderson | B. 1923, Plainfield, NJ, USA. D. 2014, Harding Township, NJ, USA. | Chair | c. 1970 |

Carina Seth Andersson studied textiles before a desire to work with forms led her to the National School of Glass in Orrefors in southern Sweden. She later attended the University of Arts, Crafts, and Design in Stockholm, before establishing her own ceramics and glassware practice in 1993. Based in Värmdö, an island in the Stockholm archipelago and flagship location of ceramics in Sweden since the 1820s, Andersson's practice consists of elemental pieces characterized by an attention to detail and a pared-back approach focused on proportion and utility. The Pallo Vase (above)—*pallo* is Finish for "ball"—features a spherical form and generous neck, meaning it is both practical and elegant;

the blue edition was a collaboration with Italian furniture maker Poltrona Frau. Throughout her career, Andersson has collaborated with a number of Scandinavian brands, such as Iittala, Arket, and Marimekko. In 2016 she was commissioned to produce a range of fine stemware in collaboration with the Swedish company Skruf as a gift to King Carl XVI Gustaf for his seventieth birthday; while the bodies of the cups differ in volume and shape, each glass shares the same foot design, transforming its proportions. Andersson's works are part of a number of permanent collections, including the Stedelijk Museum, Amsterdam and Designmuseum Denmark, Copenhagen.

| 2017 | Blue Pallo Vase | B. 1965, Stockholm. | Carina Seth Andersson |

Wendy Andreu studied metalwork at the École Boulle in Paris, where she developed her technical skills and appreciation for craft. She went on to study at the Design Academy Eindhoven, and her graduation project in 2016 included a collection of water-proof fashion and home accessories—a poncho, backpack, and hats among other pieces—made from a textile she developed herself. Using a technique she calls *regen*, "rain" in Dutch, the double-sided material combines cotton rope and silicone by coil-ing natural fibers around a laser-cut steel mold before cover-ing it in latex. The molds can be reused multiple times, adding to the material's sustainable value. The same experimental tech-nique is used to great effect in the sculptural Dragon Chair and Ottoman (above), where Andreu has arranged rope in an organic, swirling pattern over timber formwork. Fused by silicone, the materials mix together to create a soft composite that retains its structure once the formwork is removed, giving the chair its dramatic form. This time-consuming process reflects Andreu's interest in a sustainable, slower approach to design and manu-facturing, where material experimentation is a way to challenge industry norms concerning the way things are typically made.

| Wendy Andreu | B. 1990, Oloron-Sainte-Marie, France. | Dragon Chair and Ottoman | 2020 |

Antonia Astori graduated from the Industrial and Visual Design department at the Athenaeum of Lausanne in 1966, before founding design company Driade in 1968 with her brother Enrico and his wife Adelaide Acerbi, a graphic designer. At Driade, Astori was responsible for furniture design and project coordination, and she became well known for her modular pieces. Known as "open works," Astori's furniture systems—like the iconic Oikos system (1972) in which a shelving unit also becomes a partition wall, for example—encourage the participation of the user to complete the object through use. The Didymos Oval Table (below) is crafted from Carrara marble; its oval form dramatically overhanging its sculptural base is intended to leave no diner with an uncomfortable spot at the table. Astori also designed smaller objects for Driade, such as the monochrome White Snow porcelain dinner set (1991) that is still in production today. In 2004 she founded AstoriDePontiAssociati with Nicola de Ponti, an interior design studio best known for their store designs for French clothing company Marithé + François Girbaud, with whom she has a long-standing partnership of more than thirty years. Astori believes that design is an expression of life experience and not something that can explicitly be taught.

| 2014 | Didymos Oval Table | B. 1940, Melzo, Italy. | Antonia Astori |

Designer Jane Atfield's RCP2 project, a series of recycled plastic furniture, is entirely made of plastic bottles that once contained various cleaning products. The board used in the RCP2 Chair (right) is made by heating and compressing plastic chips so that they bond together, resulting in flat components that simply screw together. Manufactured by Atfield's own company, Made of Waste—an organization that sources, distributes, and promotes recycled materials—the chair has relatively high machine costs, associated with molding the plastic, which informed its simple shape. Atfield was one of the first designers to champion changing perceptions around sustainable design, choosing to emphasize rather than disguise her recycled materials' mixed coloration. Atfield studied architecture at the Polytechnic of Central London (now the University of Westminster) followed by furniture design and production at the Royal College of Art. It was there her experiments with recycling plastics began, through her incorporation of found objects and leftover materials from factory processes into her designs. Atfield developed the RCP2 process after acquiring an old plywood press, which allowed her to breathe new function into discarded plastic objects. She received considerable accolades at the time for pioneering this environmentally friendly approach. Atfield has also worked as a consultant for IKEA and Habitat, and her pieces can be found in the collections of a number of London institutions, including the Victoria & Albert Museum and the Design Museum.

| Jane Atfield | B. 1964, London. | RCP2 Chair | 1992–95 |

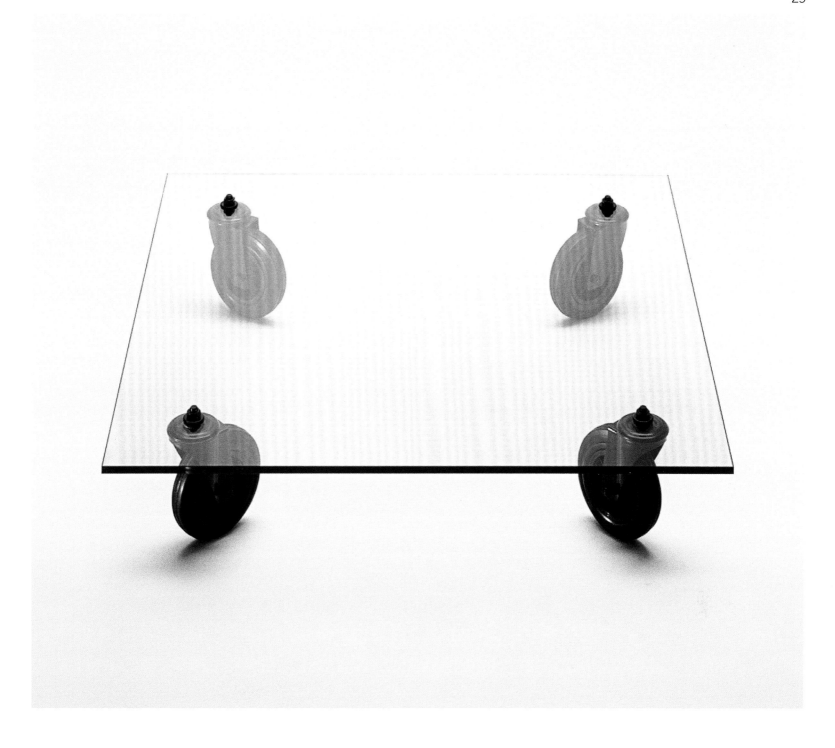

Gae Aulenti embraced the expressive handcrafted aesthetics of Italian Art Nouveau, touting the Neo-Liberty movement in post-war Italy in the pages of *Casabella* magazine, which was edited by architect Ernesto Nathan Rogers with whom Aulenti worked for ten years as art director. Concurrently, she ran her own design studio, which she founded in 1954 upon graduating from the Politecnico di Milano. In 1972 she was included in the seminal exhibition *Italy: The New Domestic Landscape* at the Museum of Modern Art in New York, cementing her reputation internationally as part of the Italian Radical Design movement and distinguishing her as one of very few women of her generation in Italian design to have received this level of recognition. Throughout her career, her witty designs were in production with manufacturers such as Knoll, Olivetti, and Kartell, among others. In 1980, she designed the Tavolo con Ruote (above) for FontanaArte, which perched a thin sheet of glass atop four oversized rubber wheel supports; a degree of humor is to be found in the combining of these heavy-duty components with a mere sheet of glass. Throughout her career, Aulenti would complete more than two hundred architectural commissions, including the transformation of the Musée d'Orsay in Paris, which won her the Légion d'Honneur in 1987—the first woman to be awarded the prize.

| 1980 | Tavolo con Ruote | B. 1927, Palazzolo dello Stella, Italy. D. 2012, Milan. | Gae Aulenti |

Tomoko Azumi studied architecture at Kyoto City University of Arts before working as an architect in Tokyo for three years. In 1992 she moved to the UK to study furniture design at the Royal College of Art (RCA) in London; the Victoria & Albert Museum (V&A) purchased her Table=Chest from her graduation show in 1995. Studio AZUMI was established with her then partner Shin Azumi, the duo setting out to subtly change people's behavior in a playful, elegant way across a wide range of products, from everyday objects like a salt and pepper shaker to the sculptural LEM Stool for Lapalma (2000), which is also in the permanent collection of the V&A. In 2005, Azumi set up her own design firm, TNA Design Studio, which flows across disciplines, producing furniture, product, exhibition, and retail interior design. The Flow Chair (right) was designed for English furniture company Ercol—Azumi is only the second woman after Paola Navone (see p. 167) to design for the company—and is demonstrative of Azumi's focus on ergonomics and careful fabrication. The curvaceous chair is designed to be elegant from all angles and easily stackable. The backrest is crafted from three finger-jointed steam-bent beech wood sections, an approach Azumi devised in close collaboration with the Ercol factory. Azumi has also taught widely, including at the RCA and the Vitra Design Museum summer workshops in Boisbuchet, France.

| Tomoko Azumi | B. 1966, Hiroshima, Japan. | Flow Chair | 2015 |

Across Southern California, the advent of the outdoor swimming pool brought with it a need for poolside furniture to complete an emerging mid-century American lifestyle of leisure. Cleo Baldon was already the owner of a successful landscape design business, Galper-Baldon Associates, before she founded a sister company, Terra, to manufacture furniture to accompany some of the 3,000 swimming pools she herself designed. Baldon's interest in integrating technology, materials, and manufacturing techniques with modern design led to several achievements, including a patent for the first prefabricated fiberglass Jacuzzi. Baldon studied interior design at Woodbury University, Burbank, California, but turned to furniture design after being unable to find furnishings she felt were suitable for the interiors that she was designing. She decided to make them herself, and acquired a foundry to fabricate the bespoke metal frames for which her pieces are known. With her practice based in Venice Beach, Baldon drew on the ubiquitous Spanish colonial motifs of Los Angeles, combining wrought natural wood and leather upholstery, as seen in this typical Counter Stool (above). Baldon published two books with her husband, novelist Ib Melchior: *Steps and Stairways* (1989) and *Reflections on the Pool* (1989), which documented swimming pools in the California region.

| c. 1970s | Counter Stool | B. 1927, Leavenworth, WA, USA.
D. 2014, CA, USA. | Cleo Baldon |

Taking their name from the British group Archigram's journal *Zoom*, the Italian radical design studio Archizoom Associati presented a colorful assault on the notion of "Good Design." Their conceptual projects were cynical critiques of consumer logic, but also the growing dominance of Rationalism and rise of Fascism in Italy during the 1960s. The Mies Chair and Ottoman (above) remix the iconic early modernist language of Lilly Reich (see p. 188) and Ludwig Mies van der Rohe's chrome frame furniture and Le Corbusier, Pierre Jeanneret, and Charlotte Perriand's (see p. 181) use of cowhide. As the only person in the group who could sew, Lucia Bartolini, who joined Archizoom in 1968, produced much of

the work for the group's project *Dressing is Easy*, presented as a stop-motion animation at the Triennale di Milano in 1973, curated that year by Ettore Sottsass. True to typical form, the project rejected tradition, proposing a do-it-yourself system of clothing largely made from repurposed domestic materials, such as bedsheets. Bartolini would marry fellow Archizoom member Dario Bartolini in 1969. A photograph from the wedding shows the couple wearing hats, both in the shape of ziggurats but with Lucia's inverted; when fit together, the conjoined headdresses emitted light—a fitting gift from their Archizoom colleagues.

| Lucia Bartolini | B. 1944, Italy. | Mies Chair and Ottoman | 1969 |

Egg Collective began through informal weekly dinner meetings between its three founders, Stephanie Beamer, Crystal Ellis, and Hillary Petrie. The trio had met while studying architecture at Washington University in St. Louis, Missouri before pursuing separate careers in different parts of the country after graduation. They worked together but from their individual locations for five years, before formalizing their ambition to synthesize the different disciplines involved in the design and fabrication process, choosing the name Egg Collective to symbolize the group's creative design incubation while also referencing a naturally occurring sculptural form. All of their woodwork is fabricated, finished, and assembled in-house at their base in New York, allowing them to maintain close attention to craft. Core designs like the Kenny Dining Table (above) establish confident forms that are then iterated using a variety of materials, such as the walnut top and base seen here. Egg Collective's showroom provides a domestic-scale interior setting to exhibit their work alongside emerging and mid-career designers. The group has been influential in promoting the work of women in the industry, as organizers for three outings of the exhibition *Designing Women* for the non-profit arts organization NYCxDESIGN and held at their Tribeca, New York studio.

| 2018 | Kenny Dining Table | Beamer B. 1984, Wichita, KS, USA. Ellis B. 1984, East Moline, IL, USA. Petrie B. 1983, Downers Grove, IL, USA. | Stephanie Beamer, Crystal Ellis & Hillary Petrie |

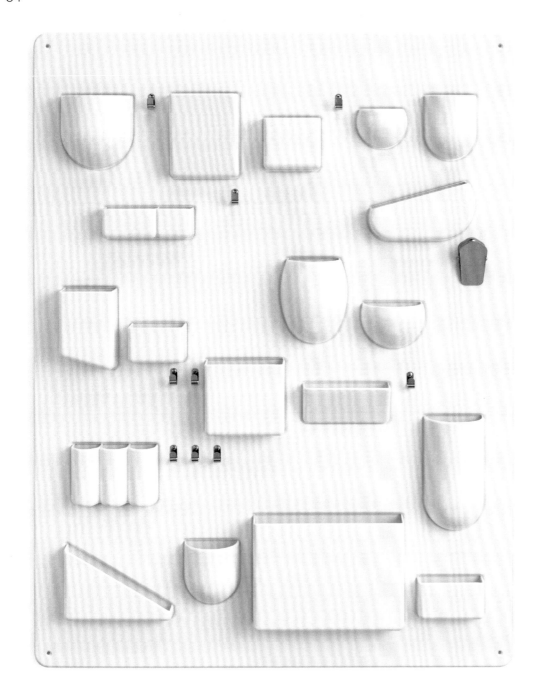

For designers in the 1960s, plastic offered a new way to create playful, unusual shapes in a multitude of electric colors. This is fully realized in Dorothee Becker's one and only plastic design—the Uten.Silo (left), a wall-mounted organizer for household items, first launched as the Wall-All. Becker was self-taught, having been discouraged from studying design by her family. Instead she studied languages in Europe, before migrating to California with her husband, the graphic and industrial designer Ingo Maurer. There she was inspired by the pedagogy of Italian physician and educator Maria Montessori to create the first Uten.Silo as a wooden toy in which different shapes filled corresponding holes in a board. Her children didn't take to it, so the design morphed into a container with a smooth, molten surface, the individual "pockets" reminiscent of the drawers in her father's drugstore. The final design for Uten.Silo was first presented at the 1969 Frankfurt Trade Fair, financed by Becker's husband who believed the thirty-two-pocket wall organizer—made in bright, shiny colors of black, white, orange, and red—would be a great success; which it was, until the cost of plastics shot up as a result of the 1970s oil crisis. Becker spent much of the rest of her career running a homeware store and designed only three other products for Maurer's company Design M: two Perspex light shades and a vase. The Vitra Design Museum reissued the Uten.Silo in 2004.

| Dorothee Becker | B. 1938, Aschaffenburg, Germany. | Uten.Silo | 1969 |

In 1957 Liisi Beckmann moved to Milan, establishing a successful career there designing for numerous Italian design firms. Her designs, however, remain mostly invisible, with the exception of the Karelia Easy Chair (below) designed for Zanotta in 1966. Its undulating form of expanded polyurethane foam covered in vinyl has become an iconic piece, inspired by the coves of Karelia, the region of Finland in which Beckmann grew up and the chair's namesake. Beckmann had a deep affinity for Karelia, which is described as the cradle of the Finnish population in the epic poem *Kalevala*, which Beckmann could recite from memory. Forced to leave the area after the Russians invaded in 1939, Beckmann went on to train at the Helsinki School of Arts and Design where she studied millinery and clothing design, but also secretly attended art and design courses without her family's knowledge. First working for La Rinascente Development Studio where she cultivated her animist approach, Beckmann's design pieces from this period are now held in the Helsinki Design Museum, although traces of her other work are hard to find, not least because she returned to painting in the 1970s, when she retired from design.

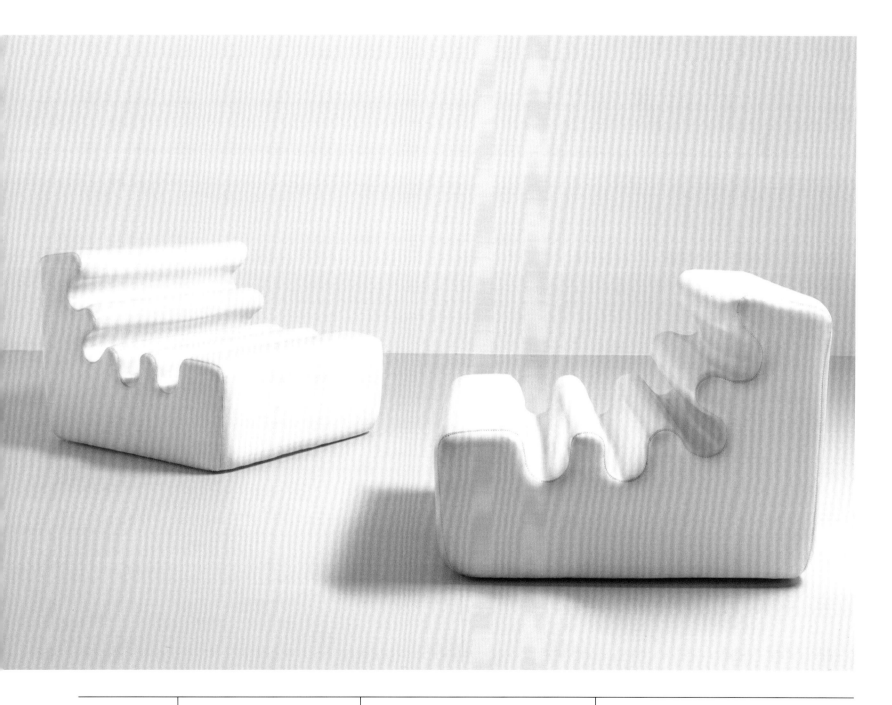

| 1966 | Karelia Easy Chair | B. 1924, Kirvu, Finland. D. 2004, Orimattila, Finland. | Liisi Beckmann |

A cross between a hedgehog and small car, the Super Lamp's joyous, polychromatic appearance encapsulates the antiestablishment approach to design of the Memphis Group—headed by Ettore Sottsass in Milan and active from 1980 to 1987. Manufactured by Fausto Celatti, the lamp (above) works like a pull-along toy and as such has been described as one of Memphis's more comical products. Martine Bedin drew the design for the lamp two years before she joined the group, and it debuted in their first exhibition in 1981. Made from painted steel sheets, the lamp rejects the trends of the time toward functional, industrial products, instead embracing intuitive, playful motifs. Bedin describes Memphis's work as an alternative to Postmodernism, looking beyond the academicism of architectural styles to make work that is entirely non-institutional and creatively free. Bedin's designs have remained anti-establishment and anti-industry, and although they often attract high prices, they are conceived as conceptual pieces rather than for mass production. Having studied architecture in Florence, Bedin's style is heavily shaped by key instigators of Florence's Radical Architecture Movement of the collective Superstudio with Adolfo Natalini, who was her professor. She joined the Memphis Group with designer Nathalie du Pasquier (see p. 91); two of only a few women in the group.

| Martine Bedin | B. 1957, Bordeaux, France. | Super Lamp | 1981 |

Based in New England, furniture designer Vivian Beer established her eponymous design studio in 2008. She works predominantly with metal and concrete to create fluid, sculptural forms whose industrial edge plays with the bounds of traditional craft and contemporary design. Having studied sculpture at the Maine College of Art in Portland, Beer decided to focus her material scope through graduate studies with the Cranbrook Academy of Art's metalsmithing department. Since then, Beer has continued rigorous research as core to her design practice, and undertook a research fellowship focused on the history of American industry at the Smithsonian National Air and Space Museum in Washington, D.C. Much of Beer's work has an architectural, hard–soft quality, playing with design tropes borrowed from pop culture, especially car and fashion design, to create richly colored, beguiling forms. The Current Chair (left), for example, exhibits a rippling silhouette that emulates flowing water, belying the strength of the formed steel from which it is made. It is painted in soft blue automotive paint—a material that allows Beer to achieve slick surface finishes and she has said: "Muscle cars and cosmetics have a lot in common ... [they both] combine physical beauty and functional efficiency, the emotional and the physical, the performed female." Beer's work is held in a number of collections, including the Museum of Fine Arts, Boston, and the Metal Museum, Memphis.

| 2004 | Current Chair | B. 1977, Bar Harbor, ME, USA. | Vivian Beer |

Architect, interior designer, and furniture-maker Mercedes "Ched" Berenguer-Topacio is one of the most prominent names in contemporary design in the Philippines, having run her successful furniture company for more than fifty years. Berenguer-Topacio studied abroad at the New York School of Interior Design where she received her degree in interior design. She bucked convention of the day and founded her own firm, Berenguer-Topacio Design Corporation, with her husband, Hector Topacio. She focused on using traditional materials to create modern forms, starting mainly with residential projects and showroom staging for home furnishings stores, designs primarily geared toward the expanding middle class in the Philippines. This led to her own line of furniture, made from local materials—like the woven cane seen in the Metal Klismos Chair (left)—aimed at creating what she described as "furniture art." Winning a Best of NeoCon Award in 1991, the chair was also a commercial success. Berenguer-Topacio was a key figure in making interior design as a profession more pervasive in her country, first by helping to establish the Philippine Institute of Interior Design and then, from 1954 onward, by teaching at the University of Santo Tomas in Manila, the first school in the Philippines to make interior design a formal course of study. Recognized internationally, her work was notably sold in Paris by Andrée Putman (see p. 183). She is the only Asian designer to have received the prestigious Roscoe Award—an annual program honoring interior designers in the U.S.—and moreover on two consecutive occasions.

| Mercedes "Ched" Berenguer-Topacio | B. 1929, Arayat, Philippines. D. 2019, Bacolod, Philippines. | Metal Klismos Chair | c. 1990 |

With extensive knowledge of industrial weaving, textile designer Otti Berger opened her own studio in Berlin, where she established profitable relationships with a number of manufacturers. As the first woman to successfully gain a patent for one of her textile designs, she was among the most accomplished of the Bauhaus alumni. At the Bauhaus, Berger had been interim head of the weaving department; she was originally recommended by Gunta Stölzl (see p. 217) to succeed her full-time, but the new director of the school, Ludwig Mies van der Rohe, overlooked Berger for the role in favor of his partner Lilly Reich (see p. 188). Born in present-day Croatia, Berger studied at the Collegiate School for Girls in Vienna and later the Royal Academy of Arts and Artistic Crafts in Zagreb. She developed a reputation for her bold use of color and geometry in her patterns; her output was short-lived, as after only four years running her own company, Berger, as a Jewish person, was banned from trading in Germany. Awaiting an American visa, she traveled to London, where she designed three textiles that were put into production by textile manufacturer Helios, and also worked for Marianne Straub (see p. 218). Berger returned to Croatia to attend to her sick mother, where she was captured by the Nazis, and later died in Auschwitz.

| c. 1929 | Rug | B. 1898, Zmajevac, Croatia. D. 1944, Auschwitz. | Otti Berger |

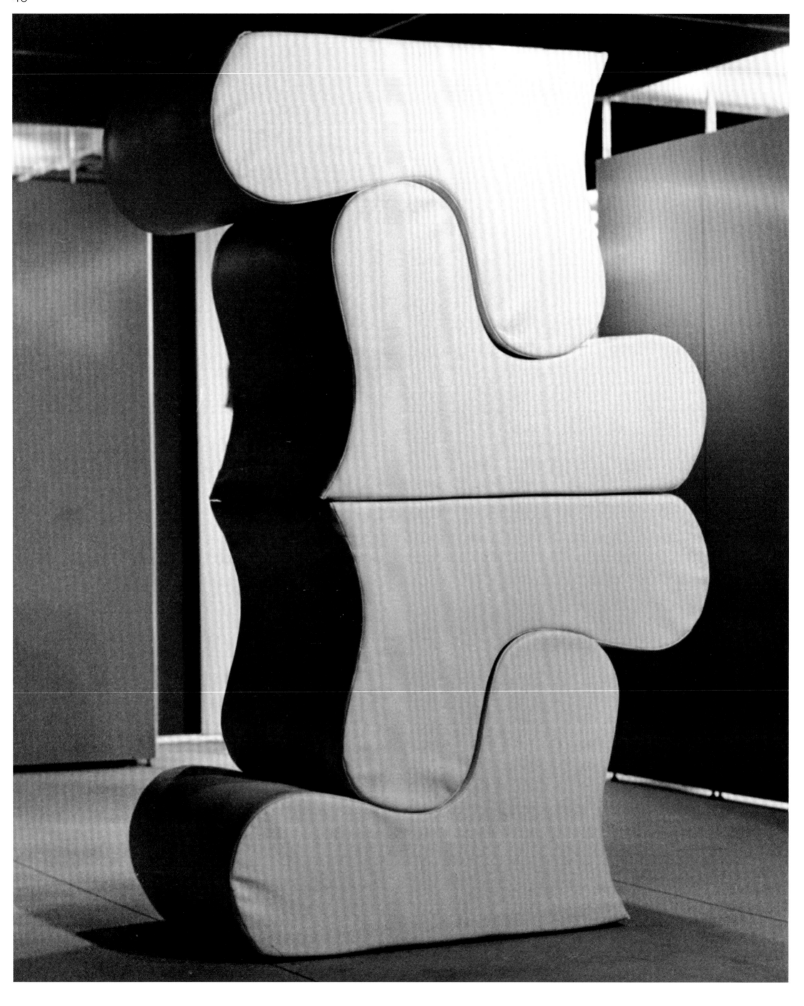

Susi Berger and her husband Ueli Berger crafted the prototype for their Soft Chair (opposite and above) in their own living room, carving its form from a slab of polyester foam acquired at a local mechanic's. Like many of the couple's designs, the chair was created entirely at a 1:1 scale. The vinyl-covered Soft Chair was produced in a variety of bright colors and became an icon of Swiss furniture design, combining the Bergers' shared DIY sensibility and graphic aesthetic. Susi Berger initially undertook an apprenticeship in graphic design under Walter Ottiger and Ernst Jordi, before attending the Kunstgewerbeschule in Bern where the Bergers first met as students, graduating in 1962.

Producing more than sixty furniture designs over the course of their careers, the Bergers put only about half into production, led by their belief that only a new idea justifies a new piece of furniture. Known for their unusual perspective, the pair regularly displaced objects moving them from one context to another, as in their design for a kitchen table that repurposed a manhole cover as a tabletop. While they were experimental to the extreme, the Bergers both took production seriously, meticulously resolving any design details before pursuing fabrication, which enabled successful long-term partnerships with manufacturers including Röthlisberger, with whom they worked for thirty years.

| 1967 | Soft Chair | B. 1938, Lucerne, Switzerland. | Susi Berger |

Melbourne-based design office SBW Australia was established in 2011 by Laelie Berzon and Lisa Vincitorio, both of whom were already working in the furniture industry. Vincitorio had formerly designed for Alessi—the youngest designer ever to do so—after studying industrial design at Royal Melbourne Institute of Technology, and Berzon studied visual arts and interior design. Their studio name, Something Beginning With, was inspired by a childhood car trip game in which players observe something In the landscape to be identified by their fellow passengers, giving just the first letter as clue. The game reflects Berzon's and

Vincitorio's attentive approach to their practice, which they manage from concept stage through to marketing and sales. While the pair collaborates on each aspect of the business, Vincitorio leads product development and manufacturing, while Berzon focuses on design direction, merchandising, and sales. Each object is made in Melbourne by local craftspeople, including the Halo Chair (above), notable for its elegant curved back, the signature gesture of the Halo series—which includes a lounge chair, high chair, sofa, as well as side and coffee tables—made distinct through the repetition of an arc form.

| Laelie Berzon & Lisa Vincitorio | Berzon B. 1983, Melbourne, VIC, Australia. Vincitorio B. 1983, Melbourne, VIC, Australia. | Halo Chair | 2017 |

Designer Nikita Bhate, alongside her partner Pascal Hien, works under the moniker SĀR, creating products that draw on cultural elements of Bhate's native India combined with Western conventions as testament to India's long history of cultural exchange. Originally from Pune, Bhate received her masters in product design at Istituto Europeo di Design Madrid, which exposed her to European design perspectives. Her unique design vocabulary developed during a series of apprenticeships in Spain, Portugal, and Italy, where she worked at Fabrica, the design and research program in Treviso set up by Luciano Benetton and notable for its esteemed alumni, all of whom are under twenty-five. Each of studio SĀR's pieces are made in India, and reflect SĀR's commitment to sustainability, storytelling, and collaboration. The Tankan Lounge Chair (below), for example, is made from rigid wrought iron shaped to highlight the fluidity of its molten state. Fabricated by Indian blacksmiths known as *lohar*, the chair's resultant hammer marks were left unpolished and visible to honor the local craftspeople and their authorship. The chair reveals Bhate and Hien's interest in the sensory nature of materials, put to use in a "playful and minimalist" way, qualities Bhate states are a reflection of her own personality.

| 2017 | Tankan Lounge Chair | B. 1990, Pune, India. | Nikita Bhate |

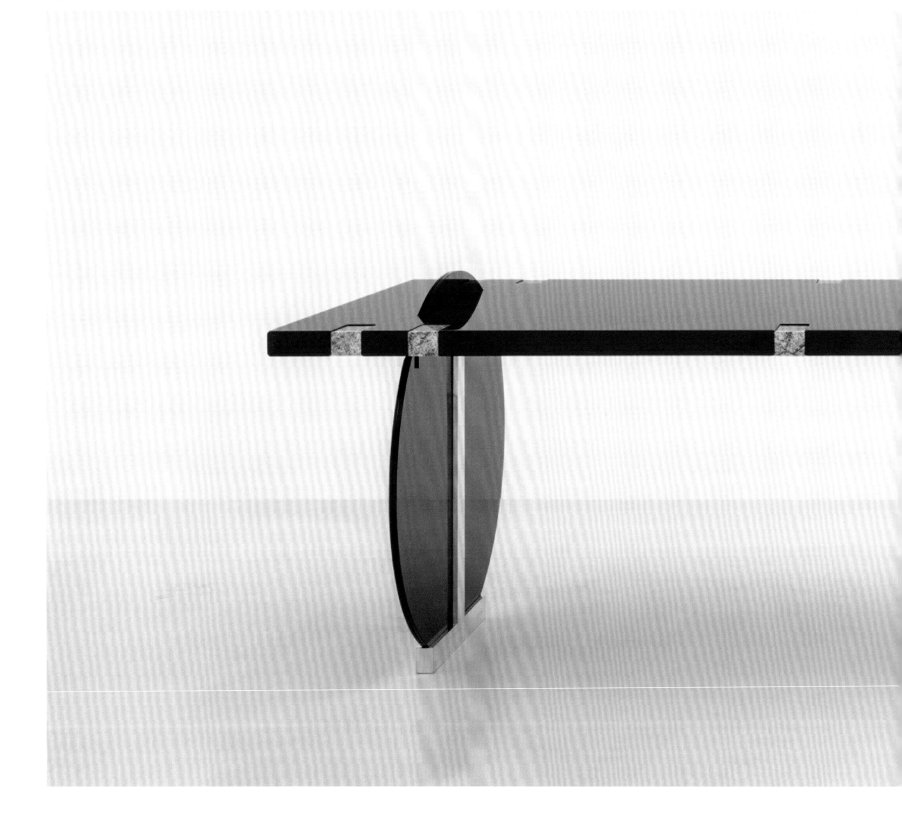

Using found and discarded objects as her material palette, Milan-based Ilaria Bianchi's design methodology centers on the cyclical relationship between waste and reuse. Her graduate collection at London's Central Saint Martins, named Cast-Away Furniture, experimented with broken furniture elements to create a new range of furnishings, including a console crafted from polystyrene, a material which Bianchi describes as having "a certain aesthetical likeness to marble." Having first trained as an industrial designer at the Politecnico di Torino, Bianchi established her own studio in 2016. Her instinctual approach to design challenges the value we collectively—as a society—place on materials using a prcess of "adhocism," which draws on ideas in the seminal 1972 text by

Charles Jencks and Nathan Silver. The Blueprint Table (above) is created entirely from leftover materials from past projects by interior design office Dimorestudio, in Milan, embodying this approach by using the occasion of improvisation that accompanies recycling found materials. The piece, largely made from marble, includes two glass tabletops that Bianchi repurposes as legs for her table by using simple polished brass joins to create points of intersection between planes of glass and stone. With fellow Italian designers Agustina Bottoni, Astrid Luglio, and Sara Ricciardi, Bianchi established design collective The Ladies' Room in 2016. Her work has been widely exhibited, including at the Victoria & Albert Museum, London and the Triennale di Milano.

| 2017 | Blueprint Table | B. 1989, Pisa, Italy. | Ilaria Bianchi |

Ayse Birsel first studied industrial design at Middle East Technical University in Ankara before traveling to the U.S. on a Fulbright Scholarship, where she earned her master's degree in design at the Pratt Institute in New York. One of her first postgraduate commissions was the Orchestra collection of desk accessories and storage solutions for Knoll, which she designed in collaboration with industrial designer Bruce Hannah. Despite seeing herself as an "outsider," Birsel has in fact been responsible for some of the most widely used products globally, from the progressive office systems she designed for Herman Miller to the Zoë Washlet created for TOTO; touted as the most comfortable toilet in the world,

it won Birsel the Industrial Design Excellence Award from the Industrial Designers of America in 1996. Birsel founded the design company Birsel+Seck with her partner Bibi Seck in 2014. Their Toogou Armchair (below) is part of their M'Afrique collection, and features a sculptural form handwoven from a polyethylene yarn normally used for fishing nets. Birsel is the author of *Design the Life You Love* (2015), a book focused on human-centered design, a topic central to much of her public speaking. A number of her designs are featured in the permanent collections of the Museum of Modern Art and Cooper Hewitt, Smithsonian Design Museum in New York, and the Philadelphia Museum of Art.

| Ayse Birsel | B. 1964, İzmir, Turkey. | Toogou Armchair | 2009 |

While still a student of the Faculty of Architecture at the Federal University of Rio de Janeiro, Aída Boal designed and built a number of houses in Rio de Janeiro with two other students, leading to her father, a builder, commissioning a project upon her graduation. He invited her to design and construct a four-story building on the condition that the site foreman employed was younger than she, thinking that otherwise the work would be erroneously credited to him. Although Boal described herself as both a sculptor and painter, she primarily worked on architectural projects throughout her career, designing a number of significant works, including more than forty prefabricated hospitals built in Amazonas state in the 1960s. During the same decade, Boal built her own residence in Petrópolis, near Rio de Janeiro, where she also set up a wood workshop to fabricate furniture for the property, stating that "with a chainsaw, it is possible to make a sofa." While her early work prioritized clean, straight lines, she later began to embrace curves, using timber native to Brazil, such as jacaranda, to create pieces that she named after friends and family, including the Angela Chair (right), which is made of solid rosewood and a straw seat and backrest.

| 1995 | Angela Chair | B. 1929, Rio de Janeiro. D. 2016, Rio de Janeiro. | Aída Boal |

Lina Bo Bardi began her design career as an editor at *Domus* magazine in Milan, working alongside Italian architect and designer Gio Ponti, before moving to Brazil in 1946 with her husband the journalist, publisher, and art critic Pietro Maria Bardi. Bo Bardi embraced her new home; she sought to foster artisanal craftsmanship in the production of Brazilian consumer goods, which she promoted through her magazine *Habitat*. Her association with the Museu de Arte de São Paulo—where her husband was the director—meant Bo Bardi had an influential voice in design discourse; in one notable instance she exhibited as part of the inaugural São Paulo Art Biennial the work of Swiss architect Max Bill, who later delivered a critique of Brazilian Modernism. A number of her initial pieces of furniture were designed in the interwar period in Milan. The Bowl Chair (opposite and above)—still produced by Arper—quickly became a recognizable icon of Brazilian Modernism, described by Bo Bardi as being reminiscent of "half an orange." Bo Bardi was not afraid to negotiate uncomfortable ideas, or to design challenging furniture. The chairs she installed in the theater of SESC Pompéia cultural center (1977–86) in São Paulo—one of her most significant buildings—have solid timber backs intended to keep the audience alert and engaged.

| 1951 | Bowl Chair | B. 1914, Rome. D. 1992, São Paulo, Brazil. | Lina Bo Bardi |

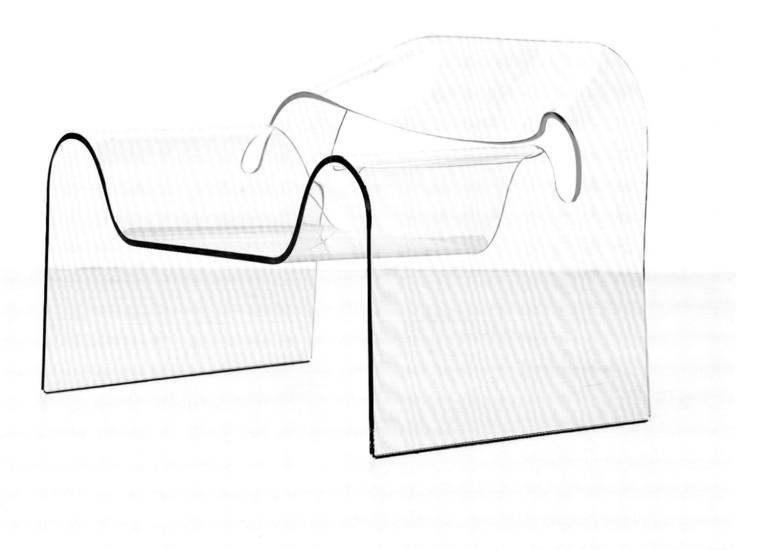

The near transparency of the Ghost Chair (above), described as a "habitable sculpture," belies its ingenuity as a piece of engineering; where glass connotes weightlessness and fragility, it now holds the body. Cini Boeri designed the seat as a provocation to see if the manufacturer FIAM could in fact fabricate it. Her concept was made a reality by bending a single sheet of ½ inch-thick (12 mm) crystal glass cut using laser technology. It took two years for Boeri to develop the work in collaboration with her assistant, Tomu Katajanagi, and it has since become an icon of Italian design. An architect and furniture designer, Boeri was interested in housing from a young age, believing the function of the house is to create a setting in which people live their lives, both independently and together. Boeri's book, *The Human Dimension of Home Living* (1980), reiterates her interest in design as a means to create freedom for the individual, joking that her designs have caused the breakup of numerous marriages. After graduating from the Politecnico di Milano in 1951, Boeri worked with design pioneers Gio Ponti and Marco Zanuso, before starting her own firm in 1963. Through form and materiality, Boeri emphasizes the relationship between an object and the process by which it is made; for Boeri, economic, long-lasting design is analogous to beauty.

| Cini Boeri | B. 1924, Milan. D. 2020, Milan. | Ghost Chair | 1987 |

Hedwig Bollhagen's mother kept her occupied with handicrafts and pottery—dainty dollhouse china—from a young age, an introduction which heavily influenced the East German ceramicist's approach to design. While still a student at a technical college, Bollhagen caught the attention of Dr. Hermann Harkort—owner of Velten-Vordamm, a stoneware ceramics factory near Berlin—who hired her as supervisor of the painting division, which involved Bollhagen overseeing the work of around one hundred "paint girls," despite being only twenty years old herself. The interwar years focused Bollhagen on creating simple, affordable ceramics. In 1934 Bollhagen became the artistic director of the ceramic workshop—previously owned by Margarete Heymann-Loebenstein (see p. 121). Bollhagen resisted Nazi attempts to co-opt the company, working with painter and ceramicist Charles Crodel, who was then deemed a proponent of "degenerate art," to sustain the pottery throughout numerous periods of political uncertainty. The ceramic 766 Watering Can (below) is notable for its absence of a handle, instead featuring two ergonomic indentations. Despite her influential legacy, Bollhagen herself described her work as "just pots."

| 1955 | 766 Watering Can | B. 1907, Hanover, Germany. D. 2001, Marwitz, Germany. | Hedwig Bollhagen |

Marianne Brandt's talent was quickly recognized at the Bauhaus, where she was invited to join the male-dominated metal workshop. Despite often being asked to complete menial tasks due to her gender, she not only went on to lead the metal workshop, but also produced some of her most recognizable and commercially successful designs during this period. Her light fittings were used in the Bauhaus building in Dessau designed by Walter Gropius, for whom Brandt worked in Berlin right before she graduated in 1929. Brandt also created memorable collages and photographs; a characteristic self-portrait of Brandt at the Bauhaus "Metal Party" shows her wearing a disk-like head piece and large sphere hung from a tubular choker necklace (both metal). This playfulness contrasts with much of her industrial design, which explored the principles of New Objectivity, where objects are a pure expression of their function. Brandt's gleaming metal and stark geometries were radical, and have since come to define the Bauhaus aesthetic. An archetypal example is the silver and ebony kettle (below), which comprises many functional details, such as an off-center lid, designed to prevent the common problem of drips. Having returned to her hometown of Chemnitz at the outbreak of World War II, Brandt found herself caught in East Germany and unable to continue her work in industrial design.

| Marianne Brandt | B. 1893, Chemnitz, Germany. D. 1983, Kirchberg, Germany. | Kettle | 1925–26 |

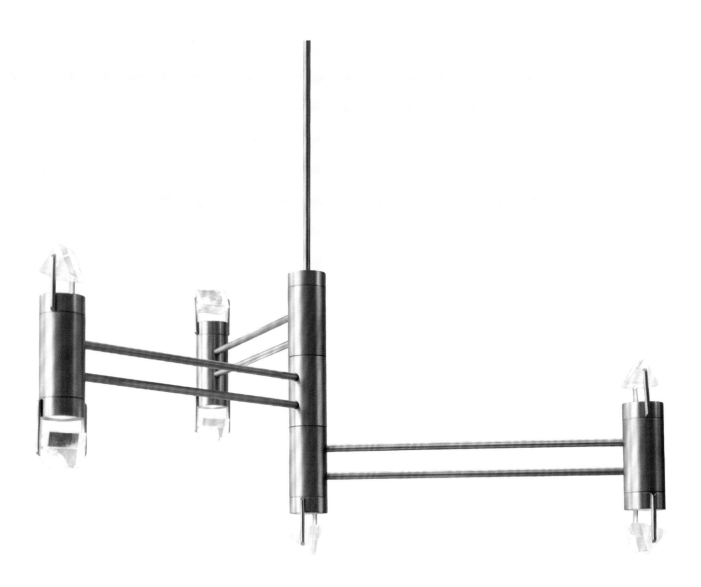

Bec Brittain began her career studying product design at the Parsons School of Design in New York before transferring to philosophy, later changing to architecture at the Architectural Association in London. Her desire to make things on a scale at which she could pay close attention to details cemented her switch from architecture to lighting, and in 2011 she founded her own studio in New York. Her first product was the modular SHY light, which composed LED lighting tubes with metal fittings to form a geometric shape inspired by crystalline structures.

A period working in high-end hardware led to Brittain's discovery of metal, which brought the complexities of engineering—and her keen interest in problem solving—together with lighting's decorative effects. Designs like the Aries IV.I (above) use simple components to enable various and ongoing iterations of the same design. Based in Long Island City, Brittain designs and engineers her own products, which are all locally made, and assembled in her studio. This way of working is enabled by her refusal to scale up, preferring to maintain a small, hands-on, closely knit studio.

| 2017 | Aries IV.I | B. 1980, Washington, D.C. | Bec Brittain |

In 1929 Gegia Bronzini founded a small weaving school in the rural neighborhood of Marocco outside of Venice. The school soon became a production workshop, and she opened a store in the Piazza San Marco, before establishing an outlet in Milan in 1939, and another one in Cortina after World War II. Originally from Milan, Bronzini moved to the Veneto region with her husband, an agronomist. Bronzini, fascinated by the work of the female farmers in the area, was inspired to purchase a loom. She began experimenting with color and texture, incorporating unusual materials such as broom bristles and corn husks into natural silk and linen yarns. Bronzini made all of her fabrics on six hand-looms; she believed that mechanical looms produced dull, flat textiles. The heavy silk seen here (right) features bands of horizontal stripes in rich hues. Joined by her daughters Marisa and Michaela, Bronzini established close relationships with the community of women in the Venetian countryside, some of whom she taught to weave on looms while researching traditional handweaving techniques. Described in 2020 by *Domus* magazine as a "textile diva," Bronzini also created furniture for many notable Italian designers, including Ico and Luisa Parisi (see p. 178). She exhibited widely with her first show in 1946 as part of the Rhodia stall at RIMA (Riunione Italiana per le Mostre di Arredamento)—a popular furnishings exhibit organized by the Triennale di Milano—which showed her work alongside that of Italian textile designer Fede Cheti and architect and designer Lina Bo Bardi (see p. 49). When Bronzini died in 1976, management of the business transferred to her daughter Marisa, who is also an accomplished weaver.

Gegia Bronzini

B. 1920, Milan. D. 1976, Venice.	Striped Fabric	1964

Textile artist Barbara Brown created some of the most original and vibrant prints of the early postwar period. She studied at the Canterbury College of Art in Kent, before moving on to the Royal College of Art in London, where she was still a student when she sold her first fabric to Heal's Fabrics, for whom she produced designs over the next two decades. Described by Heal's as their "Golden Girl," Brown's time at the company followed that of Lucienne Day (see p. 77). Her painterly style lent her designs a three-dimensional quality, imbuing her prints with a sense of motion. Their names also reflect the era in which they were created, such as Frequency (below), influenced by Op Art (short for optical art), known for using optical illusion in everything from visual art to fashion and homewares in the 1960s. From graphic, geometric shapes to abstracted botanical forms, Brown achieved her illusions by using mathematical formulae to compose vivid colors. Her later work adopted a monochromatic palette, which in the 1970s defined futuristic aesthetics. In 2017, the Whitworth Gallery in Manchester held the first retrospective of Brown's work. In addition to her career in textiles, Brown taught at numerous British art colleges, including Medway, Guildford, and Hornsey.

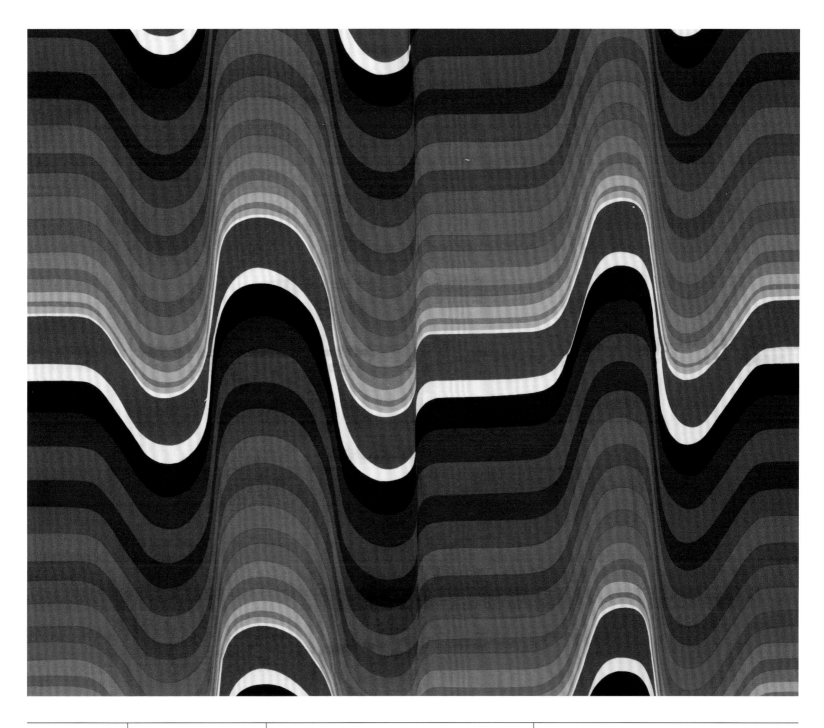

| 1969 | Frequency Fabric | B. 1932, Manchester, England, UK. | Barbara Brown |

Since graduating from the Royal Danish Academy in Copenhagen in 2012, Maria Bruun has established a number of different platforms to promote her own designs as well as those of others. As co-founder of REFORM Design Biennial, a group promoting the interdisciplinary work of young designers, Bruun curates the work of emerging talents and, alongside architect Anne Dorthe Vester, runs the design studio MBADV. Their sculptural pieces often work as both artworks and furniture, described by the duo as "functional hybrids"—dually exhibited in gallery settings but also meant for use. For example, her Mirror Mirror series consists of a series of mirrors that wrap around the corners of a room, creating a continuous reflective surface across multiple planes and providing access to continually shifting viewpoints—Bruun has described the work as an "abstract art piece that becomes functional." Bruun has extensive experience in wood workshops, and her sensitivity to craft methods and craftspeople is an essential influence on her work, whose exploratory approach to materiality and technique playfully updates mid-century Danish design for the twenty-first century. For Bruun, objects are meant to be touched. The Bigfoot Furniture range (below) balances the weight of its heavy, sturdy proportions with the smooth, elegant surfaces of the ash wood from which it is made.

| Maria Bruun | B. 1984, Copenhagen. | Bigfoot Furniture | 2015 |

Southern California is the birthplace of many American design icons. Los Angeles-based designers Rachel Bullock and Molly Purnell cite the region's light as inspiration in their work together as LAUN. Echoes of the city's modern architecture, Hollywood glamor, and Southern Californian casual spirit reverberate through their pieces, most of which are made for outdoor use. The tubular aluminum material of the Ribbon Chair (above) keeps the design light, and the way in which Bullock and Purnell repeatedly layer the bent metal tubes allows for customization; the form can be expanded or contracted with the addition or subtraction of tubes to create custom seating widths. Both designers are trained architects—they met as graduate students at the University of Texas in Austin—but Purnell had a more circuitous route into the field after initially studying sculpture at Reed College in Portland. It wasn't until the pair had a chance conversation about the lack of outdoor furniture options that they decided to collaborate. Both had experience making furniture for themselves, so were able to prototype designs in their spare time in Purnell's laundry room—hence the name of their studio, LAUN, which also plays on the word "lawn" in reference to the outdoors.

| 2020 | Ribbon Chair | Bullock B. 1985, Detroit, MI, USA.
Purnell B. 1982, Madison, WI, USA. | Rachel Bullock &
Molly Purnell |

Marie Burgos's furniture designs and product line are inspired by her appreciation of mid-century design and the aesthetics of both the natural landscape and built environment of the Caribbean island of Martinique, her ancestral home. A certified master in feng shui, the ancient Chinese art of cultivating harmony through ordering one's surroundings, Burgos pairs opposites, such as clean lines with curves, hard textures with soft, to achieve a sense of balance. The Milo Chair (below), for example, combines hand-crafted wood legs with raspberry-hued velvet upholstery; its plush, curvy form is suggestive of a hug. Born in Paris, Burgos traveled widely after obtaining a degree in business management. She studied interior design at New York University and founded her own interior design company in 2007. Focusing on high-end residential design and hospitality interiors, Burgos later expanded to the West Coast, establishing a studio in Los Angeles in 2018 where she often collaborates with her husband Francis Augustine, a photographer, who shoots all of their designs. She is a member of the Black Artists and Designers Guild.

| Marie Burgos | B. 1971, Paris. | Milo Chair | 2018 |

The work of Danish designer Louise Campbell is imbued with the rational thinking, detail, and craft characteristic of Danish design, but still embraces new technologies with designs—as she puts it, "[with] one foot on an airplane and the other solidly planted in the Scandinavian nature." Based in Copenhagen, Campbell grew up between Denmark and the UK, graduating from the London College of Furniture in 1992, before returning to continue her studies in industrial design at the Danish Design School. Campbell's own eponymous studio, founded in 1996, has a reputation for producing playful, experimental projects that revolve around new and unusual interpretations of everyday objects. Her works are produced both under her own name and for commercial manufacturers, such as Georg Jensen, for whom she designed a cutlery set (above), which she describes as a "modern tool kit." Created over a three-year research period, the set is composed of simple silhouettes cut from matte stainless steel. Campbell is influential in contemporary Danish design, and has held a number of leadership positions, from her tenure as Chairman of the Committee for Design and Crafts at the Danish Art Foundation to her service on advisory boards for the Danish Design School and Royal Danish Academy in Copenhagen.

| 2014 | Cutlery | B. 1970, Copenhagen. | Louise Campbell |

The minimal Rocking Beauty Hobby Horse (below) was designed to challenge children to rethink the relationship between horse and rider, encouraging them to use their imagination to think of themselves perhaps as pilots or astronauts instead. The manufacturer, Creative Playthings, founded in 1951, produced modern, educational toys primarily made out of wood. In the 1960s, the company's art director Philip Johnson—not to be confused with the architect—tasked designer Gloria Caranica, a recent graduate from New York's Pratt Institute, to design her take on the classic rocking horse. Caranica's original design comprised a bent birch plywood base with an interlocking curved seat and a handle formed from a bright red ball—not recognizably a horse, it was an elegant, modernist abstraction. Johnson had long been credited with the design until manufacturer Design Within Reach tried to relaunch the product in 2006, describing the toy as an anonymous piece of folk art. Intervention by online toy fans succeeded in restoring credit back to Caranica, and Industrial Woodworking Corporation instead reissued the design. Caranica designed a number of toys for Creative Playthings, including variants of the Rocking Beauty, as well as securing patents for designs that she created for other companies like Kiddie Products and the Quaker Oats Company right up until the late 1990s.

| Gloria Caranica | B. 1931, USA. | Rocking Beauty Hobby Horse | 1964–66 |

A self-taught designer, Etel Carmona discovered her love for woodcrafts while restoring vintage pieces during her own home renovation. Carmona is notable not only for her entrepreneurship through her company ETEL, founded in 1993, but also for her environmental activism. Born in the mining region of Minas Gerais, Carmona moved to São Paulo at seventeen to study. In the late 1980s she started modest weekend workshops dedicated to teaching young people woodwork, informed by the design and furniture-making skills she developed for her personal use, and later developed and refined through her collaboration with the Brazilian master craftsman known as Moacir. Carmona found it difficult to obtain certified sustainably sourced wood to work with, and so set out to investigate the entire supply chain. Her research resulted in the establishment of furniture company Aver Amazônia, headquartered in the city of Xapuri. The company managed its own forest, planting trees for eventual use in Carmona's own designs and those of others. The generously proportioned 22 Chair (above), for example, is available in four different native wood species and upholstered in warm leather. ETEL now reissues mid-century classics, such as the Rio Chaise Longue by Oscar and Anna Maria Niemeyer (see p. 170) and work by Brazilian modernist Jorge Zalszupin.

| 2008 | 22 Chair | B. 1949, Minas Gerais, Brazil. | Etel Carmona |

Having inherited her attention to detail and passion for design from her engineer father, who meticulously designed and furnished their houses growing up, designer Maddalena Casadei studied architecture at the University of Ferrara, known for its focus on construction and composition. While she now runs her own studio, she attributes importance to collaboration and exchange, which she experienced at the Domus Academy in Milan, where she worked with colleagues from all over the world. She also learned the value of teamwork as a former professional volleyball player. Before setting up her own practice in 2017 in Milan, beginning in 2004 Casadei worked at James Irvine Studio, founded by the late British designer, for nine years. In her own studio, she produces objects that create what she describes as a "tranquil intrusion," designs that elevate the experience of everyday life whilst remaining relatively anonymous. Casadei designed the sleek metal Verso Table (above) around the idea of conviviality; depending on how the expressive legs—one side rounded and the other cut with a flat facet—are mounted, the table's profile is transformed. Designed for Fucina, where Casadei is also art director, the Verso Table joins the Symposia collection, a series that also includes Paris-based furniture designer Jun Yasumoto's and Cecilie Manz's (see p. 159) own tables.

| Maddalena Casadei | B. 1976, Forli, Italy. | Verso Table | 2019 |

Like many young Italian designers in the early postwar period, Anna Castelli Ferrieri was heavily influenced by European architecture circles, made evident through her co-organization of the 1949 meeting of the Congrès Internationale d'Architecture Moderne (CIAM) and her work editing architectural and product design magazine *Casabella*. She began working for the Italian postwar Neo-Rationalist Franco Albini, whom she called her "maestro," and his partner, Franca Helg (see p. 120). At a time when her modernist (male) peers prized functionality, Castelli Ferrieri believed that beautiful objects were inherently useful. She was the first woman to graduate in architecture from the Politecnico di Milano and founded the plastic furniture fabrication company Kartell with her husband Giulio Castelli. She later became the company's design director, and was instrumental in recruiting a range of innovative designers, including Joe Colombo and the Castiglioni brothers. Many of her pieces are still in production, including the popular Componibili Modular Storage System (above). First shown at the Salone del Mobile in Milan in 1967, it was one of the first products made using the progressive technology of injection-molded ABS plastic, and was designed with an interlocking shape that allowed multiple components to stack.

| 1967 | Componibili Modular Storage System | B. 1918, Milan. D. 2006, Milan. | Anna Castelli Ferrieri |

In 1999, having recently finished a large-scale client-led project, designer Carol Catalano wanted to focus on something in-house with greater creative freedom, and so entered the International Furniture Design Competition held in Asahikawa, Japan. Requiring a full-scale prototype, she built her Capelli Stool (below) in her garage, and it became a winning entry. Inspired by the intertwined fingers of clasping hands, the design gracefully interlocks two plywood-molded pieces in an elegant construction that requires no fastenings. Awarded the silver medal, Catalano was the only American winner among eight successful entries, chosen from seven hundred international submissions. A year after winning,

Catalano licensed the stool to Herman Miller. Catalano credits her creative ambition to a six-week confinement she endured in her childhood recovering from rheumatic fever, where her only solace was drawing from bed. Going on to study at the Rhode Island School of Design, she discovered industrial design and pursued a hands-on approach, working directly with materials in the school's wood, metal, and machine shops. She founded Catalano Design in Boston in 1987, where she continues to develop products guided by her philosophy that remarkable design is led by user-centered research, and requires a combination of art, science, and craft.

| Carol Catalano | B. 1975, Portsmouth, NH, USA. | Capelli Stool | 1999 |

Jungyou Choi is the founder of the Seoul-based Studio Word, created in collaboration with her husband Kyuhyung Cho in 2018. The couple named the studio after the song "Words," by Gregory Alan Isakov, chosen because it describes how the meaning of words can change depending on context. The duo apply this logic to design, which they believe has the capacity to evolve and transform with time. While still in its infancy, Studio Word has had a prolific output of designs ranging from furniture and lighting to textiles and cutlery. Choi studied Man and Well-Being at the Design Academy Eindhoven (DAE), a course founded by Ilse Crawford (see p. 72), followed by studies in Design for Luxury and Craftsmanship at the École Cantonale d'Art de Lausanne in Switzerland. Choi credits her time at DAE's atelier as formative in her craft-based approach to materials. She has enjoyed making things since childhood, but found that by the time she was formally studying she had forgotten how to draw and model by hand. Her experience at the atelier reignited her love for the handmade. The studio has collaborated with brands such as Menu, Iittala, and Hermès; the Word Table Light (above), produced by Dims., is crafted from corn PLA (polylactic acid)—a plastic substitute—its white, luminous fluted form taking inspiration from classical Greek columns.

| 2019 | Word Table Light | B. 1982, Jinju, South Korea. | Jungyou Choi |

The period of reconstruction after World War II provided a number of opportunities for young designers, some of whom had their designs mass produced, consequently making them instant household classics. Such was the case for Polish designer Maria Chomentowska, who worked for more than twenty-five years in Warsaw's Institute of Industrial Design (IWP) furniture department. Founded in 1950 by Wanda Telakowska, the IWP aimed to foster links between designers and industry. Chomentowska's wooden Chair Model 200-102 (above) succinctly demonstrates her design clarity. Chomentowska studied at the Women's Architecture School, Warsaw before World War II, and in 1945 began working in the Office for the Reconstruction of the Capital as an architect's technician. She initially studied painting at the Academy of Fine Arts in Warsaw, but moved to the department of architecture where she studied interior design under groundbreaking designer Jan Kurzatkowski. Over the course of her career at the IWP, Chomentowska became passionate about designing for children, conceiving a range of bent plywood classroom furniture based on ergonomic and scientific research. In recognition of her pioneering work, Chomentowska was awarded the lifetime achievement award from Poland's Ministry of Culture and Art on two occasions, in 1957 and 1969.

| Maria Chomentowska | B. 1924, Warsaw, Poland. D. 2013, Lublin, Poland. | Chair Model 200-102 | c. 1950s |

Karen Clemmensen first trained as a mason before studying architecture at the Royal Danish Academy in Copenhagen, after which she worked part-time for Copenhagen's municipal architect, in part because of the lack of her own architectural commissions. Clemmensen and her husband Ebbe established a design partnership, integrating Japanese spatial concepts and early American modernism with the Danish tradition of good craftsmanship to create a new style of furniture and architecture. After visiting Masao Nakamura's Zui-Ki-Tei tea house at the Museum of Ethnography on a trip to Stockholm, the Clemmensens acquired a model tea house, which they methodically studied to better understand the principles of Japanese design. Clemmensen's graphic sensibility, for which she won awards, is evident in elegant watercolors that describe the couple's simple and functional architectural vision, characterized by dramatic eaves, light wooden construction, and the use of atriums. Together the Clemmensens built a number of churches, including the restoration of the Church of Kliplev with Clemmensen's father, the architect Holger Mund. Less well known is the couple's furniture; the Safari Lounge Chair (below) is the Clemmensens' take on Danish designer Kaare Klint's 1933 chair of the same name, which was based on versions he had seen used on safari in Africa.

| 1958 | Safari Lounge Chair | B. 1917, Copenhagen. D. 2001, Denmark. | Karen Clemmensen |

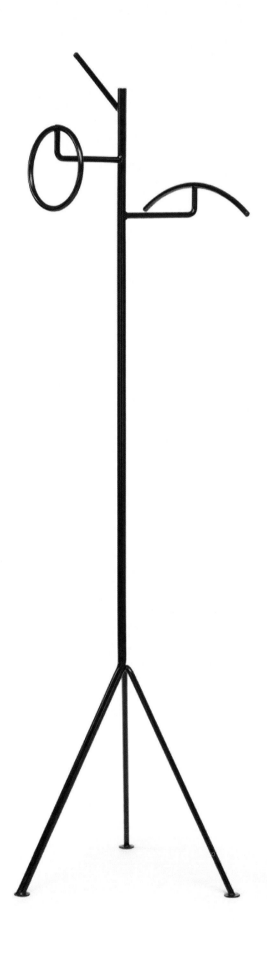

Originally from New York, Muriel Coleman studied Fine Art at Teachers College, Columbia University before moving to Paris to train as a painter under Cubist André Lhote. During World War II she worked for the U.S. wartime intelligence agency, the Office of Strategic Services (which would later become the CIA), analyzing photos of the French coastline in preparation for the Normandy landings. Following her service, the combination of a lack of funding and scarce availability of raw materials led Coleman to use her family's farm-tool manufacturing business to produce her first designs. Coleman's knowledge of metalwork enabled her to transform discarded materials such as scrap metal into elegant furniture designs. Her signature shelving units of the 1950s, first produced for San Leandro-based California Contemporary, combined steel rebar and wood to make sleek, functional pieces in which the insertion of slim metal rods eliminated the need for large quantities of wood to create structure. This combination became a ubiquitous feature of mid-century Californian design, and is a hallmark—alongside pieces like the light, minimal Coatrack (left)—of the work of the Pacific Design Group, of which Coleman was a member. Later in her life, Coleman was an active contributor to the San Francisco Bay Area's art communities as President of the East Bay Artists' Association and as a trustee of the Oakland Museum of California.

| Muriel Coleman | B. 1917, New York. D. 2003, Oakland, CA, USA. | Coatrack | c. 1952 |

Kim Colin's training as an architect informs the backdrop to her London-based studio Industrial Facility's approach, which carefully considers objects as a product of the context in which they are made, combining simplicity with utility and intellectual rigor. Colin founded the studio with her partner Sam Hecht in 2002. While Hecht was recognized as a Royal Designer for Industry in 2008, it took a further seven years for Colin to be awarded the same—regardless, she was the first woman product designer to be recognized in the organization's history. As the name suggests, Industrial Facility embraces modern industry, defying the typical suspicion that associates it with cheap mass production, and thoughtless consumption. Their twenty-first-century interpretation of craft advocates for a return to care and detail realized through contemporary industrial manufacturing techniques. The Branca Chair (above) is a good example; manufactured for Italian brand Mattiazzi and made from sustainably sourced wood, it is inspired by the twists and turns of tree branches. Produced robotically, the chair is indicative of Industrial Facility's interest in the way technology can shape the future of design. The studio's spin-off project, Future Facility, is dedicated to exploring the Internet's increasingly influential role in defining the relationship between products and people.

| 2010 | Branca Chair | B. 1961, Los Angeles. | Kim Colin |

The Brazilian northeast remains both geographically and climatically different from the urban centers of its coastal cities, where the majority of the country's modernism was shaped. One of Brazil's great modern designers, Janete Costa, grew up in Recife in the northeastern state of Pernambuco, and studied architecture at the School of Fine Arts of Pernambuco before finishing her training in Rio de Janeiro, where she moved and started her young family. Spending most of her working life in the state of Rio de Janeiro, Costa eventually moved back to the northeast with her second husband, Acácio Gil Borsoi, with whom she ran the architecture practice Borsoi Arquitetura and together the couple opened a gallery, Galeria Amparo 60. Completing more than fifty new buildings over the course of her career, Costa also worked as an interior designer and architect, restoring historic structures, including a number of churches and cultural buildings. She also designed products—such as the Borsoi Table (above) with a red lacquer compartment—to furnish these buildings, leading her to open a furniture store, Escala, in Rio's neighboring city of Niterói. Her significant influence was made evident through Brazilian architect Sergio Rodrigues' Janete Table, made as a tribute to Costa. In 2012, the City Hall of Niterói opened the Museum of Popular Arts Janete Costa, named in her honor.

| Janete Costa | B. 1932, Garanhuns, Brazil. D. 2008, Olinda, Brazil. | Borsoi Table | c. 1960s |

Pointing to new forms of experimentation within everyday life, Matali Crasset characterizes design as a form of research that refuses shape, amalgamating influences from handicraft, electronic music, graphics, and scenography to inform her designs for furniture and interiors. Her designs are playful, such as the Foglie Lamp (below) for Pallucco, which is modeled on forms found in nature (*foglie* means leaves); its shape resembles a branch that splits in two, then forks again, bending and straightening as it goes. Crasset's design, which she describes as "humble yet helpful," echoes the principles of her childhood growing up on a farm in the north of France, where she states work and life were one and the same. Crasset trained as an industrial designer at the École Nationale Supérieure de Création Industrielle, joining Philippe Starck's studio in 1993, where she became head of the Thomson Multimedia project. She left to establish her own studio with her husband Francis Fichot in 1998. Crasset has exhibited her work internationally, designing across a range of scales from tableware to interiors for luxury hotels. Crasset's functional designs are unapologetic in their search for new typologies articulated around modularity, flexibility, and networks, and have earned her numerous awards, including the Légion d'Honneur in 2017.

| 2010 | Foglie Lamp | B. 1965, Châlons-en-Champagne, France. | Matali Crasset |

Ilse Crawford's furniture set for Portuguese manufacturer De La Espada, Seating for Eating (above), in many ways encompasses the London-based designer's entire philosophy. Described as a "family" of furniture, the seven pieces that make up the set create a range of different ways to organize people around a table. Crawford is always thinking about wellbeing when designing both

furniture and spaces. Her observational and analytical skills, which she credits to her economist father, have led to her integration of design with academia, pioneering the Man and Well-Being course at Design Academy Eindhoven, which she led for more than twenty years. A celebrated interior designer, Crawford is influenced by her Scandinavian heritage and what she explains as "the sensory

thing, in thinking about it from a human context ... the thing that touches you." Having considered becoming an architect after studying architectural history, Crawford pursued a career in journalism, becoming the founding editor of *ELLE Decoration*, a post she held for ten years. After she left to establish her own design practice, Studioilse, Crawford's seminal early projects included Babington House (2001) in Somerset, England for the Soho House group—the property notable for its plush but informal and homey interior, a rule-breaking concept at the time—and later her sleek yet down-to-earth TwoTwoSix Hollywood Road apartment (2010) in Hong Kong.

| 2009 | Seating for Eating | B. 1962, London. | Ilse Crawford |

Part of a celebrity social milieu, designer Gabriella Crespi was frequently visited by the likes of Audrey Hepburn, Gianni Versace, and even Qatari royalty at her combined home and showroom. The Milanese designer studied art at the Accademia di Belle Arti di Brera, before training as an architect at the Politecnico di Milano, an unconventional choice of course for a woman in the 1940s. Her eye for beauty was matched by her technical skill—she acquired patents for all the mechanisms used in her sculptural cabinets—made evident through her handcrafted yet sleek and often futuristic aesthetic, which blurred the boundary between functional modern design and sculptural abstraction. At sixty-five, Crespi left for India, where she lived in the Himalayas for twenty years. She cited "the universe" as inspiration for her aesthetic, and Crespi's furniture drew heavily on motifs found in nature. Upon returning to Italy in 2005, Crespi wrote about her spiritual experience in India in her only published work, a book called *In Search of Infinity: Himalaya* (2007). Before her death in 2017, she returned to design, elevating simple materials by shaping them into bold, geometric silhouettes. Later works, such as the Scultura Coffee Table (below), resurrected the luxurious and elegant forms of her early projects; in this table the upper slab slides to reveal the lower.

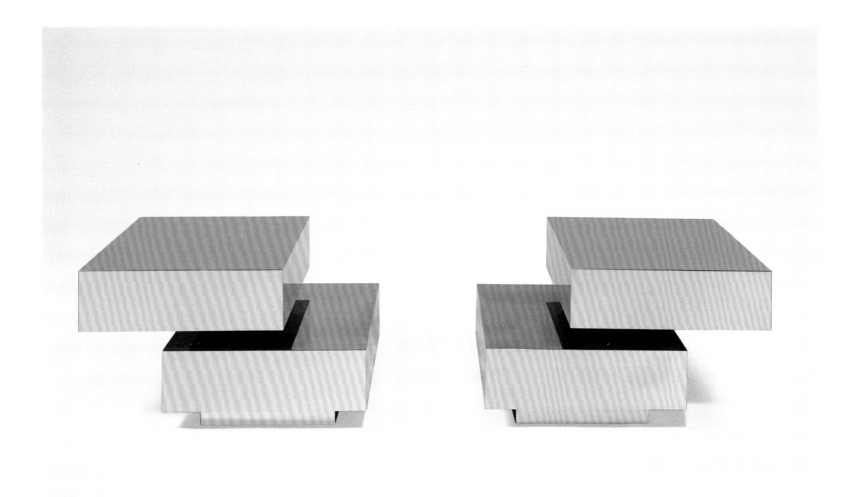

| Gabriella Crespi | B. 1922, Milan. D. 2017, Milan. | Scultura Coffee Table | 1970 |

Mid-century Italian furniture is the product of a relatively small group of designers and historians who made their name rethinking modernism in the postwar period, shaping a new era of Italian design. A good example of this is Raffaella Crespi's Lounge Chair (above), manufactured by Mobilia, which features a simple silhouette and a rosewood frame with gently undulating armrests. Crespi, who was not only an accomplished designer but also a writer and academic, publicized Italian Rationalism in the pages of magazines. She even founded a number of them, including *Italia Nostra*, and was one of the founders of the Associazione per il Disegno Industriale. A born Milanese, Crespi studied architecture at the Politecnico di Milano, and concentrated on planning as a Professor of Architectural Technology and Industrial Design at the University, a position she held for more than twenty years. Crespi also founded the Terragni Foundation in Como to commemorate the work of Italian modernist architect Giuseppe Terragni (1904–1943). Crespi's building and research was motivated by her interest in how new industrial technologies and building methods could inform urban recovery in Italian cities. She became an authority and wrote a number of books on this topic, which later led to her appointment as President of the Order of Architects of Milan, the first woman to hold the position.

| c. 1960s | Lounge Chair | B. 1929, Milan. D. 2011, Milan. | Raffaella Crespi |

Designers Helena Jonasson and Veronica Dagnert named their practice studio vit, *vit* meaning "white" in Swedish, after a book of the same name by Kenya Hara about the value of simplicity—fitting, given that their designs are underpinned by a shared belief in sustainable, thoughtful design that "makes space for daily life." While Dagnert's background is in fashion and communication, Jonasson was trained as an industrial designer; this collaboration allows both to branch out from their respective disciplines. From their London studio the duo create refined, nuanced products that express "a reduction and stillness," core values for their shared work. The Inox Table (below) embodies these ideas; its cylindrical base made from shiny corrugated metal—a material that is usually associated with building construction—contrasts with its raw steel top finished in a gentle, milky white lacquer, establishing aesthetic tension between the polish and cloudiness of the respective materials. The design elevates the everyday, offering its user "a daily dose of poetry." For Jonasson and Dagnert, the visual lightness and simplicity of the Inox Table inherits certain qualities of Scandinavian design, where every detail, large and small, is afforded the same attention.

| Veronica Dagnert & Helena Jonasson | Dagnert B. 1974, Lund, Sweden. Jonasson B. 1978, Ängelholm, Sweden. | Inox Table | 2018 |

Lucienne Day studied textiles at the Royal College of Art in London, where she met her husband, the designer Robin Day. The couple both taught before establishing independent design careers alongside each other. Day's best-known creation, the Calyx Textile (above), was first introduced at the Festival of Britain in 1951 to adorn a modern interior designed by her husband. At the time, the British textile company Heal's Fabrics—who had put the print into production—were shocked when the pattern, then considered a radical composition, became a bestseller, before evolving to become an era-defining motif. Day mixed her signature contrasting color blocks with playfully drawn interpretations of natural forms with energetic lines that appeared to dance off their fabric substrate in a range of textile designs throughout the 1950s. Day's fresh, colorful abstractions, coupled with her keen insight into consumer needs, made her one of the most successful print designers of her era. In the 1960s, she moved away from botanical forms, producing increasingly stylized prints that traded larger graphic shapes for the spidery lines of her earlier prints. Pioneering the use of synthetic fibers, such as Rayon, in the production of more affordable textiles made Day a household name; in 1987 she was the first woman to be appointed Britain's Master of the Faculty of the Royal Designers for Industry.

| 1951 | Calyx Textile | B. 1917, Coulsdon, England, UK. D. 2010, Chichester, England, UK. | Lucienne Day |

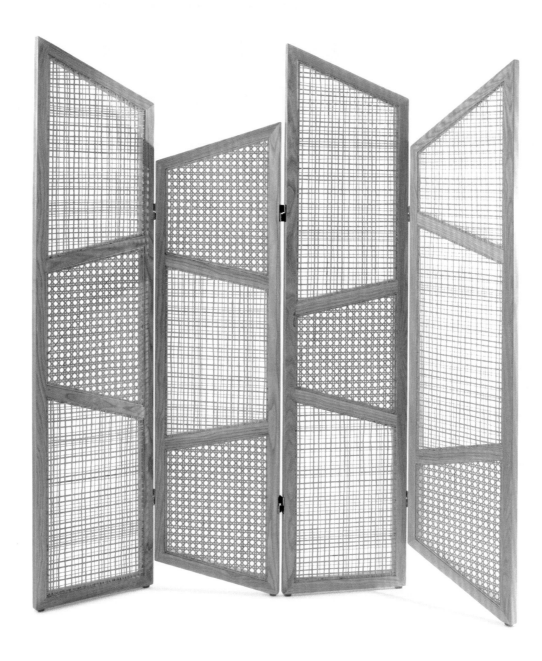

As an infant, Lebanese designer Nada Debs was raised in Japan, returning to Beirut in 1980 to study at the American University of Beirut. She went on to study interior architecture at the Rhode Island School of Design and remained in the U.S. for three years before moving to London, where she began designing and producing custom furniture. In 2000, Debs returned to Lebanon and established her home and showroom, Nada Debs Furniture & Design Beirut. Debs's global travels and cosmopolitan background inform her interest in fusing cultures in her work, often mixing intricate craft-based designs. The handmade is central to Debs's effortlessly tactile work, informed by her belief that craftsmanship transcends geography, language, and culture. Given their minimal but also surprising forms, Debs credits her clean-lined, functional furniture and homewares with combining the Japanese sensibility of her upbringing with the decorative Middle Eastern Arabesque patterning of her heritage. The Summerland Paravan (above) exemplifies this fusion through its exuberant, angular form crafted from textured straw in varied patterns, then woven on an ash wood frame. Debs often uses mother-of-pearl inlay in her pieces to decorative effect, such as in her Fragmented Clock (2012), whose totemic form with diamond motif is handcarved from maple.

| Nada Debs | B. 1960, Beirut. | Summerland Paravan | 2019 |

Qiyun Deng trained as an industrial designer at the Guangzhou Academy of Fine Arts, later graduating from the École Cantonale d'Art de Lausanne in Switzerland in 2013, where she studied product design. After returning to her native China, she joined the interdisciplinary design studio Benwu, which is based in Beijing and Shanghai. For her diploma project, Deng created a set of disposable tableware, called Graft, made from compostable PLA bioplastics. By crafting each utensil in the form of a plant or vegetable—spoons with a carrot-shaped handle, for example, or an artichoke petal-shaped bowl—Deng melded material, in this case revealing its source in its design, with function, inviting the user to question the value of the object and reconsider its disposable nature. The Soft Pack Sofa (below) was designed as homage to the iconic Maralunga Sofa (1973) by Italian industrial designer Vico Magistretti. Like the Maralunga, which is characterized by its adjustable head and armrests, the malleable form of the Soft Pack Sofa allows the seat to mold around its occupant, creating a range of flexible seating positions. The Soft Pack Sofa was displayed at the Cassina showroom during Salone de Mobile in 2014. In her role as senior product manager at Benwu, Deng specializes in developing products for the consumer market, predominantly through cutting-edge materials and technologies.

| 2014 | Soft Pack Sofa | B. 1983, Foshan, China. | Qiyun Deng |

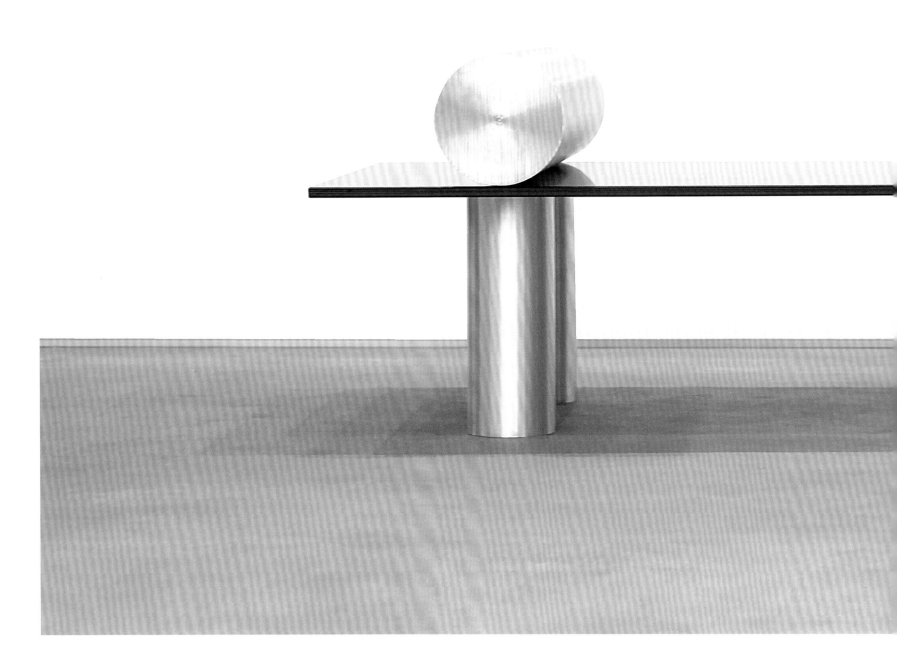

Marie Dessuant co-founded Studio Dessuant Bone with graphic designer Philip Bone in 2014; the duo met in 2010 while working at Fabrica, the influential research center in Treviso, which supports young designers through a collaborative program of workshops and lectures, all within a seventeenth-century villa owned by fashion magnate Luciano Benetton. Based in Paris, the studio's

Fabrica influence lived on through Dessuant and Bone's emphasis on collaborations with designers from different disciplines. The Day Bed (above) was born from such collaboration, as part of the studio's Art Industrial series made with Belgian metal and glass manufacturers Allaert Aluminium. With glass and metal as core materials, the Day Bed benefited greatly from the company's

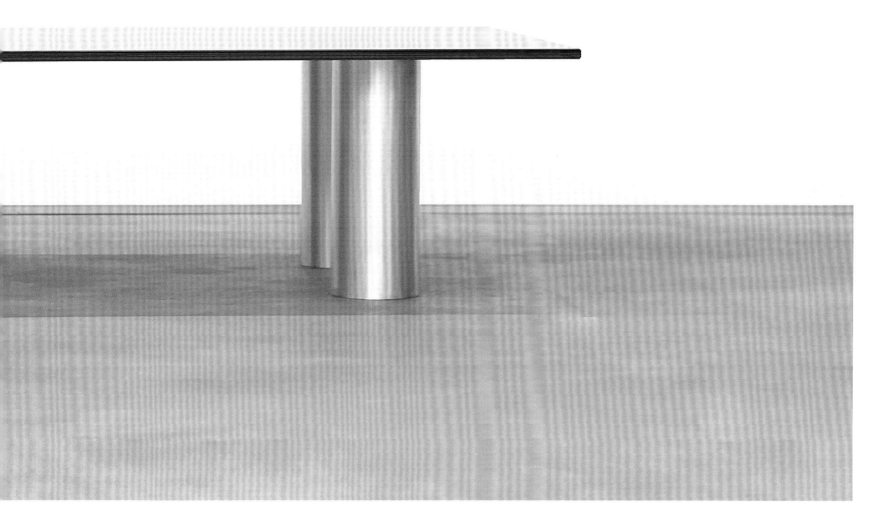

expert fabrication history dating to 1955. Dessuant studied product design at the École Supérieure des Arts Décoratifs de Strasbourg in France, graduating in 2008, after which she spent time working abroad, notably in Shanghai. In 2010 she won the Cinna-Ligne Roset award for her lavender blue-lacquered MDF Étagère de Coin Corner Shelf, whose boxlike form perched on stilts looks like a work of micro architecture. Prior to establishing Dessuant Bone, she worked as head of design at UK-based maker and retailer Another Country for a number of years, specializing in furniture and homewares drawing from Shaker and British countryside vernaculars.

| 2017 | Day Bed | B. 1984, Paris. | Marie Dessuant |

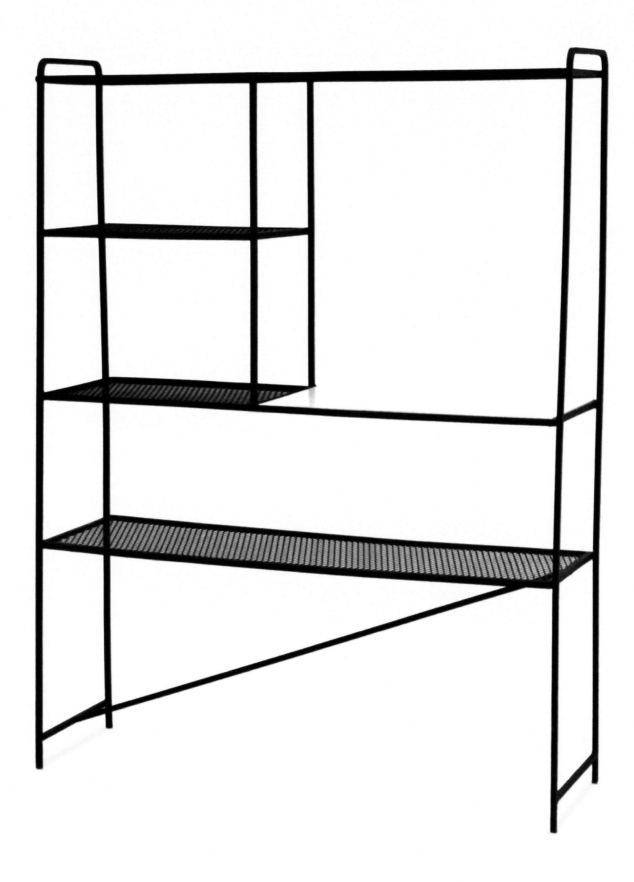

In 1954 *Life* magazine stated that Freda Diamond had done more than any other designer to furnish American homes, naming her the "Designer for Everybody." Diamond believed that design should reflect existing and often conservative tastes of the consumer, while introducing new manufacturing techniques, making her a commercial hit. She sold over 75,000 units of her wrought iron furniture for Baumritter in 1954 alone, including this mesh-shelved unit with a single laminate section (opposite). Diamond studied at the Women's Art School at Cooper Union, New York, where she later taught. After continuing her education in Europe, Diamond sought experience in department stores, working at

William Baumgarten and Stern Brothers, before leaving to set up her own studio and design for others, including Herman Miller. Her focus on designing for the home and concern for the tastes of the average American housewife led to her appointment alongside Virginia Hamill (see p. 114) as a consultant at the glass company Libbey. Diamond undertook a year-long survey to discover female consumer preferences for glassware; later 25 million of her glass pieces were sold within ten years. Continuing her work in consultancy immediately after World War II, Diamond advised Italian craftsmen on what to produce for an American market, a role she later undertook for the governments of Israel and Japan.

| 1954 | Shelving | B. 1905, New York. D. 1998, PA, USA. | Freda Diamond |

Under the tutelage of Bauhaus master Joseph Ittens, Friedl Dicker-Brandeis developed the belief that art was a form of emotional expression and spiritual progression. Studying with Ittens at his private school and later at the Bauhaus, where she also taught, Dicker-Brandeis worked across typography, photography, and textiles, and later set up a series of design studios of her own, focusing on architecture and interiors. While she was at the Bauhaus, the painter Paul Klee introduced her to educational concepts advancing childlike imagination as a fruitful tool for her own artistic exploration. This chair (below) was designed for a children's home in collaboration with her business partner Franz Singer. Following an invitation to teach art to kindergarten teachers in Vienna, Dicker-Brandeis later moved to Prague. Deported in 1942 to the Theresienstadt ghetto in Czechoslovakia, Dicker-Brandeis carried with her art supplies with the intention of providing children with a form of therapy in order to help deal with the upheaval of deportation, having the children sign their work as a testament to their existence. She hid more than 5,000 artworks inside a suitcase when she was deported, this time voluntarily, to Auschwitz-Birkenau in an effort to reunite with her husband. She died at the concentration camp in 1944 aged forty-six.

| Friedl Dicker-Brandeis | B. 1898, Vienna. D. 1944, Auschwitz. | Chair | 1930 |

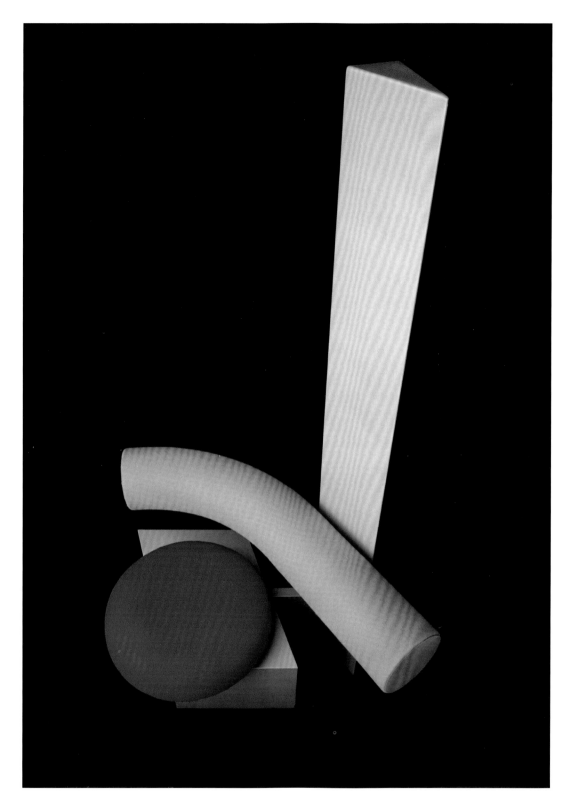

The Moveable Chair (left) designed by British artist and designer Jane Dillon (née Young) was first displayed, against the advice of her tutor, at her graduate show at the Royal College of Art (RCA) in London in 1968. Not interested in replicating what Dillon refers to as "chairness," the piece is a study in dynamic ergonomics, its four parts swiveling as the user changes position. Excited by the new dyes available at the time, Dillon had the chair fabricated in bright pink—it was later put into production by Planula, who produced several color variations, and Joe Colombo had it reproduced in *Domus* magazine. While on a travel scholarship in Italy, Dillon worked as a color consultant at Olivetti for Ettore Sottsass. Sottsass was so impressed by her proposal for a new palette for a range of modular furniture that he had fifty copies of her book-like document silkscreen printed. Dillon met her husband Charles in Italy—he was among numerous RCA graduates working in the country at the time. Returning to London, the duo founded Studio Dillon in 1972, and had many of their ideas put into production by well-known furniture retailers, including Habitat and Herman Miller. Dillon returned to the RCA where she taught for more than thirty years and became an Honorary Fellow in 2006. Her complete studio archives are held by the Victoria & Albert Museum in London.

| 1968 | Moveable Chair | B. 1943, Manchester, England, UK. | Jane Dillon |

French-born Senegalese designer Aïssa Dione founded her textiles studio Aïssa Dione Tissus in 1992. The workshop is located in the town of Rufisque, close to Dakar, and is known for producing contemporary fabrics using traditional weaving techniques. Tissus studied fine arts in Paris before relocating to Senegal to develop her work as a painter. A career in interior design began somewhat by chance after she offered to redecorate the office of a client who had purchased one of her works. The fabrics used in her interiors were quickly in demand, and she established a makeshift studio at her home, creating textiles with the assistance of a single weaver on a hand-built loom. Her studio now employs more than one hundred people who practice traditional Manjak weaving methods, a disappearing craft that has its origins in Guinea-Bissau. Through her work with local artisans, Dione has returned emphasis to Senegal's rich textile heritages, which dates back to the fifteenth century. Much of her fabric, including Kara (above), is characterized by vivid, bold geometric patterns in earth tones. Alongside her own range based in Senegal, Dione has also created fabrics for luxury brands, including Peter Marino, Rose Tarlow, Hermès, and Fendi, and does so through her showroom in Paris.

| Aïssa Dione | B. France. | Kara Fabric | 2019 |

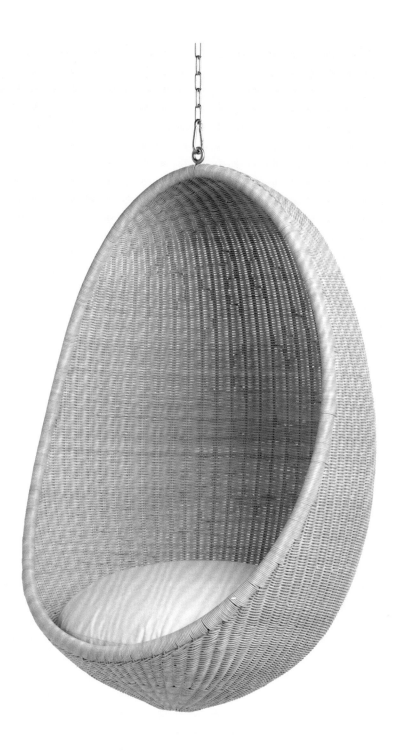

Nanna Ditzel's designs elegantly translate artistic ideas into functional objects; for her, chair design had the potential to be both practical and poetic. Ditzel's technical expertise from her training as a cabinetmaker contributed to her ability to realize many of her gravity-defying proposals. She went on to study formally at the School of Arts and Crafts and the Royal Danish Academy in Copenhagen, developing award-winning designs for jewelry, tableware, and textiles. Ditzel originally partnered with her husband Jørgen Ditzel, who passed away in 1961 at only forty years old. Together, the couple designed the wicker Hanging Egg Chair (above). Like much of the their work together, it pairs an evocative form with a simple twist of technical fabrication; the free-spirited design, a kind of hanging basket pivoting on a cord, was a move away from what the Ditzels recognized as a dogmatic functionalism of Danish design at the time. In 1968 Ditzel married Kurt Heide, an English furniture dealer. The pair moved to London, setting up the furniture house Interspace, where Ditzel began experimenting with new materials, including fiberglass, that could be shaped to make the curvaceous forms popular to the era. Her designs, and varied output, remain in demand; and her daughters continue her legacy by managing the design studio she bequeathed to them.

| 1959 | Hanging Egg Chair | B. 1923, Copenhagen.
D. 2005, Copenhagen. | Nanna Ditzel |

A celebrated illustrator, Helen Dryden popularized what was considered a European style of illustration in America, working for publications including *Vogue*. She later moved into industrial design through her connections with the American Union of Decorative Artists and Craftsmen, becoming Art Director of the Dura Company in Ohio. Dryden's sense of style and brand appeal helped market mass-produced items at the height of the Great Depression. The Art Deco-style chrome and brass Candlesphere Candleholder (above) is one of two items created for Italian manufacturer Revere. Dryden was an artistic child, growing up in Baltimore where she was mostly self-taught, detached from the traditions of design which she referred to as an "unconscious reflection of an admired master." While decorative, her illustrations used bright colors and clean lines, which hinted at her later advocacy for modernist simplicity across a number of design fields; she even published articles on car design in trade magazines. She also wrote on behalf of one of her employers, the car company Studebaker, for whom she designed the Studebaker President (1936), leading to her reputation then as the highest-paid "woman artist" in America. Despite such success, Dryden inexplicably disappeared from public view toward the end of the 1930s, citing a "personal shock."

Helen Dryden

| B. 1882, Baltimore, MD, USA. D. 1972, Brentwood, NY, USA. | Candlesphere Candleholder | c. 1937 |

Socialite Helen Hughes Dulany only established a career in design in her mid-forties after a move to Chicago in 1920, where she fell ill and began modeling objects out of clay to pass the time. She first designed furniture for her personal apartment, using her own money to fabricate each piece. She eventually opened a factory of her own to put a number of these designs into production, and established Helen Hughes Dulany Studio, selling to clients and department stores all over the country. Like a number of women in design during this period, Hughes Dulany was also an inventor. She pioneered a new way of backing glass with metal, and, like her contemporary Belle Kogan (see p. 139), also used Bakelite—an early plastic more commonly employed in the auto and electric industries—for its heat-resistant properties, as seen in her Coffee Service (below). Her work is characterized by its use of stainless steel, which, coupled with geometric forms, was at the time seen as both futuristic and also emblematic of the modern home. This modern aesthetic led to commissions by large companies such as General Electric and the Burlington Zephyr trains, who sought to update their image. Because of her prominence, her divorce in 1936 attracted significant public attention, ultimately overshadowing her designs and resulting in the closure of her studio.

| 1934 | Coffee Service | B. 1885, Bismarck, ND, USA. D. 1968, USA. | Helen Hughes Dulany |

Nathalie Du Pasquier's Postmodern style is a riot of color, capturing three dimensions in a flat plane, as can be seen in both her painting and textiles. Her furniture, however, is almost the reverse, with three-dimensional objects constructed from flat, assembled paintings that abstract everyday objects into exuberantly patterned surfaces. Covered in her distinctive, almost anarchic

graphics, the Royal Sofa (above) was created in collaboration with George Sowden and is an example of Du Pasquier's work with the Memphis Group, led by Ettore Sottsass. Embracing Sottsass's anti-academicism, Du Pasquier admired how design could leave things to interpretation of the audience. With no formal training, Du Pasquier came to design through drawing. She spent her

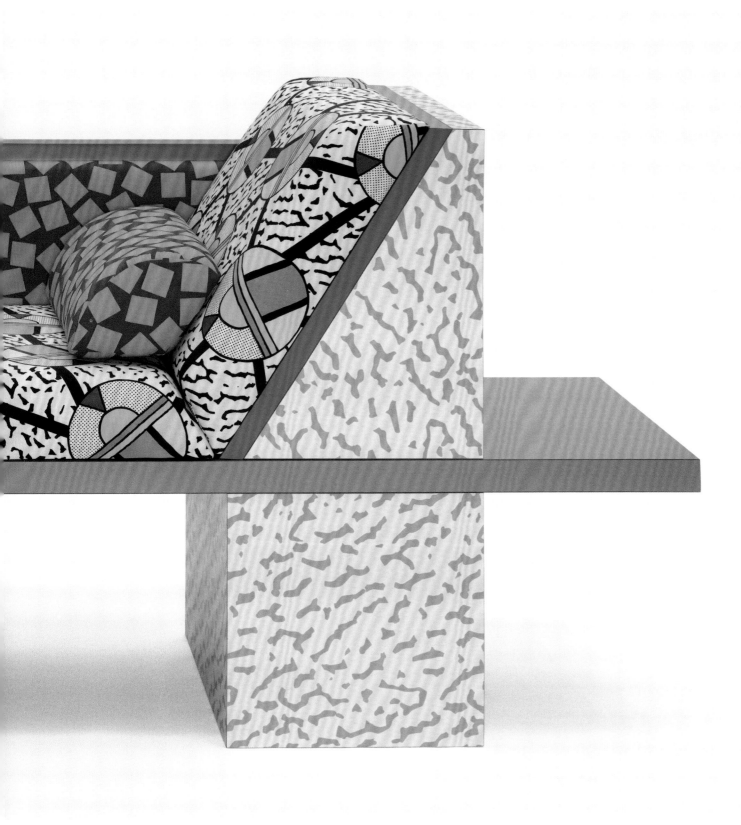

upbringing in the French port town of Bordeaux. Living in Gabon when she was eighteen allowed Du Pasquier to absorb the graphic signage and bright aesthetics of street life that later, after moving to Milan in 1979, became present in her work. At the time, Milan was a city shaped by industry, offering an entirely distinct built environment that inspired Du Pasquier's search for her own sense of modernity. After what Du Pasquier refers to as "the excitement of the 1980s," she returned to painting, publishing her drawings and exhibiting her work internationally, including at the Palais de Tokyo, Paris and Pace Gallery, London.

| 1983 | Royal Sofa | B. 1957, Bordeaux, France. | Nathalie Du Pasquier |

Ray Eames, alongside her husband Charles Eames, designed some of the world's best-known architecture, furniture, textiles, graphics, and industrial design objects. The development of the Lounge Chair (opposite), made from three independently moving plywood shells clad in leather cushions, took several years. The Eameses applied their pioneering technique for meticulously molding plywood not only to furniture design, but also to making medical splints during World War II. The success of the chair was part of a longstanding relationship with manufacturer Herman Miller, and it remains as popular today as when it was first produced. Ray Eames studied painting at the Art Students League in New York with Hans Hofmann before attending the Cranbrook Academy of Art, where she studied under textile artist Marianne Strengell (see p. 219). There she met Charles Eames, head of the new industrial design department, and the couple married and moved to Santa Monica, California, where they built their own Modernist home, the steel-framed Case Study House 8 (above), also known as the Eames House. The Eameses' technical innovation of materials paired with their humorous and often whimsical forms created a whole new visual language for American design. Ray continued their legacy for a further ten years after Charles's death in 1978.

| 1956 | Lounge Chair | B. 1912, Sacramento, CA, USA. D. 1988, Los Angeles. | Ray Eames |

The studio of Dutch designer Kiki van Eijk is full of energy, experimentation, and joy, qualities evident in her quirky Soft Table Lamp (left), which celebrates human touch. Made from white ceramic, it appears pillowy and soft, as if a textile cushion. Having enjoyed making from a young age, van Eijk's first real encounter with design came through family friends, one a furniture designer and another a painter, the latter teaching her how to cast bronze and make molds. Setting up her own painting atelier at sixteen, van Eijk was encouraged to study industrial design by one of her drawing teachers. Upon visiting the Design Academy Eindhoven, in the Netherlands, she was surprised to find that it felt like an art school, but with a rigor that suited her technical and solution-driven approach. There were few design studios in the Netherlands when van Eijk graduated during the early 2000s recession. With no money or projects, van Eijk, along with her partner Joost van Bleiswijk, who she met at the academy, built a workshop in a garage and slowly acquired new tools. The pair edited each other's work while maintaining their own distinct design identities. Today, van Eijk works largely from a farmhouse in Eindhoven, where the expansive property houses a workshop, showroom, and library. She works with a team of craftspeople to make her products—varied to the extreme, including lighting, carpets, and household objects—by hand.

| Kiki van Eijk | B. 1978, Tegelen, Netherlands. | Soft Table Lamp | 2010 |

Yeşim Eröktem established her practice called DAY studio with Doğanberk Demir in 2015 after meeting as students at the Istanbul Technical University. Their work is guided by traditional Turkish manufacturing practices, as well as the local landscape. An early design for an elegant marble platter, for example, was based on the marquetry techniques used to construct the Hagia Sophia mosque. The iridescent Volume Side Table (above) is a larger-scale implementation of this concept, with its robust marble top supported by a playful concertina base; the form of the latter takes its inspiration from the paperlike, folded metal construction of local street vendor structures. Eröktem also studied industrial design at École Cantonale d'Art de Lausanne, Switzerland, graduating in 2014. With DAY Studio—"DAY" being a combination of the pair's first-name initials—Eröktem and Demir sought to develop their own design language. For Eröktem, design is a constant opportunity to flex her curiosity about the role objects play in shaping people's lives. Alongside her design practice, in 2016 Eröktem began working toward her doctorate from the Özyeğin University in Istanbul, for which her research looks at the emerging number of self-employed designers and design studios in Istanbul, and their relationship to the design profession in Turkey.

| 2016 | Volume Side Table | B. 1988, Istanbul, Turkey. | Yeşim Eröktem |

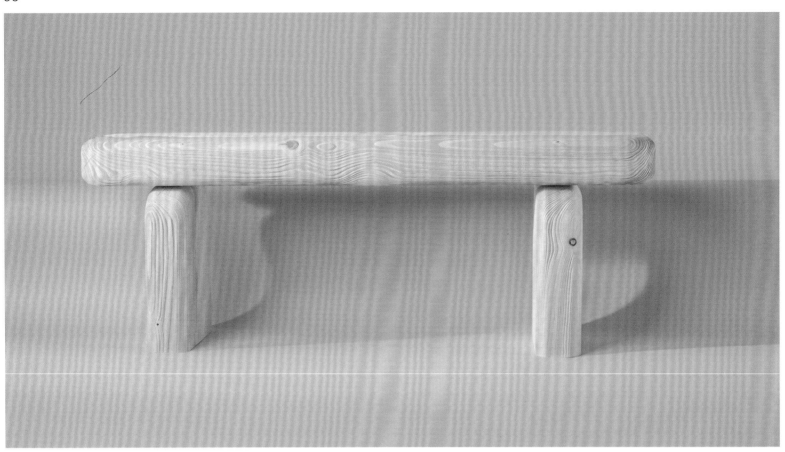

The Dune collection (left), described by designer Lisa Ertel as a family of archaic seating, is made from solid spruce wood, sandblasted to create a textured surface throwing the wood's grain into relief. This transforms the annual rings of a tree that reveal its age into a tactile surface. The German-born designer based the forms of Dune on traditional German *Ruhsteine*, stone benches placed on the side of roads where historically travelers would stop to rest. The light color of the Dune pieces contrasts with the distinctive outlines of their rings, creating an interplay between shadows on the surface of the furniture. Dune was designed while Ertel was still a student of product design at the Karlsruhe University of Arts and Design. She has since evolved her practice, creating work that mixes natural materials and traditional craft techniques with distinctly artificial ones, achieved through new technologies and industrial processes. She continued to work with her alma mater, where she has co-founded the materials-driven open research platform Bio Design Lab in collaboration with the ZKM | Center for Art and Media in Karlsruhe. She established the Fan Collective with a group of eleven friends, together realizing projects, events, and exhibitions at the intersection of art and design. In 2020–21, Ertel was an artist-in-residence at the Jan van Eyck Academie in Maastricht, the Netherlands.

| 2017 | Dune Furniture | B. 1990, Karlsruhe, Germany. | Lisa Ertel |

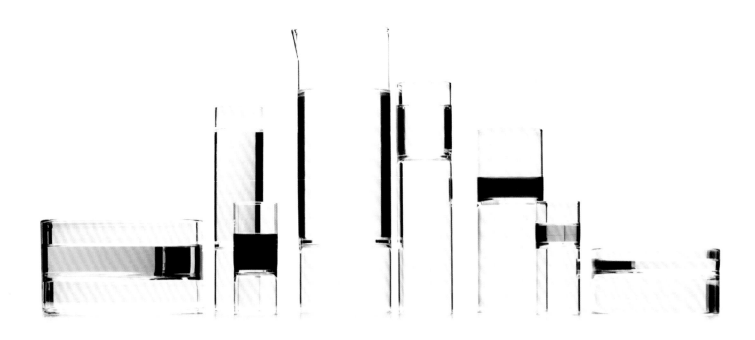

American industrial designer Felicia Ferrone founded her eponymous brand fferrone in 2010. Ferrone studied architecture at Miami University, Ohio before moving to Milan, where she became interested in the blurring of disciplinary boundaries between design and architecture while working as an architect. Her work deploys simple gestures to elegant effect in her glassware and furniture, drawing on Italian design's strong relationship to cultural heritage reinterpreted for her American context. The Revolution Wine and Water Glasses (which are held in the permanent collection of the Art Institute of Chicago) combine Ferrone's interest in handcraft techniques with the ingenuity of an unexpected design feature. The glasses (above) are mouth blown by master glassblowers in the Czech Republic, with the glasses playing on the adage "is the glass half empty or half full?" by combining an exaggerated hollowed base with an elevated beverage compartment, such that liquid inside appears to float. It was the first of Ferrone's creations that allowed her to develop a full understanding of the design process, and begin working for herself. Ferrone is interested in the capacity of design to bring people together, not just through the use of design objects, but through the process of their making. She is director of graduate studies and Professor of Industrial Design at the University of Illinois at Chicago.

| Felicia Ferrone | B. 1972, Chicago. | Revolution Wine and Water Glasses | 2001 |

The idea for the Lira Coffee Table (below) was born during the COVID-19 pandemic, when designers Andrea Flores and Lucía Soto were inspired by the actions of residents of Mexico City who, during periods of lockdown, took to their rooftops for fresh air. The pair designed the table to bring color and joy to a new activity that had suddenly become defining of everyday life in the city. Flores and Soto set up their studio, Comité de Proyectos, in 2014, working across interior and product design. The two came together through their shared belief that design should enhance a user's quality of life. The Lira Coffee Table is representative of much of their work in its fusion of the contemporary and traditional, and the way it honors local craftsmanship, while emphasizing socially responsible production and affordable pricing. Made for the outdoors with a corrosion-resistant, powder-coated metal frame, it features a round marble top. Other pieces highlighting local craft include the woven-fronted Mexico Sideboard (2020) crafted by wicker-caning artisans. The duo also produce smaller objects, like their modern take on the *anafre*, a traditional ceramic kitchen tool used to heat tortillas; their version also doubles as a fruit bowl when not in use. Both Flores and Soto studied industrial design in Mexico City, with Flores completing her higher education at the Istituto Europeo di Design Barcelona.

| 2020 | Lira Coffee Table | Flores B. 1979, Mexico City. Soto B. 1986, Mexico City. | Andrea Flores & Lucía Soto |

The Handicraft Monofilo Armchair (above) looks like a scribble rendered in three dimensions; its sinuous frame effortlessly twists to outline the contours of the woven seat, appearing improbably delicate for a functional item of furniture. Created by hand from nylon thread wrapped around an iron rod frame, the Monofilo was first produced in black and white, and later in blue and red. Inspired by the intertwining shapes large soap bubbles make when intersecting with one another, the chairs were fabricated by artisans in Florence for the Mostra dell'Artigianato exhibition in 1954. Each chair has its own distinctive form, and is individually named: the Butterfly, Napoleon, Fischer, Antiques, Basket, and

Silvano. The Monofilo was reminiscent of much of the tensile architecture that was emerging at the time and was the creation of two architects and an artist—Sergio Conti, Luciano Grassi, and Marisa Forlani respectively—who undertook the project as part of their experimental architecture practice, specializing in renovating historic structures, which they founded in Florence in the early 1950s. Forlani wrote books about the restoration of old buildings in Tuscany and was married to her co-founder, the better-known Conti, yet little other biographical information about the artist exists. The Monofilo chair is today held in the collection of the Triennale di Milano.

| Marisa Forlani | B. 1928, Bologna, Italy. | Handicraft Monofilo Armchair | c. 1953–55 |

The flowing form of Stockholm-based Monica Förster's Glide Lounge (below) for Tacchini is inspired by her observation of melting snow in her native village in Lappland, near the Arctic Circle. Surrounded by nature in childhood, Förster developed a hands-on approach to making things with her mother and father. She studied painting and art history in the city of Umeå, after which she moved to Stockholm to work as a graphic designer and continue her studies at Beckmans College of Design and the University of Arts, Crafts, and Design. Early success came when a major furniture company showed interest in her graduate project, a glow-in-the-dark toilet seat. Recognizing that she wanted the freedom to continue making her experimental designs, she established her eponymous studio, Monica Förster Design, in 1999. While running her own practice, Förster is concurrently the creative director of Bosnian furniture company Zanat, whose unique woodcarving technique is registered as an Intangible Cultural Heritage asset by UNESCO. Working with an international team of designers alongside craftspeople at Zanat, Förster aims to integrate a wide range of cultural perspectives while promoting socio-economic development.

| 2006 | Glide Lounge | B. 1966, Lappland, Sweden. | Monica Förster |

While undertaking her degree in architecture at Mackenzie Presbyterian University in São Paulo, Carol Gay participated in a workshop with renowned Brazilian designers Fernando and Humberto Campana in 1999 through 2000; it inspired her to reorient toward furniture and product design. Since establishing her eponymous practice in 2000, Gay has gone on to develop a multidisciplinary approach with prolific output across furniture, product, and lighting design. Gay interprets traditional objects with quirky twists, as in her sculptural lampshade made from playing cards or her distinctive, amorphic glassware. She generally works with local manufacturers, seeking new ways to combine artisanal skills with unlikely materials to create modern and sustainable products. Her NoAr range consists of a high-backed chair, swing seat, bench, and lounge seat (below). For the latter, Gay draped a stainless-steel frame with recycled industrial tire rubber, which from afar creates a graphic silhouette that on closer inspection has a relaxed, almost slouchy feel. Formed of a series of rubber ribbons, the NoAr Lounge Chair demonstrates Gay's ability to manipulate humble materials in sophisticated and surprising ways. Coming full circle, Gay has directed workshops at the Brazilian Museum of Sculpture and Ecology, or MuBE, where her first workshop with the Campana brothers originally took place.

| Carol Gay | B. 1976, São Paulo, Brazil. | NoAr Lounge Chair | 2010 |

Johanna Grawunder uses light as if it were a raw medium, like glass or metal. While she is best known for her monumental light installations, she spent the majority of her early career working as an architect in the studio of Italian architect Ettore Sottsass. For Grawunder, the sculptural qualities of light shape her architectural projects in the same way that lighting can define interior space or furniture. Having been made partner by Sottsass in 1989, Grawunder established her own practice in 2001, where she began to develop her signature pieces favoring luminous, electrified colors. The XXX Table (below), manufactured by Glas Italia, exemplifies Grawunder's interest in the way translucent materials like colored glass can transform through the interplay of light and shadow. Her more recent work integrates contemporary technology and color, focusing on the novel visual effects afforded by digital colors. She describes her fascination with the "language of technology," rather than technology itself, manipulating light as a means to discover colors that don't exist in material form. American-born, Grawunder now works between San Francisco and Milan, where her studio combines the latest technologies from California's flourishing engineering and aerospace industries (important in California's Light and Space sculptural movement) with the historical legacy of Italy's design heritage.

| 2009 | XXX Table | B. 1961, San Diego. | Johanna Grawunder |

In 1967, Swiss designer Trix Haussmann and her partner Robert Haussmann founded the Zürich-based studio Allgemeine Entwurfsanstalt to create work whose use of materials and style playfully referenced architectural and art history. In the 1970s the couple put a name to their evolving aesthetic that celebrated artifice and illusion: Critical Mannerism, denoting a design-led approach that played with ambiguity, contradiction, and chance. Trained as an architect at ETH Zürich, Haussmann has gone on to complete more than 650 furniture, architectural, and interior design projects, which have collectively come to define postmodern Swiss design. The pop-inflected theatrics of the Haussmanns' work are designed to shock with classical and familiar forms twisted beyond the natural. The Lehrstück II (left) interprets an antique column, but distorts its classic form through a series of drawers when opened. The couple paired their designs with a conceptual manifesto, which included the "Log-O-rhythmic Slide Rule," a design tool which consisted of a list of one hundred adjectives and one hundred adverbs used in architectural discourse that could be slid up and down to make ten thousand new possible combinations in all. Now in their eighties, the pair continue to use design as a way to bend reality, adding ornament to modernist iconography. Their oeuvre is recognized by the Swiss Federal Office of Culture, who awarded the pair the Grand Prix Design in 2013.

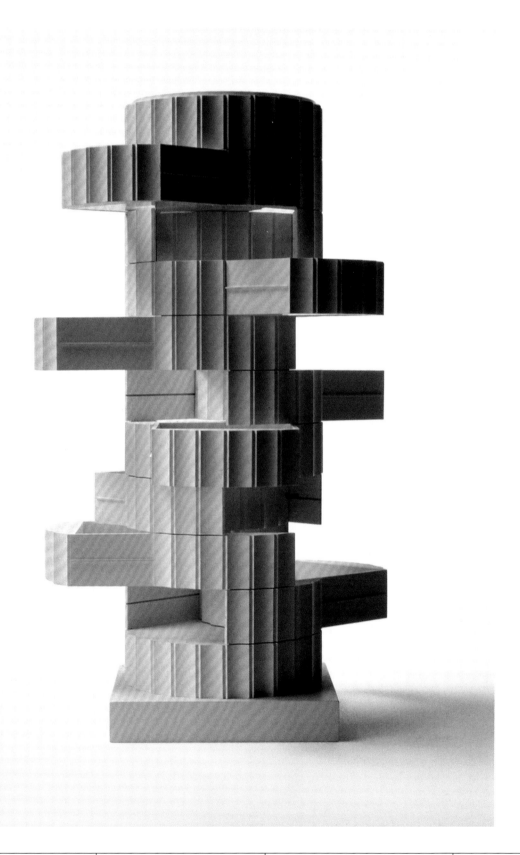

| 1978 | Lehrstück II | B. 1933, Zürich. |

Trix Haussmann

Mette Hay cofounded the design company HAY with her husband Rolf Hay in 2002; the pair met when both were working for a firm that represents Italian furniture brand Cappellini in Denmark. Having identified a gap in their native market for high-quality, accessible design objects, HAY today runs the gamut in scale from dishwashing sponges—rendered with charming smiley faces— to modular sofas in pleasing shades. Indeed, the couple cite the iconic mid-century design duo, Ray and Charles Eames (see p. 93), as an influence, particularly in respect to their sense of fun and use of color. At HAY, Mette primarily works on the development of housewares (above) with her team and designers from around the world; the playful Sowden Kettle, for example, was conceived by the Milan-based designer George Sowden, and is indicative of HAY's signature use of contrasting hues and clever detail, seen in its oversized handle and neat button. The Hays have a knack for identifying interesting design partners like Sowden, including Ana Kraš (see p. 141) and Inga Sempé (see p. 208). HAY headquarters in Copenhagen is situated in the same building as their flagship store; for Hay, connecting with customers fosters the brand ethos that good design should be available to the largest audience possible.

| Mette Hay | B. 1978, Herning, Denmark. | HAY Accessories | 2020 |

The ubiquity of refined white clay in the mid-century, used in popular ceramics from Europe and China, inspired ceramicist Edith Heath to harvest her own native clay, as she thought the imported material "gutless." Heath mixed an earthy, more durable clay—as seen in this early Tea Pot (above)—that is now itself ubiquitous across America through Heath Ceramics, based in Sausalito, California, one of the most successful potteries in the U.S. Founded in partnership with her husband Brian Heath in 1947, Heath Ceramics was run by the couple for close to sixty years. Heath was born to Danish parents and grew up in a large family as part of a farming community in Iowa. She studied art education before enrolling part-time at the Art Institute of Chicago. Alongside the forming technique of slipcasting, Heath embraced methods of production like hand-jiggering or jollying to produce her unpretentious designs at scale in the Heath factory; clients such as the City of Seattle, for example, specified Heath ashtrays for all public buildings in the city. From the late 1950s, Heath also fabricated architectural tiles. She was the first non-architect to be recognized by the American Institute of Architects when she was awarded the Industrial Arts Medal in 1971 for her red-brown tile cladding of the Pasadena Art Museum in California.

| 1947 | Tea Pot | B. 1911, Ida Grove, IA, USA. D. 2005, Tiburon, CA, USA. | Edith Heath |

Nicknamed by a colleague the "Grand Lady of Architecture," Franca Helg established a lifelong collaboration with architect Franco Albini, setting up an office together in the early 1950s. Shaped by her training at the Politecnico di Milano, where she would go on to teach, Helg first began working on both architectural planning and industrial design. With Albini she designed buildings in the tradition of Italian Rationalism, focusing on the application of new technologies—often integrating the infrastructure of a building with its structure—to shape reconstruction projects in Italy's postwar period. The logical consistency and historical integrity of Helg's built work translates into her furniture designs, which explore trapezoidal shapes coupled with traditional Italian craft methods to make simple expressive patterns and forms using raw and inexpensive materials. The Primavera Armchair (below)—made by Vittorio Bonacina—is a design demonstrating new methods of weaving rattan and wicker. With this design Helg pushed the boundaries of the traditional material and its means of production to play with the rhythm of a twisting base that unfolds to reveal the voluminous shape of the seat itself. Although the pair took the position that no design should be attributed to an individual author, it is Albini rather than Helg who is credited with the majority of their joint design work.

| Franca Helg | B. 1920, Milan.
D. 1989, Milan. | Primavera Armchair | 1967 |

Margarete Heymann-Löbenstein had a fast-paced career in ceramics, opening and closing two factories before the beginning of World War II. Her work focused on simple shapes, composed mostly of circles and triangles, compatible with emerging mass production techniques. Adorned with luminous blues and yellows, the geometries of her early tea services reflect the modernism of the Bauhaus, where she spent a year studying under Gerhard Marcks. Leaving the school after disagreements with her tutors, she founded the Haël-Werkstätten pottery, largely producing tea sets (above), which have become an icon of German modernism. The pottery employed over 120 people and exported to both the U.S. and U.K. Following the loss of her first husband and the defamation of her designs, labeled "degenerate" by the Nazis, Heymann-Löbenstein was forced to sell the pottery at a loss and moved to the UK with her two sons—the pottery was taken over by Hedwig Bollhagen (see p. 51). In the UK, she designed tableware at the Minton Factory in Stoke-on-Trent, but was let go because her Constructivist style was at odds with the traditional forms of English ceramics. Ostracized from both the Bauhaus canon and the British pottery community, she abandoned ceramics, settling with her second husband in London, where she used broken pottery to make paintings.

| c. 1930 | Tea Service | B. 1899, Cologne, Germany. D. 1990, London. | Margarete Heymann-Löbenstein |

Austrian-born, and America-based, designer Franziska Hosken was pioneering in multiple respects. In 1944 she became one of the first women to receive a Master of Architecture degree from Harvard's Graduate School of Design, where she studied under the tutelage of influential figures like Walter Gropius and László Moholy-Nagy, and in 1947, together with her husband James Hosken, she founded the successful furniture business Hosken. An early piece, Hosken's perforated metal and wooden Bar Cart (below) had an elegant steel-tube frame, and was featured in the trade publication *Furniture Forum* in the late 1940s. Despite its success, the company was short-lived, closing in 1951 when

Hosken had her first child. In addition to her work in design, Hosken was a writer and social activist. After the company's closure, she continued her work in design as an architectural photographer, journalist, and teacher, publishing numerous books, including her tome on urbanism, *The Language of Cities* (1968). After an extensive period of travel in which she observed the living conditions of women across Africa and in Afghanistan, Hosken published reports that put the issue of women's health on the agenda of major health organizations globally. In later life, Hosken pursued yet another line of work as a notable artist, while continuing to distribute a feminist newsletter well into her eighties.

| Franziska Hosken | B. 1920, Vienna. D. 2006, Lexington, MA, USA. | Bar Cart | 1947 |

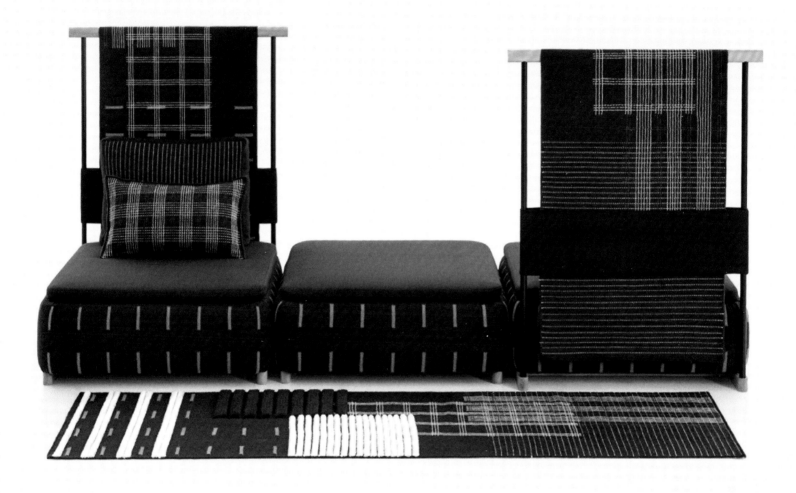

Architect Rossana Hu and her husband and partner in practice Lyndon Neri explore what they refer to as a transitional style between old and new and across continents, rejecting the idea that they represent simply a modern Chinese aesthetic. Trained in the United States, Hu is part of a Chinese diaspora that has returned to China, interested in incorporating the global with the local. As such Hu relies on broad research to combine existing, older techniques and methods with modern materials and forms. Neri and Hu worked together at architects Michael Graves & Associates before founding their own design and research office, Neri & Hu, in 2004.The couple also opened Design Republic, a retail store in Shanghai that brings together the work of designers from all over the world. Hu embraces a synthesis between interior design and architecture, arguing for a greater integration of intellectual discourse in the former, and a more holistic approach to the latter, which she reflects in furniture like the LAN Sofa (above). The modular sofa can be adapted to suit a multitude of spaces, configurations, and uses. The piece blends Eastern and Western design sensibilities; the deep indigo hue references Chinese home decoration traditions while the extended fabric back component emphasizes the sofa's Spanish manufacturer, GAN's, history as a textile brand.

| 2018 | LAN Sofa | B. 1968, Taiwan. | Rossana Hu |

Growing up in the shadows of Naples' Mount Vesuvius, Marialaura Rossiello Irvine was inspired by the area's rich cultural heritage. She studied architecture at the University of Naples Federico II—the oldest public university in the world—under Riccardo Dalisi, where her love and deep respect of history first influenced her work as a designer. She went on to get her degree in strategic design at the Politecnico di Milano, producing work that often applies tradition to modernity. The Fusto Bookshelf (above) demonstrates this humorously with its referential nod to the archetypal column, while dramatically changing its scale and context—the modular system, made from cement, uses columnar supports to prop up flat slabs, allowing for table, console, bookcase, or pedestal configurations. At once functional, fantastical, and full of irony, the Fusto system, produced by Forma & Cemento, riffs on an eternal form of architecture. Irvine's cross-disciplinary philosophy was developed with her partner, the late London-born designer James Irvine, after she joined his studio, Studio Irvine, in 2011. Since James Irvine's passing, Marialaura has continued his legacy. The practice now works across multiple disciplines, including interior design and strategic design for clients such as Mosaico+, Thonet, Muji, and Offecct.

Marialaura Rossiello Irvine

| B. 1972, Naples. | Fusto Bookshelf | 2020 |

Shinobu Ito graduated in textile design at Tama Art University, where her work looked at the structural dimensions of fabrics. Heavily influenced as a student by postmodern Italian design, Shinobu later moved to Italy to attend the Domus Academy in Milan, where she met her husband and business partner, Setsu Ito, who at the time was working as a tutor at the school. The pair were attracted to the city as a place of design history, but also of innovation and experimentation, so in 1997 they established a studio in Milan. They set out to integrate aspects of Japanese culture into their European-influenced work, prioritizing what they describe as the Eastern relationship to nature with a Western focus on people. Across their practice—which ranges from tableware to furniture and lighting—the Itos state that for them, design should "feel the rhythm of the universe." This perspective yielded modular pieces such as the Au Seating (below) designed for Edra, a lightweight system composed two forms that take the shape of the Japanese yin/yang sign when nestled together. An interest in natural forms extends to the Itos' concern for the environment; they believe in using science and technology to recycle materials for a secondary use.

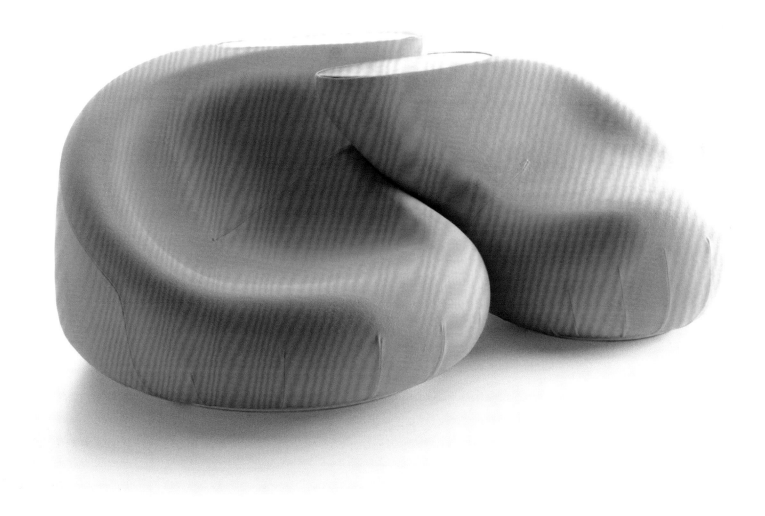

| 2003 | Au Seating | B. 1966, Tokyo. | Shinobu Ito |

Interior designer Sarita Posada and product designer Sophie Lou Jacobsen met on Craigslist after Posada posted an ad seeking assistance with a project, and Jacobsen, new to New York after moving from London, answered, finding in Posada a good friend and collaborator. Together they founded Studio Sayso—a combination of their names—with the goal of cultivating joy through well-crafted, thoughtfully produced objects. Their shared affinity for simple, playful shapes and bright colors finds form in products that are both affordable and accessible. Sayso's first range, Collection 01, is inspired by two of their biggest influences: Hungarian–French designer Mathieu Matégot (known for his rattan and steel-tube furniture) and Swiss architect Mario Botta. The series was produced in collaboration with craftspeople in Medellín, Colombia, and the collection's color-blocked palette was inspired by the vibrantly painted houses of Medellín—Posada's hometown. Lamp 01 (left) features a pleated shade and solid geometric base, while Chair 01 mixes powder-coated steel tubing with rattan, a material commonly used in Colombian furniture. Centering usability, the duo is invested in rethinking familiar furniture tropes to create modern pieces whose materiality honors history.

| Sophie Lou Jacobsen & Sarita Posada | Jacobsen B. 1987, Seattle. Posada B. 1987, Medellín, Colombia. | Lamp 01 | 2018 |

Grete Jalk is one of the most prominent twentieth-century Danish designers who has shaped modern design aesthetics. Formed of two conjoined pieces, the GJ Chair (above) is an elegant experiment in folded plywood. Presented at the 1963 International Furniture competition organized by British newspaper the *Daily Mail*, the chair was quickly acquired by the Museum of Modern Art, New York as part of their permanent collection. A piece of post-war design innovation, the chair—developed in collaboration with cabinetmaker Poul Jeppesen, and later mass produced by Lange Production from 2008—was instrumental in transforming manufacturing processes in Denmark. Jalk attended the Danish Design School in Copenhagen followed by an apprenticeship with cabinetmaker Karen Margrethe Conradsen. Her first-hand experience making furniture inspired her interest in low-cost solutions for modern living. Embracing societal progress, she also designed a self-supporting "den" (1947), which combined an all-in-one sofa bed, storage space, and desk for professional women. Throughout her career Jalk sought to make modern design more broadly accessible, including via her editorial work at the magazine *Mobilia* and her curatorial work organizing exhibitions featuring Danish design that traveled across the globe.

| 1963 | GJ Chair | B. 1920, Copenhagen. D. 2006, Denmark. | Grete Jalk |

Nata Janberidze and Keti Toloraia studied interior design together at the Tbilisi Academy of Arts, collaborating on ad hoc projects before founding their own interior and product design studio in 2007. Their practice, called Rooms Studio, draws on Asian and European storytelling traditions as inspiration, reflecting the geography and cultural rituals of their home country of Georgia. Much of their work is made from natural materials such as stone and marble, exhibiting primitive, elemental shapes that reference the bold architectural forms of Soviet style, resulting in pieces that feel simultaneously archaic and modern. "You can't wipe away the past," Janberidze has said. "You have to use it, change it, make peace with it." The Spiral Floor Lamp (left), featuring alternating matte and shiny surfaces to create a striped pattern, is a good example. Made from metal it seems quixotic for its sculptural form yet is also sturdy and functional. The Life on Earth collection featured twelve furniture pieces all handcrafted from the green and golden rock diabase—said to carry healing properties and bring good fortune, according to Georgian legend—and a series of sculptural terra-cotta objects, the latter featured in a showcase of female designers organized by the Egg Collective (see p. 33) at the 2018 NYCxDesign festival.

| Nata Janberidze & Keti Toloraia | Janberidze B. 1981, Tbilisi. Toloraia B. 1981, Tbilisi. | Spiral Floor Lamp | 2017 |

Chicago-based architect, designer, and educator Ania Jaworska creates work that is attentive to connections between art and architecture. The Unit 6 (Armchair) (above) is part of a collection of eight pieces of lacquered fiberglass and wood furniture, called SET, which all share simple yet exaggerated, physically imposing forms. Unit 6 was designed to intensify its user's body-consciousness in a humorous way, a challenge to the overde-termined design icon of the domestic chair. For Jaworska, SET pushes scale and form to a place almost in conflict with, or else prescriptive of, function. Jaworska holds a master's degree in architecture from the Cracow University of Technology in Poland, after which she relocated to Detroit to study at the Cranbrook Academy of Art. Since 2010, she has been an assistant professor at the University of Illinois at Chicago School of Architecture and runs her own eponymous practice. She has presented her work internationally in significant exhibits including the Venice Architecture Biennale, Chicago Architectural Biennale, and Lisbon Architecture Triennale, and was also a finalist for MoMA PS1's Young Architects Program in 2017—for which she proposed four individual pavilions comprised largely of reusable fabric and aluminum pole framework for the PS1 courtyard in New York.

| 2016 | Unit 6 (Armchair) | B. 1979, Stary Sącz, Poland. | Ania Jaworska |

Hilda Jesser-Schmid, along with Jutta Sika (see p. 212), is one of 180 women canonized by the Austrian Museum of Applied Arts (MAK) as having played a role in the development of Viennese arts and crafts through the influential Wiener Werkstätte. Jesser-Schmid studied at the Vienna School of Applied Arts under the school's founder, architect Josef Hoffmann, with whom she also collaborated through decorating a number of his glass pieces, while her own work of this period primarily focused on fashion and fabric design. She was also a prolific designer of tulle embroidery, working principally with elaborate, abstract plant motifs. Jesser-Schmid went on to work for the Wiener Werkstätte, where she expanded her expertise, creating ceramics, glassware, lamps, leather goods, toys, metal works, and wall paintings. Her rare ceramic works of this period are characterized by their emphasis on utility, with muted color and decoration combinations, like this box-shaped bowl (below), which features angular handles and is glazed in shades of yellow and green. She left the Wiener Werkstätte in 1922 after an argument with Philipp Häusler, and was appointed assistant professor at the Vienna Kunstgewerbeschule where she herself had once been a student. Jesser-Schmid taught until 1967, although was forced by the Nazis to briefly give up her post during World War II.

| Hilda Jesser-Schmid | B. 1894, Marburg an der Drau, Austria. D. 1985, Vienna. | Bowl | c. 1928 |

Voluminous round shapes define the lamps of Finnish designer Lisa Johansson-Pape. One of the country's leading designers of the twentieth century, Johansson-Pape co-founded the Illuminating Engineering Society of Finland and was a staunch advocate of Finnish design abroad, writing and lecturing on lighting in Japan. While she spoke often of functionality, believing the lamp a technical instrument for holding light, Johansson-Pape described herself as a "light artist." She was able to balance designing for the consumer market while introducing experimental techniques. While working for the glass manufacturers Iittala, she worked directly with the glassblowers to arrive at new collaborative forms that would inform new designs. Having studied furniture design at the Central School for Arts and Crafts in Helsinki, Johansson-Pape switched to lighting design during World War II when she found employment with the Stockmann-Orno lighting factory. Johansson-Pape designed a number of lamps there—including the cream Pendant Lamp (right)—working mainly in enameled metal, acrylic, and glass, and eventually became the company's artistic director with the ambition to bring "good light" to every Finnish home. Her use of simple forms conveyed her desire for design to be "neat and correct," but Johansson-Pape also had a keen eye for detail; in combination these features lend her lights both delicacy and warmth.

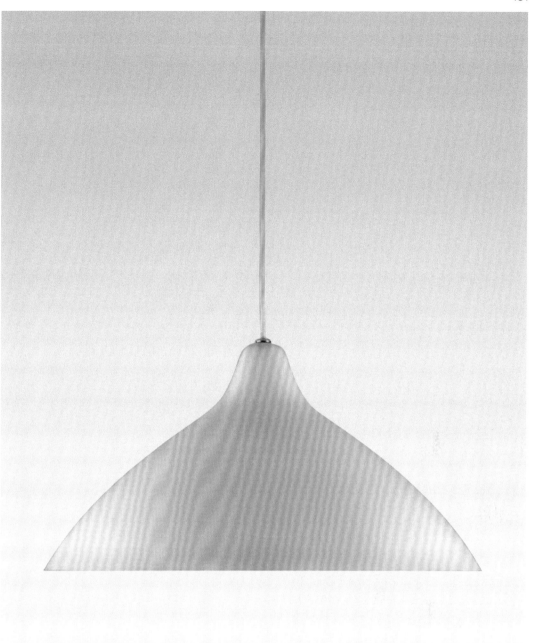

| 1947 | Pendant Lamp | B. 1907, Helsinki. D. 1989, Helsinki. | Lisa Johansson-Pape |

The Polder Sofa (above) manufactured for Vitra utilizes prolific Dutch designer Hella Jongerius's expertise in weaving and textiles, having previously spent ten years as art director for colors and materials at Vitra. In her book, *I Don't Have a Favourite Colour* (2016), Jongerius describes the research-led design methodology she developed at the Swiss furniture company, where she combined complex, highly engineered construction techniques with low-tech traditional crafts to make products that were contemporary and long lasting. The Polder Sofa, which comes in many colors, such as blues and greens, demonstrates this approach through its combination of different weaves in a low, asymmetrical form—polder refers to the flatlands common in parts of the

Netherlands. After graduating from Design Academy Eindhoven in 1993, she founded Jongeriuslab, where she continues to develop approaches to surfaces and color not only in textiles, but also in ceramics and furniture. In search of ways to make increasingly sustainable products, Jongerius prefers to work for companies with whom she has a long-established relationship. Originally based in

Rotterdam Jongerius sought to scale down, moving her studio to Berlin to stimulate new creativity without a large team around her. The size of her projects, however, has not diminished; her commissions remain varied to the extreme, from meticulously handcrafted one-off pieces to the outfitting of cabin interiors for Dutch airline KLM.

| 2005 | Polder Sofa | B. 1963, Utrecht, Netherlands. | Hella Jongerius |

The imaginative, sculptural quality of Turkish designer Merve Kahraman's work is influenced by nature, mythology, and in the case of the Cassini Floor Lamp (left), outer space. The lamp is named for the Cassini-Huygens project, a joint mission between the European Space Agency, NASA, and the Italian Space Agency to send a probe to Saturn. Its carved marble base supports the main structure of the lamp, which cantilevers to hold a white glass sphere encased in a wooden disk clad in cane, evoking the planet's ring. Kahraman came to design unexpectedly, having first studied molecular biology and genetics before enrolling in an interior design summer school in Milan. This led to degrees in interior design at the Istituto Europeo di Design in Milan and product design at Central Saint Martins in London. Following graduation, Kahraman worked for a number of architecture and design studios internationally, seeking to integrate industrial with spatial design. Based between New York and Istanbul, Kahraman draws inspiration primarily from her travels; she sketches her ideas before developing prototypes, which she then likes to "live with." Kahraman believes that because she spends times with her pieces before making modifications, her designs can cultivate an emotional bond of sorts between an object and its owner.

| Merve Kahraman | B. 1987, Ankara. | Cassini Floor Lamp | 2019 |

Ilonka Karasz was a prolific designer across a range of media, including textiles, furniture, lighting, ceramics, metalwork, and even toys. Karasz started young, submitting designs to national competitions run by various periodicals, and held her first solo show at the age of sixteen. After the death of her father in 1913 she relocated with her sister Mariska to New York, where they became part of the active art scene surrounding their bohemian Greenwich Village home. Karasz had a remarkable ability to shift between media, made evident through her textile designs that debuted as illustrations on the cover of the *New Yorker*, for whom she would go on to produce 186 covers between 1929 and 1972.

Karasz's liberal use of bright colors and fluid lines in her illustrated works are at odds with her early tea sets and furniture designs, such as her 1930s armchair (above), which reflect a more functional aesthetic rooted in Bauhaus geometry and craft techniques. The breadth of her output and style is a testament to her skills as an innovator, but also as a businesswoman who advocated for designers within an emerging market of industrial and contemporary design. In 1915 she set up the Society of Modern Art, a collective of European-American designers, and later was the founding director of the Design Group, a collective of industrial designers, craftspeople, and artists.

| c. 1930 | Armchair | B. 1896, Budapest.
D. 1981, New York. | Ilonka Karasz |

London-born designer Anna Karlin frames her journey in design by citing New York City—where she is now based—as a place of endless exploration and inspiration. After working for design agencies on projects in varying disciplines, Karlin moved to New York and set up her own practice. Her studio works across a range of media including jewelry, interiors, furniture, tabletop objects, and art direction for clients including Adidas and Fendi. Karlin is a self-taught furniture designer, and her multidisciplinary approach is underpinned by her broader training in the arts, having completed a foundation course at Central Saint Martins in London, followed by a degree in communication design at Glasgow School of Art, where she was encouraged to experiment with different materials and fabrication techniques. Karlin's Lady Lamp (left) is crafted from cast aluminum, brass, and glass; its hand-blown, tear-shaped lantern tilts, as if to appear quizzical, atop a pyramid base. Each of Karlin's designs—from totem-like brass-plated steel stools designed to be dotted around a room like chess pieces on a board to Windsor-style wooden chairs and a curving chaise longue supported by a sculptural, oversized steel sphere at one end—is created in-house through close collaboration with fabricators and craftspeople to retain the integrity of her ideas throughout the design process.

Anna Karlin

| B. 1984, London. | Lady Lamp | 2019 |

In the mid-twentieth century Bodil Kjær started to design products that, compared to the predominating furniture designs on the market, which to her felt outdated, better suited the evolving visual language of the buildings she was designing. Having studied architecture at the Royal College of Art and the Architectural Association in London, Kjær designed public interiors throughout the 1950s, developing her distinct principles for solving what she saw as emerging functional and aesthetic problems of the era. Kjær returned to Denmark to study interior design under Jørgen Ditzel and Finn Juhl, and in 1960, after spending a year in the U.S., set up her own studio in Copenhagen. Her furniture designs from the early 1960s were originally devised without commercial intent, but due to their popularity among other well known architects—including Paul Rudolph and Marcel Breuer, who specified different pieces to furnish their own buildings—Kjær's lamps, glassware, and furniture were put into production by C.I. Design. The desk (below) from her best-known series Elements of Architecture was featured in three early James Bond movies. Kjær later joined the engineering firm Arup to work on designing flexible office environments. She continued to work between Denmark and the U.S., where she was a tenured professor at the University of Maryland.

| 1959 | Office Desk | B. 1932, Hatting, Denmark. | Bodil Kjær |

Florence Knoll studied under Eliel Saarinen at the Cranbrook Academy of Art before attending the Architectural Association in London. The outbreak of World War II saw her return to the U.S., studying and working with Ludwig Mies van der Rohe, Walter Gropius, and Marcel Breuer. She began to design furniture after establishing the Knoll Planning Unit in 1946 with her husband, Hans Knoll, who had started his own furniture manufacturing company in New York after arriving from Stuttgart. In her position as co-director of Knoll Associates, Knoll was able to commission designs by some of her friends and acquaintances—Saarinen and Mies, as well as Harry Bertoia—that have come to define the pioneering

modernism of the age. Indeed, her quip that "good design is good business" understates her critical eye, keen understanding of consumer needs, and ability to identify talent. Under her steward-ship, designers like Anni Albers (see p. 20) and Lella Vignelli (see p. 232) created some of their most iconic pieces. The Sofa 1206 (above) is emblematic of her notion that furniture should form the background of an interior: or, as she said, "fill-in-pieces that no one else wanted to do." The elegant, streamlined sofa was meant as a perch, its light frame and modularity distinguishing it from the deeper, plumper alternatives that were common at the time.

| Florence Knoll | B. 1917, Saginaw, MI, USA. D. 2019, Coral Gables, FL, USA. | Sofa 1206 | 1954 |

Commonly cited as the godmother of industrial design in the U.S., Belle Kogan trained at the Pratt Institute, developing a strong relationship with the Quaker Silver Co. before becoming the first American woman to open her own design firm in 1931, where she employed an all-female team. Kogan began her trade in silver, due in part to her father's jewelry business, which she ran for ten years. Kogan was one of the first—along with her contemporary Helen Hughes Dulany (see p. 89)—in the U.S. to use the material in her homeware designs, including for her silver Serving Dish (below) for silversmith manufacturer Reed & Barton, for which ornamental detail is subordinated to functional shape. Kogan also worked in aluminum, ceramic, and glass, and experimented with early plastics for clocks and Bakelite jewelry, amassing numerous patents of her own. Her largest collaboration was with the Red Wing Pottery, for whom she designed a range of 100 pieces, known as the Kogan 100. Despite such success, she constantly sought to change her industry and the limiting perceptions associated with women practitioners; Kogan spoke out widely about the role of the modern designer, and in 1936 became a founding member and chair of the American Designers Institute in New York, a predecessor of what is now the Industrial Designers Society of America (IDSA).

| c. 1930 | Serving Dish | B. 1902, Ilyashevka, Russia. D. 2000, Israel. | Belle Kogan |

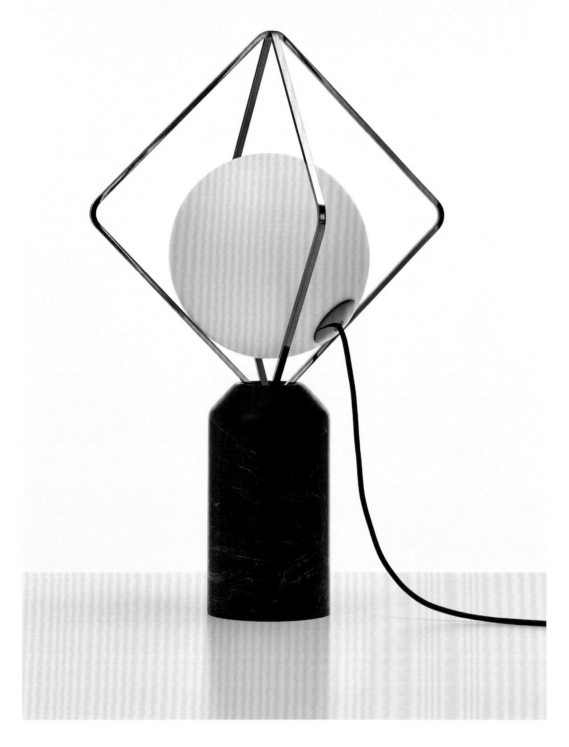

Czech designer Lucie Koldová was motivated to study design as a way to make things for everyday use. She graduated from the Academy of Arts, Architecture, and Design in Prague, before taking a job in Paris with artist and industrial designer Arik Levy. Koldová established her own eponymously named studio in 2012, at the same time beginning her collaboration with Brokis, the contemporary Czech glassware manufacturer known for their traditional techniques. Koldová describes glass as a Czech legacy, a material heritage she respects in her own approach by combining classic craft techniques with cutting-edge technologies. Since 2014, Koldová has worked as the art director of Brokis, continuing the company's strong tradition of hand-blowing, a technique it has perfected over its two-hundred-year-long history. Koldová is fascinated by glass's contrasting qualities of fragility and resilience, which she emphasizes in her lighting designs, which play with translucency to cultivate different atmospheres. She often works with bold colors, unusual proportions, and material juxtapositions, as seen in her Jack O'Lantern (left), which positions a matte orbed globe—also available in shades of smoky gray and soft pink—inside an elegantly geometric copper or chrome frame atop a marble base.

| Lucie Koldová | B. 1983, Cheb, Czech Republic. | Jack O'Lantern | 2018 |

The Serbian designer Ana Kraš graduated from the University of Applied Arts in Belgrade with a degree in interior architecture and furniture design. Influenced by her engineer father, Kraš is attracted to the problem-solving aspects of design. In 2011, she relocated from Belgrade to the U.S., expanding her creative design practice to include photography and illustration. The graphic character of her work is demonstrated in the maple wood Slon Round Table (below) manufactured by Matter Made—*slon* is the Serbian word for elephant—with a black-and-white striped tube base and a warm, earthy-hued slab on top. While Kraš drew a lot as a child, her design ideas now begin with text; she keeps sketchbooks close at hand so she can write down ideas as they come. Kraš prototypes her ideas in three dimensions before committing them to paper. This slow, craft-based approach underpins much of her work, and is reflected in the methodical wrapping of recycled textiles around sculptural, powder-coated steel armatures to create her signature Bonbon Lamps produced by Hay. These bold, colorful lampshades are handwoven with discarded yarn used in the fashion industry.

| 2015 | Slon Round Table | B. 1984, Belgrade, Serbia. | Ana Kraš |

Teresa Kruszewska studied at the Interior Design department of the Academy of Fine Arts in Warsaw, and later at the Rhode Island School of Design in the United States. In Poland she was taught by, and later worked for, Jan Kurzątkowski, who played a formative role in shaping her design approach, which combined a concern for proportion with the ergonomics and folk patterns she observed in modern Scandinavian design. Kruszewska designed the Scallop Chair (left) for the Ład Artists' Cooperative in 1956, during a time when Poland began to open up to the West, which led to an influx of modernist influence and creativity. Kruszewka's furniture stood out at this time for her innovative use of skillfully shaped plywood, which she faced difficulty producing as local manufacturers were reticent to engage new technologies. The chair was exhibited widely, but never mass produced. Kruszewska is also known for her children's furniture designs of the same era, inspired by assisting her sister and brother-in-law, both pediatricians, with their work in a hospital. This work is best seen in the entire collection of chairs, tables, and benches that Kruszewska designed for the American Pediatric Clinic Foundation in Kraków. Kruszewska was able to create organic, sculptural furniture designs heavily based on scientific data, which she collected diligently decades before others did the same.

| Teresa Kruszewska | B. 1927, Warsaw. D. 2014, Warsaw. | Scallop Chair | 1956 |

Agata Kulik-Pomorska co-founded design studio Malafor with Pawel Pomorski in 2004, both having studied at the Faculty of Architecture and Design at the Academy of Fine Arts in Gdańsk, Poland. Together they create furniture and smaller objects, with a focus on recycling and ecology in their approach to materials. In 2012 the duo was awarded a Red Dot Award—a German prize— for the Blow Sofa, which is created entirely from inflated recycled paper bags. The PAPER+ Armchair (below) is a continuation of the theme, consisting of a washable, highly durable, and lightweight paper and foldable metal arms. The chair led to the development of a collection of furniture, each piece formed from inflatable paper bags and a metal frame. Kulik-Pomorska started her career as a designer after receiving the Award of the President of the Republic of Poland for her final degree project, which was followed by an exhibition at the Królikarnia Palace, part of the National Museum in Warsaw. The show included Malafor's Ladder (2004), comprising a 6-ft-high (2 m) ladder with a seat perched on top, encouraging users to challenge their point of view. Since then the work produced by the studio has continued to combine simple ideas with humor, often realized through a materially and economically resourceful approach that elevates everyday objects through rethinking their use.

| 2012 | PAPER+ Armchair | B. 1976, Warsaw. | Agata Kulik-Pomorska |

Anna Lindgren and Sofia Lagerkvist established their design studio, Front, in Stockholm in 2004. They experiment with high-tech materials and radical manufacturing methods to produce fantastical furnishings, lighting, and homewares ranging from an abstract Royal Delft vase formed by a computer simulated gust of wind, to a lamp rendered as a life-size black horse, replete with a lampshade on its head. The pair met while studying industrial design at the University of Arts, Crafts, and Design in Stockholm. Since then, their inventive, highly conceptual approach has infused their work with humor and play; the Furia Rocking Horse (below), for example, was inspired by the curvilinear frame of

Michael Thonet's classic Vienna Rocking Chair (1881). The rocking horse is made by hand, using the same bentwood technique as Thonet, and is similarly designed as an heirloom, with leather seat and ears, intended to be passed on through generations. Elsewhere, a series of slumbering creatures, ranging from small ceramic birds to a knitted ottoman in the shape of a bear, demonstrates Front's research-based approach, in this case focused on the relationship between humans and figurative objects. Front's work is held in a number of international collections, including at the Museum of Modern Art, New York and the Vitra Design Museum, Weil am Rhein, Germany.

| Sofia Lagerkvist & Anna Lindgren | Lagerkvist B. 1972, Stockholm. Lindgren B. 1974, Stockholm. | Furia Rocking Horse | 2016 |

The work of sculptor and designer Claude Lalanne courted controversy throughout her career with an uncompromisingly avant-garde, humorous approach. Lalanne met her husband François-Xavier in 1952; collectively known as "Les Lalannes," the duo worked separately until 1964 when they collaborated on an exhibition *Zoophites*, centered on their shared interest in nature. The bronze Table Lotus et Singe Carrée (above) finds inspiration in flora and fauna, expressed through botanical motifs that repeat throughout Lalanne's work. She considered herself primarily a sculptor and Lalanne's expressive forms always retain functionality, as evident in pieces like her iconic Ginkgo Chair (1996), whose back is modeled on a leaf form. Lalanne was initially taught metalwork by her father, before going on to study architecture at the École des Beaux-Arts and the École des Arts Décoratifs, both in Paris. After her graduation, she began making jewelry, working with molding and electroplating, using metal casts of her friends' mouths to create fantastical necklaces, earrings, and bracelets. Her work is held by institutions including the Centre Pompidou in Paris and Cooper Hewitt, Smithsonian Design Museum in New York, and favored by the likes of Serge Gainsbourg, Yves Saint Laurent, and Jacques Grange.

| 2013 | Table Lotus et Singe Carrée | B. 1924, Paris. D. 2019, Fontainebleau, France. | Claude Lalanne |

146

Although Elizabeth Eyre de Lanux's career as a designer lasted just six years, the period was fruitful; she designed a range of furniture, rugs, and lighting fixtures that employed simple forms and muted shades, defining a new age of modern comfort. Born into a distinguished family in Pennsylvania, Eyre de Lanux studied painting at the Arts Students League in New York, before moving to Paris in 1919 after marrying a French diplomat. Eyre de Lanux exhibited her own work while working alongside designers such as Eileen Gray (see p. 109), for whom she pioneered lacquer techniques incorporating the innovative use of cork, amber, and linoleum. Her own Dressing Table (opposite and above) is sheathed entirely in parchment; two boxes at the front swivel open to reveal a black lacquered interior. Eyre de Lanux's biography is filled with anecdotes of her impassioned affairs with both men and women, one of which led to a successful business partnership with the rug designer Evelyn Wyld. Other contemporaries and fellow members of Paris's high society, like Picasso, Matisse, and Picabia, were social acquaintances and influenced Eyre de Lanux's other vocation for painting. Going simply by the name Eyre de Lanux, she reported for the *New Yorker* and *Harper's Bazaar* upon her return to New York in the 1960s, and spent her later years illustrating and writing children's books.

| c. 1930 | Dressing Table | B. 1894, Johnstown, PA, USA.
D. 1996, New York. | Elizabeth Eyre de Lanux |

As a child, Francesca Lanzavecchia would collect household objects so that she could study how they were made, her attention a result of being brought up in a home in which both parents were doctors and discussion was often centered on science. She went on to study product design at the Politecnico di Milano, later attending the Design Academy Eindhoven. There she met Singaporean designer Hunn Wai, with whom in 2010 she founded industrial design studio Lanzavecchia + Wai, which has offices in Italy and Singapore (headed by Lanzavecchia and Wai respectively). The furniture and products of the studio collide material innovation with forms that often explore the physical needs of the human body and encourage interaction. Lanzavecchia explains her design process as beginning "a bit like that of the scientist in the phase of analytical observation of a phenomenon, without knowing the results of the research." This open-minded approach results in an output that is varied to the extreme, from practical but pleasing walking canes for the elderly to wool rugs emblazoned with a mutant insect. Made for Living Divani, the Pebble Desk (above) draws on the materiality of a stone, which also influences the irregular shape of the mirror. Luxurious details, such as the leather top, belie the desk's simple form and lend the piece a surrealist spirit.

Francesca Lanzavecchia	B. 1983, Pavia, Italy.	Pebble Desk	2018

Erwine and Estelle Laverne established their design practice in 1938, although it would be nearly twenty years until they released their renowned Invisible Group furniture. The transparent acrylic used in the series gave each of the four pieces—one of which is the Daffodil Chair (right)—an ethereal, nearly immaterial quality, as if each piece could disappear into its surroundings. Estelle imbued each design with a poetic sensibility through her sensitive handling of language—it was Estelle who named and wrote descriptive copy for all of the couple's works—as well as her fine arts training as a painter at the Art Students League in New York. It was there she met Erwine, whose own background in mural painting cemented the couple's reputation as artists, with one of their specialties being hand-painted wallpaper. Having created a successful design company in New York, the couple were able to acquire part of Laurelton Hall in Long Island, which they ran as an artist colony as well as their own production studio. They hosted important figures such as Alexander Calder, who designed a mobile for the estate and wallpaper for their design company. In 1952 the Lavernes were issued a cease-and-desist order by neighbors who complained they were manufacturing industrially in a residential zone. The Lavernes lost their fortune in the ensuing litigation, but their undisputed style, innovation, and humor live on in their designs.

| 1957 | Daffodil Chair | B. 1915, New York. D. 1997, Long Island, NY, USA. | Estelle Laverne |

Monling Lee of design studio JUMBO seeks to make objects that are reductive, so simple that they are almost, in JUMBO's words, "dumb." With no seams, fixings, or fastenings, JUMBO's creations deny the material from which they are made to create a sense that their designs are in some way organisms. Embracing a cartoonish appearance that abstracts form, the studio finds joy in the soft edges and clumsiness of such dematerialization, reveling in the childlike and the whimsical to produce what they call a "loveable and human response" to their furniture. Created during the lockdown of 2020, the Sport Sofa (above) is part of JUMBO's Creature Comfort collection, which researches the influence of objects on emotions by creating tension between physical and digital surroundings. The result is tactile but utterly surreal—the neoprene-upholstered sofa calls to mind an oversized tennis ball. Given how highly technical the fabrication of Lee's furniture is, it is unsurprising that she met her creative partner Justin Donnelly while both studying architecture. They began working together in 2018. Alongside JUMBO, she runs the hugely popular Instagram and website @colorindex, which documents the intersection of fashion and the built environment through color-blocked visual conversations between Lee's personal style and her surroundings.

| Monling Lee | B. 1982, Taipei. | Sport Sofa | 2020 |

In the 1950s, the Museum of Modern Art's advent of the Good Design movement through the success of its Good Design awards and exhibitions, combined with improved mass-production techniques, inspired the idea of self-assembly furniture, which is now ubiquitous. Los Angeles-based designer Olga Lee was an early proponent, designing for the short-lived Designers' Plan, a program which invited designers to make available instructions that required "a little money and a little imagination" for willing consumers to build their own furniture. She ran a successful design shop in Los Angeles with her husband, the acclaimed furniture designer Milo Baughman. Although they shared a business, the couple designed mostly independently from one another, allowing Lee's iconic eponymous aluminum lamp (right) for manufacturer Ralph O. Smith to win her sole credit for her Good Design award in 1955, as well as inclusion in that year's associated exhibition. A graduate of the Chouinard Art Institute (now the California Institute of the Arts), Lee studied interior and industrial design, going on to form part of the Californian avant-garde. After Lee and Baughman divorced, she relocated to the East Coast, establishing her own company, Olga Lee Design, through which she produced furniture commercially. Much of this output is housed in the collections of major institutions, including the Art Institute of Chicago and the Victoria & Albert Museum in London.

| 1952 | Olga Lee Lamp | B. 1924, CA, USA. D. 2014, Sarasota, FL, USA. | Olga Lee |

Designer Geke Lensink established her studio in 1988, after graduating from the ArtEZ University of the Arts in Zwolle, the Netherlands. Trained in the spirit of the Bauhaus, Lensink specialized in interior and commercial architecture for two decades before developing her own line of furniture and ceramic tableware, a goal she had wished to pursue since her early studies. Lensink experiments with emerging technologies with an aim to simplify both materiality and form, resulting in a graphic sensibility, which has been described as matter of fact. While minimalist, Lensink's work has a playful side, often using oversized silhouettes with each object almost taking on a personality as the result of her highly refined forms. She often limits her color palette to black or white, as seen in her sturdy Kitchen Stool (left), whose expanded polystyrene (EPS) elements are cut by hand. The piece is part of an ongoing project by Lensink called Souvenir, which also includes a handwoven monochrome wool rug and an oversized octagonal ceramic vase inscribed with a geometric motif, among other limited-edition objects. Lensink has also collaborated with designer Jesse Visser to create a number of pieces for Dutch brand Brothers and Sons.

| Geke Lensink | B. 1963, Eibergen, Netherlands. | Kitchen Stool | 2010 |

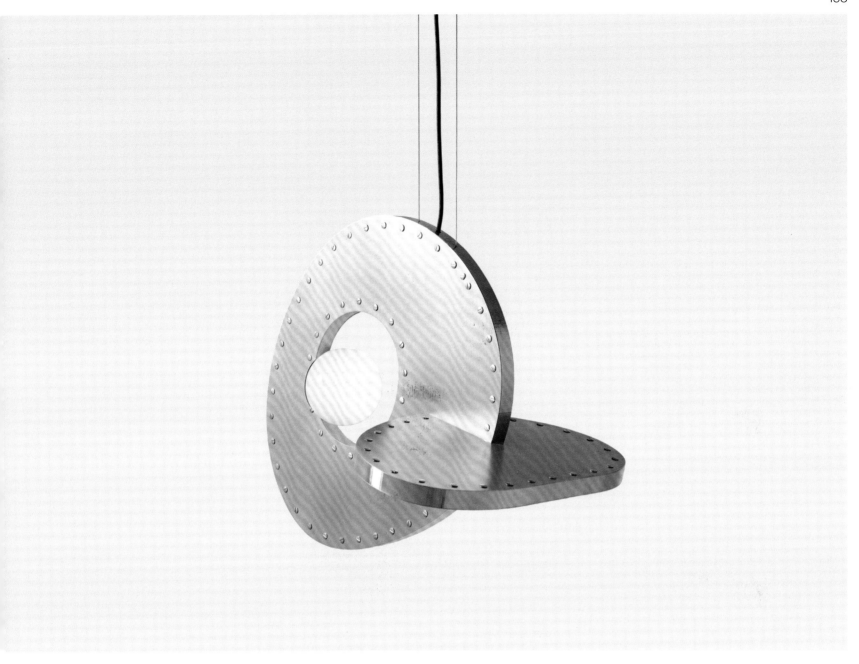

The career of lighting designer Rosie Li was kickstarted when her thesis project—the Stella sconce, notable for its Op Art-inspired geometric form—was picked up by Brooklyn-based manufacturer Roll & Hill. They were introduced to Li's work by Lindsey Adelman (see p. 17), then a visiting critic at the Rhode Island School of Design where Li was a student. Li was subsequently recruited by the company as a junior designer, where she learned all aspects of lighting production, enabling her to set up her own Brooklyn-based studio with her Roll & Hill colleague, engineer Philip Watkins. For Li, science is an applied art, and her pared-back yet optically engaging work seeks to challenge visual perception. With forms

that are both organically inspired and modular, she blurs the line between the practical and sculptural. The majority of her pieces are handmade in-house. The Pebble Hanging Lamp (above) is inspired by stacked stones, which Li interprets through rounded, interlocking planes of machined aluminum fastened together by orderly lines of rivets both functional and ornamental, recalling the aesthetic of airplane hulls. The fixture is lit from an illuminated milk glass globe suspended within the aluminum form. Designed in collaboration with architect Michael Yarinsky, the lamp is indicative of Li's ability to combine the organic and the industrial.

| 2018 | Pebble Hanging Lamp | B. 1989, Zhengzhou, China. | Rosie Li |

With dual Finnish and Italian heritage, Francesca Lindh's work expresses influences from both countries. She studied at the Liceo artistico Ripetta in Rome, graduating in 1958, and moved to Finland to continue her studies at the Institute of Industrial Arts. With her husband and fellow potter, Richard Lindh, she established a studio in 1953, working in parallel with the Arabia Company, Finland's oldest ceramic brand, where she started out making vases and dishes. It was at Arabia that the Lindhs were able to develop their own distinctive style, experimenting with new fabrication possibilities. Lindh stayed at Arabia for more than thirty years, becoming head of the art department. The stackable

Double Tea Pot (above) was co-designed by the Lindhs and has two handles and two different ways to serve tea. It was produced in the Abruzzo region of Italy, where Lindh was born, surrounded by mountains and known for its innovative ceramic, metal, stone, and wood production techniques. As a result, the tea pot combines a simple graphic form with a handicraft sensibility. This is characteristic of Lindh's designs, which demonstrate years of skill developed from embracing the wide material spectrum of clay and its raw qualities. Even their intricate, hand-rolled surface decoration pays homage to the natural, with organic forms drawn directly from nature.

| Francesca Lindh | B. 1931, Anversa degli Abruzzi, Italy. | Double Tea Pot | 1956 |

Aljoud Lootah has become one of Dubai's leading designers through work that embraces traditional Emirati silhouettes and injects them with modern elements and patterns, such as deconstructed classical Arabesque motifs, to arrive at something both contemporary and grounded in history. Trained in graphic design, Lootah moved into working in product design after joining a program called Design Road Professional (now Tanween by Tashkeel)—a year-long professional mentorship program in product design in London and Barcelona. This experience allowed her to see how her graphic design work in two dimensions could translate to three-dimensional forms. Lootah's origami-like Oru Cabinet (left) was inspired by her playing with Post-it notes, and joins a series of pieces that includes a faceted teak and copper mirror, chair, and table lamp. The National Gallery of Victoria in Melbourne, Australia acquired two items from this series, making Lootah the first Emirati designer to have her work in the permanent collection of an international gallery. An interest in exploring a new material culture within Emirati design led Lootah to establish her own studio in Dubai Design District in 2015. She works closely with artisans to identify opportunities for modernizing craft. In 2019, Sheikh Mohammed Bin Zayed Al Nahyan gifted Pope Francis a design by Lootah's studio.

| 2015 | Oru Cabinet | B. 1983, Dubai, UAE. | Aljoud Lootah |

Althea McNish injected color into postwar fashion and textiles with vibrant, natural imagery inspired by her native Trinidad. In 1951, McNish moved from the Caribbean to London upon a scholarship to study at the Architectural Association. Feeling that the structure of a degree in architecture was inhibitive, she enrolled in a print course at the London School of Printing and Graphic Arts where she met the sculptor Eduardo Paolozzi, who encouraged McNish to apply her abilities in print to textiles. McNish was one of the Royal College of Art's first Black postgraduates. Her distinct style was soon noticed by the chairman of Liberty, the famous London department store, who from 1957 commissioned numerous fabric designs, notable for their tropical motifs, and McNish developed a long-standing partnership with Zika Ascher's textile company, which supplied fabrics to the likes of Yves Saint Laurent and Dior. Golden Harvest (below)—inspired by McNish's impressions of wheat fields in Essex combined with the sugarcane fields of her homeland—became one of textile manufacturer Hull Traders' bestselling upholstery fabrics. McNish was also active within the design community, as a member of the board of the UK Design Council, and was awarded the Chaconia gold medal in Trinidad for her contributions to art and design.

| Althea McNish | B. 1924, Port of Spain, Trinidad and Tobago. D. 2020, London. | Golden Harvest | 1959 |

The Gallery dining room at Sketch, a popular tea house and restaurant in London, is saturated in dusty pink, further expressed in the now iconic velvet Charlotte Chair (above), whose shapely form cocoons diners. For designer India Mahdavi, who unsurprisingly has been dubbed the "Queen of Color," her radical use of pink in this setting is intended to convey strength, challenging the conventional association of the color with frivolity and the feminine. Mahdavi enjoys combining things that, to her mind, shouldn't go together, using her three showrooms in Paris to primarily showcase her unique approach to color. Born in Tehran, Mahdavi led a nomadic childhood living in Germany, the United States, and France, where she studied architecture at the École des Beaux Arts in Paris, from which she graduated in 1986. Mahdavi then went to New York to study graphic and furniture design at Parsons School of Design and the Cooper Union, respectively. Returning to Paris, Mahdavi directed influential French interior designer Christian Liaigre's studio before opening her own in 2000, where, contrary to Liaigre's minimal style, her projects consciously integrate pop influences and bold shapes to advance her vision of the cosmopolitan. For Mahdavi, design is about joyfulness, and imbuing tradition with a playful take on the contemporary.

| 2014 | Charlotte Chair | B. 1962, Tehran. | India Mahdavi |

Dutch designer Rianne Makkink was a practicing architect and urbanist when she took a hiatus to travel around the Netherlands on a horse-drawn cart as part of Sloom—which means "slow" in Dutch—which she initiated in 2002 with architect and educator Herman Verkerk. Through a series of activities documented in a self-published magazine and website, sloom.org, Sloom embraces "the potential of slowness" and prioritizes "moderation rather than acceleration" in architecture and urban and landscape design. Also since 2002, Makkink has run her Rotterdam-based studio, Makkink & Bey, with designer Jürgen Bey. With Bey, Makkink's work is primarily interested in context regardless of typology or scale; all their projects from product to furniture to architecture are treated with equivalence. The Pixelated Rug (right), produced for CSrugs and designed with Nai-Dan Chang, is part of a series of wool carpets made from a digital tufting method specially designed by Makkink; the decorative pattern produces a QR code that, when scanned by users, directs them to an online gallery of earlier pixelated furniture, blurring the line between the tangible and intangible dimensions of everyday life. Makkink's work brings together different forms of professional knowledge to expand the role of the designer, an approach she has taught over the years at many institutions, including the Sint-Lucas School of Architecture in Ghent, and at Ghent University, the Design Academy Eindhoven, University of Art and Design Linz, and the Delft University of Technology.

| Rianne Makkink | B. 1964, Gorssel, Netherlands. | Pixelated Rug | 2020 |

Cecilie Manz grew up around ceramics in her parents' workshop and originally wanted to be a painter. However, a self-declared furniture design "nerd," Manz instead studied at the Royal Danish Academy's School of Design, and participated in an exchange program with the University of Art and Design in Helsinki, where she sought to learn about the Finnish design tradition. After completing her studies in 1997, Manz founded her own studio in Copenhagen the following year, and established a reputation as a designer who creates pieces that are both striking and quiet, possessing an elegant simplicity that might remain in the background until one is rewarded through a closer look. The entirely collapsible Plint Coffee Table (below) exemplifies this. It is made from three types of wood—Oregon pine, Kalmar pine, and oak—and a system of soft, subtle leather hinges connects the sides and top of the table, using two wedges to brace the table's structure. Manz's work is emblematic of a new generation of makers reinventing the traditions of Danish design, while retaining a historical commitment to finely crafted forms with a high level of material integrity. Manz was named as Designer of the Year by influential French trade fair Maison & Objet in 2018, and was the recipient of the Honorable Award from the Danish Art Foundation in 2020.

| 2020 | Plint Coffee Table | B. 1972, Odsherred, Denmark. | Cecilie Manz |

Sabine Marcelis—who spent her adolescence in New Zealand—came to the field of design after an extensive period of travel, deciding to finish her studies at the Design Academy Eindhoven. Upon graduation, Marcelis founded her own studio. Based in Rotterdam, the studio comprises a young team balancing conceptual projects with commercial commissions. Marcelis enjoys working with ephemeral materials, having completed substantial projects that employ water and light to create what she describes as moments of wonder. While by contrast more solid, her furniture design also emphasizes pushing the limits of her materials and production capabilities in search of new fabrication possibilities. Marcelis's frequent use of resin highlights her attentive approach

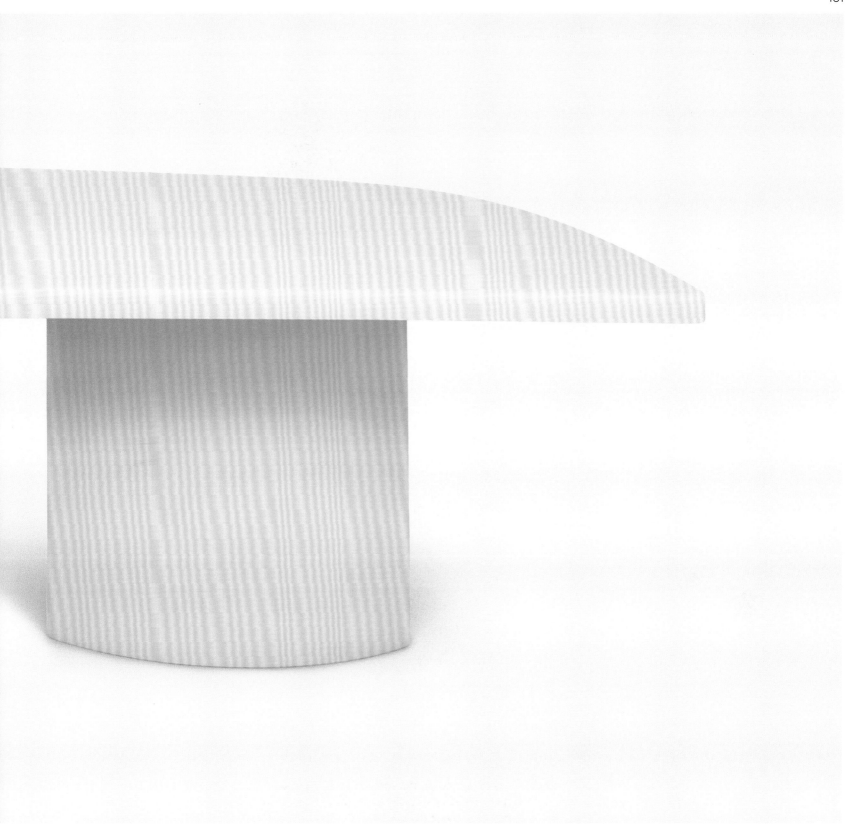

to the sensorial; the interplay between light and movement that lends her pieces their effect is driven by user activation. The SOAP Table (above) for Etage Projects is designed to take into consideration the sounds made during dining, with the softer materiality of resin dulling the noise of cutlery as it meets the table. Her other works range from studies of the optical effects achieved by materials like resin or glass to large-scale installations, such as her iridescent sundial for watch brand A. Lange & Söhne, which combines geometric elements to shape color through light.

| 2018 | SOAP Table | B. 1985, Alkmaar, Netherlands. | Sabine Marcelis |

Revolutionary in its technical transformation of the cooking process, Grethe Meyer's Firepot (below) was designed to relieve women—increasingly joining the workforce, yet still burdened with domestic duties—by shortening meal preparation time through dinnerware that could go straight from freezer to oven to table. Made from fireproof cordierite porcelain, the Firepot, manufactured for the Royal Copenhagen Porcelain Factory, made Meyer one of Denmark's most renowned designers despite her understated design sensibility. Simplicity of form and an unglazed buff porcelain finish lend the dinnerware a natural feel, like much of Meyer's other designs, which are characterized by their formal anonymity. Meyer's work reflects her belief that design must be uncomplicated and products easy to use so that owners may derive pleasure from the regularity of their use. After studying architecture at the Royal Academy of Fine Arts in Copenhagen, Meyer worked for the Building Research Institute specializing in housing. She advocated for the retention of smaller companies employing skilled craftsmen to maintain quality. However, mechanization ultimately rendered many of Meyer's products obsolete; her Firepot range went out of production in 1986 with the advent of aluminum foil trays, which reduced washing up and overtook oven-to-table dinnerware.

| Grethe Meyer | B. 1918, Svendborg, Denmark. D. 2008, Denmark. | Firepot Series | 1976 |

Hikaru Mori graduated from Tokyo University of the Arts in 1987, where she later obtained her PhD in architecture. Mori moved to Milan to study interior design at the Istituto Europeo di Design, after which she opened her own architecture and design studio in 1993. She went on to form, with Italian architect Maurizio Zito, Zitomori studio in 1996, based in Milan and Avellino, which has since undertaken a wide range of projects spanning architecture, landscape design, interiors, furniture, and lighting—from organic, aromatic cedar benches to a subterranean concrete winery. Mori's approach is informed by traditional Japanese architecture and her interest in design fluidity, particularly when navigating boundaries between interior and exterior spaces. She seeks to integrate nature into her buildings, and the spatial surroundings of objects with her products. The elegant Carmencita Lamp (below) for Nemo-Cassina, for example, is multipurpose and invites interaction. At once formal and theatrical, differently sized conical fabric shades can be positioned and oriented on the illuminated glass body to control light distribution and to express different moods. The product was awarded Best Lamp by the Wallpaper* Design Awards in 2012.

| 2012 | Carmencita Lamp | B. 1964, Sapporo, Japan. | Hikaru Mori |

Sonneberg, Germany was once the world's center of toy production, and so it's fitting that Renate Müller, who has lived in the town her whole life, grew up to be a toy designer. She assisted in her family's toy factory and studied at Sonneberg's Polytechnic for Toy Design. While studying, Müller's teacher, Helene Haeusler, began a project looking at the therapeutic effects of large-scale toys on children with physical and mental disabilities, and suggested that Müller design a range of animals. The resulting menagerie debuted in 1967 at the Leipzig Trade Fair in 1967, the same year Müller graduated, and included jute and leather seals, elephants, giraffes, bears, and hippopotamuses (above) intended for balance training and orthopedic exercise. As part of the design process, each animal was rigorously tested by psychiatric hospitals and clinics. After completing her studies, Müller worked for her family's company managing all aspects of the design and production process, and was able to bring her animal designs into production, adding new creatures annually. After the nationalization of the toy factory in 1976, Müller embarked on an independent career with her own workshop specializing in entirely handmade toys. In 1990, Müller acquired the rights to her early work and continues to produce limited quantities of her stimulating and highly tactile creatures.

| Renate Müller | B. 1945, Sonneberg, Germany. | Therapeutic Toys | 1969 |

Ignacia Murtagh works across furniture, textiles, and ceramics. Her minimal, often sculptural pieces are deeply rooted in the material culture and tradition of her native Chile. Murtagh's work, particularly in ceramic, is made in a limited palette of predominantly white to create what she describes as "silence," so as to amplify the symbolism taking shape in her work through careful and continuously contoured forms. Works like her bone china tableware collection Lof (below) use form to center spiritual traditions of Chile's indigenous peoples. Murtagh collaborated with five museums over the course of a year to analyze original artifacts that inspired eight contemporary pieces of her own, whose elegantly ballooning forms pay homage to Mapuchean ceramics. Murtagh has studied design all over the world, first at the Pontifical Catholic University of Chile in Santiago, and later at the Royal Danish Academy of Fine Arts in Copenhagen, going on to continue her education in ceramics at the Royal College of Art in London. She has since completed an apprenticeship at the Royal Crown Derby bone china manufacturers in the north of England and a residency at the Textile Arts Center in New York.

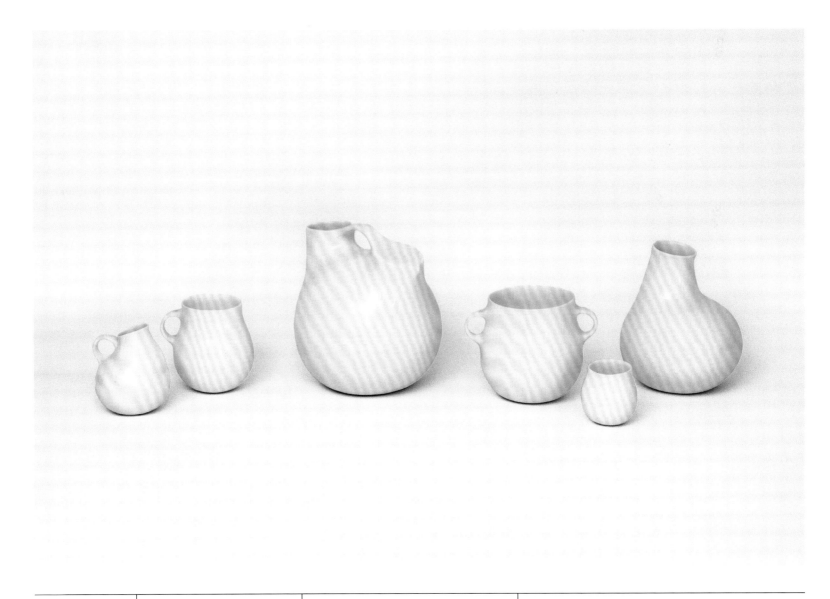

| 2016 | Lof Tableware | B. 1989, Santiago, Chile. | Ignacia Murtagh |

Mira Nakashima dedicated her practice to a single material: wood. Her pieces celebrate the knots and idiosyncrasies found in timber, reflecting the dictum of her father, George Nakashima, that there is a perfect and singular piece of wood for each design. Nakashima inherited her father's woodworking studio in 1990 after having worked with him since returning from studying architecture in Tokyo at Waseda University. Her own reverence for the material and demonstrable woodworking skills did not prevent her from being fired on a number of occasions by her father for subordination; indeed, Nakashima states she was not at first interested in assisting him, and that she was only attracted back to New Hope, Pennsylvania because he had promised to build her a house. Now a woodworker and craftsperson in her own right, Nakashima sees a parallel between furniture design and architecture, which both unite function and economy, just at different scales. Her approach has introduced more angles and curves to the work of Nakashima Studios, which, although it has now adopted a more collaborative working culture, continues to be based on the craft-based traditions of her father—the richness and texture of wood is still very much in evidence. The refined nature of Nakashima's work means it is largely shown in gallery settings or sold direct to private clients. The walnut Concordia Chair (left) was created for a group of local chamber musicians. Its flat seat and upright back mean the musicians can play exuberantly without any obstruction to bowing.

| Mira Nakashima | B. 1942, Seattle. | Concordia Chair | 2003 |

The avant-garde design group Studio Alchimia—founded by Alessandro Guerriero and Bruno Gregori in Milan—presented their handmade furniture series called Bau.Haus Uno in 1978, announcing themselves as part of the Radical Design movement in Italy. The group introduced color, pattern, and asymmetry as a counterpoint to the austere nature of Italian design at the time, which Paola Navone—the only woman in the collective—described as like "a black canvas." Navone studied architecture at the Politecnico di Torino, before traveling widely in search of alternative architectural utopias promoted by groups including Archizoom Associati and Arcosanti in Arizona. After winning the

Osaka International Design Award in 1983, Navone spent much of the 1980s and 1990s living and working part-time in Hong Kong and throughout Southeast Asia. Indeed, her designs are a mix of cultural influences, often melding North African and Asian artisanal handicrafts with modern forms. The futuristic Ghost Armchair (above) for Italian furniture manufacturer Gervasoni is notable for its reflective, foil-like upholstery and demonstrative of her aim to "expand the horizons of design." Across her three-decade career Navone has also worked as art director, interior designer, teacher, and exhibition organizer, collaborating with brands such as Driade, Abet Laminati, Cappellini, and Habitat.

| 2004 | Ghost Armchair | B. 1950, Turin, Italy. | Paola Navone |

Electric lighting was a relatively new field in homeware design when industrial designer Greta von Nessen and her husband, Walter, emigrated from Sweden to the United States in 1927. The couple quickly became industry leaders, establishing Nessen Studios in New York. After Walter's death in 1943, von Nessen revived the studio, developing a series of designs which became known for their utility and simplicity. Von Nessen often launched products in her own home, using her carefully curated interiors inspired by the modernism of the 1920s as a backdrop to showcase her company's designs. The Anywhere Lamp (above) was made from aluminum and enameled steel, and could be hung,

wall-mounted, or used as a table lamp. Its enameled shade allowed the fixture to pivot so that it could be placed "anywhere." Such versatility reflected von Nessen's interest in new materials and functional design, with the lamp becoming Nessen Studios' best-selling product. An icon of design, the Anywhere lamp—now renamed the Greta Lamp—was featured on a 2011 U.S. Postal Service postage stamp celebrating American industrial design, and von Nessen was the only woman out of twelve designers chosen for this commemoration. Several of von Nessen's lamps were featured in the Museum of Modern Art's *Good Design* exhibition (1950–51), and are included in its permanent collection.

| Greta von Nessen | B. 1898, Malmö, Sweden.
D. 1975, Murrysville, PA, USA. | Anywhere Lamp | 1952 |

Kuala Lumpur-based designer Stephanie Ng was first formally recognized in 2015 when her first piece of design, called Mick's Deck Chair, won the Furniture Design Competition as part of the Malaysian International Furniture Fair. The chair is made from red balau timber, a wood native to Malaysia, and is indicative of her use of local materials in her practice. Winning the competition bolstered her to set up her own eponymous design studio and develop a focus on lighting. Ng was raised in Vancouver, and relocated with her family to Malaysia as a teen. She studied industrial design at Swinburne University of Technology in Melbourne, Australia, attending as a mature student. Her work seeks to make

the "ordinary special." This approach can be seen in the elegant Scoop Desk Lamp (below), which feels both functional and artisanal, crafted from powder-coated aluminum with oak detailing. The minimalist curving shade rotates 180 degrees to control the direction of illumination. The lamp is part of a series that includes a pendant version—its form inspired by the shape of an ice-cream cone—and wall-mounted options. Ng's work often revels in a sense of play and craft, from a pendant decorated with crocheted angel wings to perforated leather lightshades hand-embroidered with botanical motifs.

| 2015 | Scoop Desk Lamp | B. 1985, Kuala Lumpur. | Stephanie Ng |

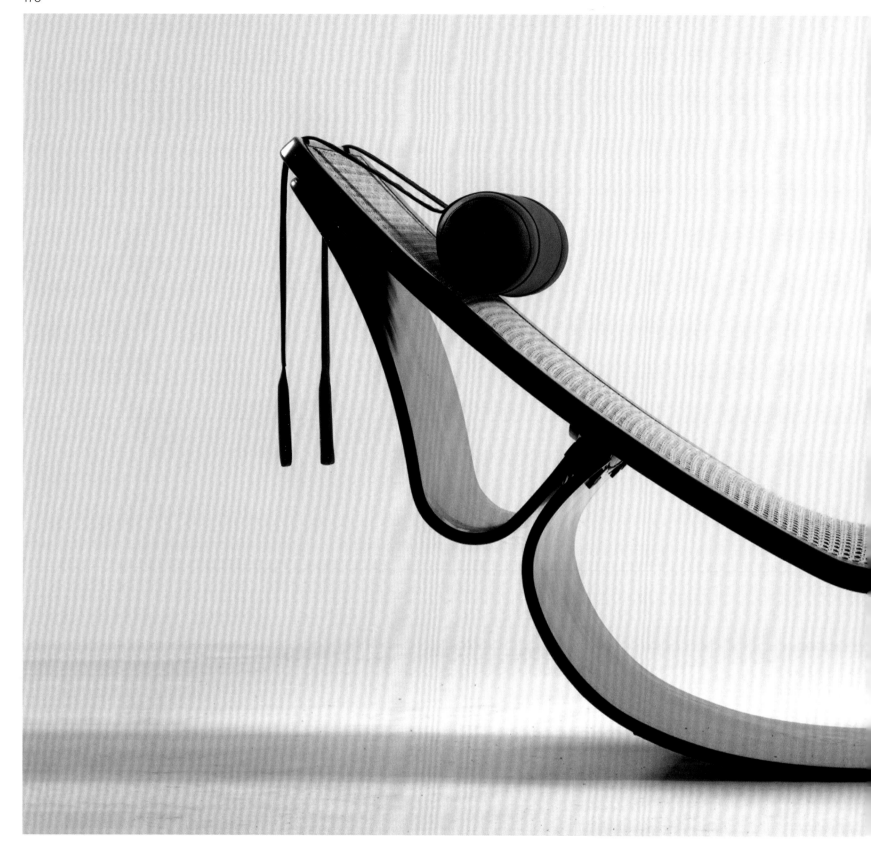

Anna Maria Niemeyer frequently collaborated with her father, the Brazilian modernist architect Oscar Niemeyer, throughout her career. Notably, she was integral to the production of his most significant project, the design and construction of the planned capital city, Brasília, built in only five years between 1955 and 1960. Niemeyer moved with a team of 120 professionals to the state of Goiás where the city was being built, and many of her early designs dressed the interiors of the new administrative buildings, which became the backdrop for pioneering modern furniture that later furnished the homes of Brazil's expanding middle class. Mixing arresting curvilinear forms with cutting-edge technologies, the father-daughter collaboration launched the furniture line

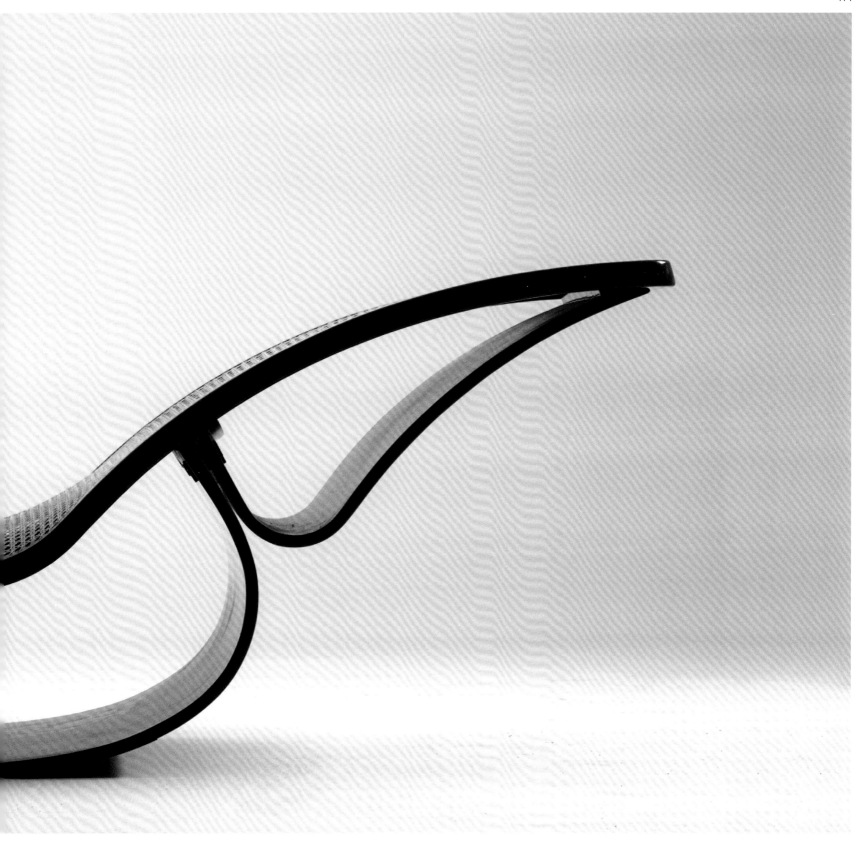

On in 1971, using a glued plywood technique developed in Sweden. The first prototype was manufactured in France due to the lack of technology available to bend steel in Brazil at the time; the Niemeyers even opened a manufacturing studio in Italy in order to fabricate some of their pieces. The Rio Chaise Longue (above) was designed for Oscar Niemeyer's personal use. Inspired by the city's curving coastline, it was named "Rio" and built from shaped plywood stained with black lacquer. Niemeyer later opened an art gallery, Galeria Anna Maria Niemeyer, in Rio de Janeiro, which was a precursor to the Niterói Contemporary Art Museum, which she founded and designed with her father.

| 1978 | Rio Chaise Longue | B. 1929, Rio de Janeiro.
D. 2012, Rio de Janeiro. | Anna Maria Niemeyer |

Plastic became widely available after World War II, and like many designers of her time, Libuše Niklová was excited by the possibilities the material offered, chiefly its ability to be molded into almost any shape and availability in a wide spectrum of colors. Before plastic's environmentally damaging properties were known, Niklová believed that the material's ubiquity would render natural materials luxuries, stating that "in the future, products from plastic will surround man like air ... the future belongs to plastic." Niklová graduated from the Secondary School of Applied Arts in Uherské Hradiště, Czech Republic, continuing to study the new industrial field of plastic molding while working for the manufacturer Fatra,

with whom she created the recognizable polyethylene animals that launched her career in toy design. Her toys are both stimulating and elegant, with simplified forms that act as sensory aids in children's development and play. Her inflatable animals, such as the joyful blue elephant (above), were designed to be sat on, emitting a sound whenever the child moved. The combination of bright colors and material innovation in Niklová's designs was a symbol of the energy of their time. She died early, at only forty-seven years old, but left more than 120 toy designs as a legacy, including nine totally new inventions and three patented designs.

Libuše Niklová

B. 1934, Zlín, Czech Republic.
D. 1981, Zlín, Czech Republic.

Inflatable Animals

1969

New York-based Dina Nur Satti draws inspiration from her Sudanese and Somali heritage, one that is rooted in ideas of womanhood and community. Her company, Nur Ceramics, established in 2016, takes its name from the Sufi concept that light can be found through one's shadow. This notion of duality reflects her thoughtful design method, which melds spirituality with a logical, hands-on approach. Creating expressive wheel-thrown and coil-built vessels in earth tones, she draws on various East African cultural traditions and natural forms—a vessel with two asymmetrical "arms" is inspired by the form of the native acacia tree, for example—and she has traveled extensively through northern and eastern Africa observing the use of clay pots in ceremonies. Satti originally earned a degree in international and intercultural studies from Fordham University in New York, and cites her search for tradition within her own legacy as leading her to work in ceramics, an artform through which she seeks to challenge ideas inherent to a Western canon of art and design by incorporating African references and storytelling. The textured Baobab Bowl (right)—as part of the Naama collection—takes its shape from the thick-trunked baobab tree. Known as the tree of life, the baobab can live for up to 5,000 years, and is a symbol of strength and grace. The eggshell finish is inspired by that of an ostrich egg (*naama* is Arabic for "ostrich"), an important motif in Nubian and Egyptian creation myths as a sign of life and rebirth. The piece is indicative of Satti's belief that ceramics can hold deep meaning and symbolism.

| 2018 | Baobab Bowl | B. 1987, N'Djamena, Chad. | Dina Nur Satti |

Modern glass production arguably only really began in Finland when the Finnish designer Gunnel Nyman joined Nuutajärvi Glassworks in 1942. Interested in the play of light in glass, Nyman enjoyed experimenting with its material properties, especially its transformation from molten to solid form. She believed an object should only be made from one material, with the addition of proportion and form used simply to amplify its natural properties. She first introduced bubbles to the surface of her designs in the 1930s, refining their shape and size in her later work for Nuutajärvi in the late 1940s. Nyman initially worked at Riimäki Glassworks while still a furniture design student at the University of Art and Design in Helsinki. Transitioning fully to glassware during World War II, Nyman began making bold geometric forms and became an early proponent of mass production. Over the course of her career she also created metalwork and lighting designs for Finnish company Taito. Throughout her life, Nyman's work was exhibited internationally, but she passed away in her late thirties, so did not live to see her posthumously awarded Gold Medal at the Triennale di Milano in 1951. Her Munankuori Bowl (below) was designed for Finnish brand Iittala. Created only a year before her death, it now resides in the permanent collection of the Museum of Modern Art, New York.

Gunnel Nyman

| | B. 1909, Turku, Finland. D. 1948, Finland. | Munankuori Bowl | 1947 |

Under the moniker Àga Concept, Moyo Ogunseinde reimagines African culture for contemporary functional products and furniture designs, inspired by her childhood growing up in Ibadan, Nigeria. Filled with nuanced references to Yoruba culture and values, the name of Ogunseinde's brand is derived from the Yoruba word for a useful object. Her designs for the Egungun collection are based on masked Yoruba figures translated into lamps and shelves to arrive at a new form of Nigerian minimalism. Àga Concept products use locally sourced woods and natural materials, which, according to Ogunseinde, "evoke the texture of Africa." The Oko Chair (right) references the use of hoes in agricultural production, the mainstay of Ibadan's economy. Ogunseinde had assumed she would become an accountant like other members of her family, but instead studied architecture at University College London (UCL). Following a period working in France and Nigeria, she continued her studies at UCL, returning to Nigeria to help her family with a number of architecture projects. Ogunseinde now works on large-scale commercial developments across West Africa, most notably founding and designing Upbeat, a trampoline park and recreation center. This dual entrepreneurial and design endeavor has led to a series of positions for Ogunseinde in Nigerian sports as a chairperson of the Lagos Gymnastics Association and a board member of the Lagos State Sports Trust Fund.

| 2017 | Oko Chair | B. 1978, Ibadan, Nigeria. | Moyo Ogunseinde |

With sweeping black folds molded into a buoyant, amorphous shape, the Savage Sofa (above) creates an unusual seat form that seems at once inviting while also entirely improbable for its material strangeness. This tension encapsulates Jay Sae Jung Oh's design philosophy of combining the aesthetic priority of art and images with the tactility of design. The first iteration of the Savage Sofa, which forms part of a series, was made while Oh was studying at the Cranbrook Academy of Art in Michigan, where she noticed dumpsters often overflowing with discarded prototypes for items ranging from patio furniture to musical instruments. She collected these objects and combined them with other refuse into an assemblage of waste that she then wrapped with natural jute cord. Oh first studied fine art in South Korea, followed by her time at Cranbrook in their 3D design department, where she embraced the school's emphasis on creative, rather than commercial, thinking. While a student, she worked for the Italian designer Gaetano Pesce, who instilled in her a strong work ethic, and encouraged her to explore a range of disciplines, from furniture design to homewares. Oh now runs her own Seattle-based practice, focused on using design as a tool to encourage people to question their relationship with everyday objects, materials, and consumption, such as used plastic.

| Jay Sae Jung Oh | B. 1982, Seoul. | Savage Sofa | 2016 |

Before the design group Movement 8 emerged in 1999, the Philippines was not recognized for its contemporary design rather It specialized in manufacturing and exporting furniture designed abroad. True to the symbol of the figure 8, signifying both eternity and a united front, the members of Movement 8 worked together to make visible original work by Filipino designers on an international stage, exhibiting globally at important convenings such as the Salone de Mobile in Milan. Interested in establishing a high-end consumer market—and in the process defining an Asian modernist aesthetic—the Movement 8 designers created bold modern forms using locally sourced materials indigenous to their country. Ann Pamintuan, a Movement 8 member, is celebrated in the Philippines for her sculptural furniture. She is drawn to organic shapes inspired by her hometown of Davao, which is rich in wildlife. She started experimenting from her home garage, where she established her company Gilded Expressions in 1993. The company found initial success producing fashion accessories; she later developed an experimental electroplating technique in metalwork, showcased in pieces such as the Cocoon Lounge Chair (below), a demi-orb with a biomorphic form made from intricately woven steel. Entirely self-taught, Pamintuan's work has been conceived wholly through trial and error.

| 2003 | Cocoon Lounge Chair | B. Davao, Philippines. | Ann Pamintuan |

Architect Luisa Parisi had a career in the Italian Navy before turning to design. Completing her studies at the Politecnico di Milano in 1948, where she was taught by renowned architect Gio Ponti, Parisi began designing interiors, furniture, glassware, and jewelry with her husband, Ico Parisi, with whom she was a member of the group Alta Quota. After they settled in Como, the Parisis' studio and showroom, La Ruota, was a meeting place for contemporary designers, creating a community of notable friends who could support one another. Ponti, for example, often promoted the group's work in the architecture and design magazine *Domus,* of which he was founding editor. Together, the Parisis produced numerous iconic pieces of furniture, including the Egg Chair (1951) for Cassina. While their early designs pursued biomorphic forms, they began using more geometric shapes inspired by architectural influences as their work grew in scale. Their rosewood and aluminum desk (above) for Mobili Italiani Moderni illustrates this evolution. Despite her fundamental role in the duo's output, Parisi's legacy has been eclipsed by that of her husband, who himself referred to her as "director and first critic."

Luisa Parisi	B. 1914, Italy. D. 1990, Como, Italy.	Desk	c. 1950s

Tamara Pérez formed the Santiago-based gt2P studio (which stands for Great Things to People) with her partner Guillermo Parada as a way to investigate their shared interest in applying digital tools usually reserved for architectural design to make objects for the home. Pérez, who is Nicaraguan-born but identifies as Chilean, studied architecture at the University for the Arts, Sciences, and Communication in Providencia, Chile. The studio, which had since expanded to four members, initially explored low-tech and analog approaches to the typically computer-aided, algorithmic Parametric style, hoping to adapt the doctrine Zaha Hadid (see p. 112) pioneered in her sleek and highly technical buildings to the design of more modest and accessible public spaces. gt2P's version of the Parametric style combined digital processes with manual intervention to create work that holds technology and the traditionally handmade in tension. Their stout Remolten Monolita Chair (left)—crafted from ceramic stoneware and re-melted lava—was designed in celebration of the studio's tenth birthday; it presents as a monolith, something the studio describes as a "petrous object built in one piece" as a memorial. The chair uses everyday methods from gt2P's daily work, combining traditional ceramic processes such as wheel-throwing, extruding, slab-rolling, kiln-firing, and, most fundamentally, hand-sculpting. The chair's title comes from the female version of the word *monolito* (monolith) in Spanish, paying homage to what they describe as "the feminine power of the studio."

| 2019 | Remolten Monolita Chair | B. 1981, Diriamba, Nicaragua. | Tamara Pérez |

Emigrating to France with her mother at the age of seven at the onset of World War II, Pergay studied costume and set design before opening her own store in the Place des Vosges in Paris. With no formal training in furniture design, she developed her skills by first working in decorative silver, designing objects to dress boutique windows in Paris, before being approached by the manufacturer Ugine-Gueugnon, who asked her to experiment with steel. The Wave Bench (below) is part of the first series of furniture that she produced in metal, and is emblematic of her sensual treatment of a material she has celebrated as "authoritative" yet "sweet." In Pergay's hands, this industrial material becomes supple and liquid. The Wave Bench appears to be made from a single sheet of metal folding back on itself at the edges of the seat, curving around to form the legs. The negative space created in the sculptural forms of this series of furniture gives a light and airy appearance despite the heft of the material. In 1977 Pergay moved to Saudi Arabia where she designed interiors for the royal family. Pergay, at the time of writing in her nineties, has returned to furniture design, most recently integrating stainless steel with hand-sculpted bronze, lacquer, and inlaid wood.

| Maria Pergay | B. 1930, Moldova, Romania. | Wave Bench | 1968 |

Le Corbusier was still dressing his modernist interiors with decorative Thonet chairs when Charlotte Perriand introduced him to the aesthetics of tubular steel. Collaborating with the famed Modernist and his cousin Pierre Jeanneret for ten years, Perriand produced a series of iconic chairs, which have become emblematic of Modernism's interest in the machine age. By the mid-1930s, however, Perriand newly embraced natural materials, refuting her own 1929 mini-manifesto "Wood or Metal?," in which she had described timber as a "vegetable substance." Instead, her straw Paillé Chair (1935) and timber Free Form furniture (1937–39) reflect an interest in merging the natural with the industrial, an approach Perriand promoted while consulting for Japanese manufacturers from 1940 to 1941. Influenced by the simplicity and geometry of the craftsmanship she saw there, Perriand's design vocabulary and manufacturing techniques evolved to incorporate Eastern references and methods. The stackable Ombre Chair (above) was made from a single piece of ply and manufactured for Tendo. Meaning "shadow," the Ombre was unveiled at the *Synthèse des Arts* exhibition (1955) curated by Perriand in Tokyo. Perriand is also responsible for a number of significant architectural projects, including the prefabricated Les Arcs ski resort (1974) in the French Alps—her largest work.

| 1954 | Ombre Chair | B. 1903, Paris.
D. 1999, Paris. | Charlotte Perriand |

Overshadowed by many of the great Modernist architects in Mexico, such as Luis Barragán and Mario Pani, for whom she designed numerous interiors, Clara Porset developed her own design style inspired by attentive study of the vernacular forms and materials found in villages across the country. Combining materials such as ixtle, jute, palm, and hemp using craft techniques, Porset made furniture particularly for those in rural locations during Mexico's post-revolutionary reconstruction period. Porset grew up in a wealthy family, which gave her the resources to travel widely, and study in Europe and the United States, including at Black Mountain College in North Carolina where she struck up a close friendship with the artists Josef and Anni Albers (see p. 20). Her socialist views forced her into exile from her native Cuba, settling in Mexico City in 1935. The Butaque Chair (left) was designed to express Mexico's complex national cultural history by combining the form of Spanish X-frame chairs and pre-Columbian ceremonial *duhos* with natural material found locally within Mexico. The chair's component parts were designed for mass-production, allowing Porset to create numerous iterations of the chair throughout her life.

| Clara Porset | B. 1895, Matanzas, Cuba. D. 1982, Mexico City. | Butaque Chair | c. 1952 |

The simplicity of Andrée Putman's designs reflects her rejection of a childhood steeped in luxury, during which at one point she emptied her entire bedroom in the family's Left Bank apartment, leaving just a Mies van der Rohe chair and Noguchi lamp. Putman developed her eye for design while working as a journalist at various fashion magazines and later as a stylist. Later in her career Putman began refurbishing iconic furniture pieces by renowned French designers such as Eileen Gray (see p. 109). Her resurrection of a lost French modernist aesthetic led to work designing interiors for hotels, shops, and private residences, and she acquired the moniker "the taste maker," not least because of her own personal style. Using and reusing materials in unusual and often surprising ways, Putman designed pieces that were both resourceful and simple, an outlook that made her quite radical at the time. Her iconic recycled aluminum Morgans chair, created exclusively by Emeco for her 1984 development of the boutique Morgans Hotel in New York, launched Putman's career internationally. Putman approached Ralph Pucci—the mannequin company for whom she had designed the Olympian Goddess mannequin (1985)—to represent her interests in the United States. A long business relationship ensued, including the production of the now classic oak-framed Crescent Moon Sofa (below).

| 2007 | Crescent Moon Sofa | B. 1925, Paris. D. 2013, Paris. | Andrée Putman |

The cold climate of designer Ingegerd Råman's native Sweden shapes her work in ceramic and glass. Combining simplicity of form with carefully chosen production techniques, her timeless pieces seem to contain the stillness of her frozen landscape. Råman began by designing textiles, before discovering pottery while assisting the Swedish architect Carl Malmsten in 1960 as he set up Capellagården, a craft school on the Swedish island of Öland. In the school's studio, Råman reveled in the tactility and sculptural capacities of clay, taking instantly to working in three-dimensions. She soon moved into glassware, establishing her own studio and developing longstanding, close collaborations with Swedish glass manufacturers Orrefors and Skruf, made deeper through her own experience working in a glass factory as part of her training at the University of Arts, Crafts, and Design in Stockholm. Råman makes functional pieces that emerge from her own needs, such as her Water Decanter (above). She has reworked her designs throughout her career, as with the Decanter, which was originally produced in 1958 and later reissued in 1981. She has undertaken a number of major design partnerships, including numerous pieces for Ikea and a collection of minimalist lights for manufacturer Örsjö Belysning with Swedish architect Gert Wingårdh.

| Ingegerd Råman | B. 1943, Stockholm. | Water Decanter | 1958 |

Mary Ratcliffe's passion for design was first nurtured in childhood in her father's home wood and metal workshops. She learned to weld by age seven, creating objects from scavenged scrap materials. Ratcliffe pursued this interest in making academically at Ontario College of Art & Design University, where she studied environmental design with the intention of becoming an architect. While working for a residential architecture firm, Ratcliffe was pulled to the field of design, realizing that it provided a more hands-on mode of expression. Ratcliffe launched her eponymous studio in 2018, focusing on making quality pieces that "can be passed down through history." She handmakes all her designs in her Toronto studio with a small team. Her work has been described as having an elegant toughness, exemplified in the Lyndoe Low Seat (below) and its juxtaposition of wood and leather: each of the chair's thirteen ash components is hand-shaped, and the buffalo-hide leather seat is knitted together with nylon cord on its underside. The piece was inspired by Ratcliffe's impressions of the residence of Leonardo da Vinci in Milan, where she observed contemporary design and traditional craftsmanship positioned together in the home; similarly, she has imbued her stool with a polished but still rustic quality.

| 2019 | Lyndoe Low Seat | B. 1989, Toronto. | Mary Ratcliffe |

Samira Rathod named the design arm of her studio the Big Piano in reference to the complexity and sturdiness of the instrument's form. She cites these elements as integral to furniture design, and creates pieces that seek to capture the piano's nuance of touch, where striking just a few keys can produce a range of sounds. This translates in practice to her selection of different materials according to their individual characteristics to achieve what Rathod describes as a balanced composition—one with "beat and rhythm." Each product is handcrafted in India, where Rathod might work with carpenters, weavers, tailors, fabricators, electricians, polishers, and painters to develop full-size prototypes with an emphasis on exposed joinery and unusual techniques. The Bloat Desk (below) is crafted from recycled teak wood and is notable for its smooth, bulbous drawer rendering the piece both fantastical and functional. The kinetic quality of Rathod's furniture resonates with her architectural practice, Samira Rathod Design Atelier, founded in 2000, where she explores experimental processes and whimsical material qualities such as broken brick or reclaimed waste steel. Her research as a faculty member of the Kamla Raheja Vidyanidhi Institute in Mumbai has a similar reciprocity with her design work, with her teaching emphasizing principles of craftsmanship.

| Samira Rathod | B. 1963, Mumbai, India. | Bloat Desk | 2019 |

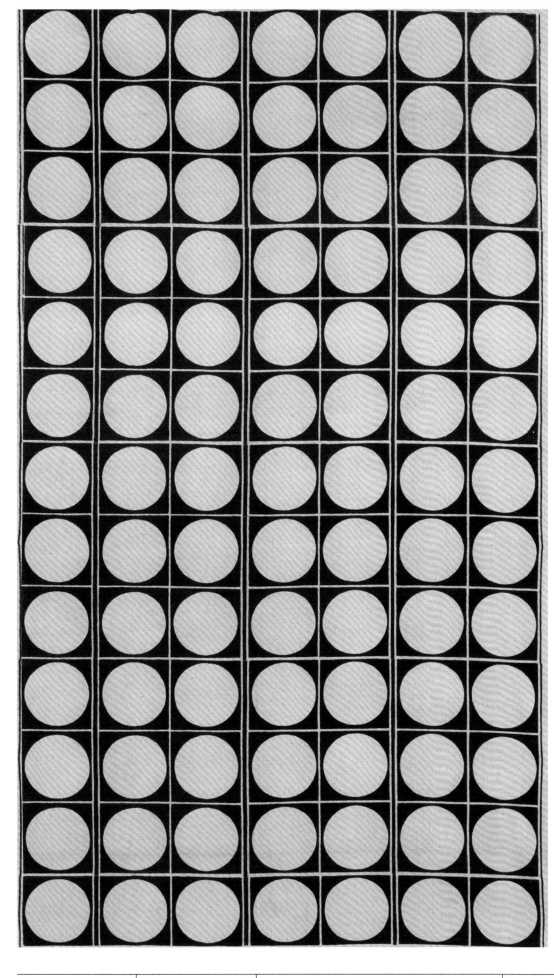

In a journey departing from the wave of migration of designers in the inter-war years from Europe to America, French-born Noémi Raymond instead traveled east. She contributed to introducing the International Style to India and Japan, where she created more than three hundred built works in partnership with her husband, architect Antonin Raymond, includ-ing houses, churches, schools, and even embassies. Born into an affluent family, Raymond was raised in New York, where she studied at Columbia University before continuing her stud-ies in Paris at the Académie de la Grande Chaumière. Returning to New York at the beginning of World War I, she initially set up her own graphic design studio before partnering with Antonin. After a period of working together for Frank Lloyd Wright on his large-scale, Japan-based projects, the duo established their own prac-tice in 1922. Raymond designed all the interiors for their practice, from fur-niture to rugs and textiles, including her Circles pattern (left). The simple design was influenced by her expe-rience with block-printed textiles in Japan, and, as she described, the "Japanese charm" of "doing away with all but essentials." In 1938, the duo returned to the U.S., establishing the New Hope Experiment—an appren-ticeship of sorts—on a farmstead in Pennsylvania. They would later return to Japan to help with the reconstruc-tion effort after World War II.

| c. 1941 | Circles Fabric | B. 1889, Cannes, France. D. 1990, New Hope, PA, USA. | Noémi Raymond |

Trained as an industrial embroiderer, Lilly Reich was an important figure in Germany's modern design movement, first as a member of the Deutscher Werkbund, where she collaborated on the interior design of the Haus der Frau (Women's House) at the group's 1914 exhibition in Cologne. Reich also managed her own studio before attending the Bauhaus Dessau in 1932 at the invitation of then director Ludwig Mies van der Rohe. Reich was only the second female master at the Bauhaus, and director of its weaving workshop for just under a year before the Nazis closed the school. In 1928, along with Mies, Reich received the commission for the German Pavilion for the Barcelona International Exhibition in 1929. The duo presented the now iconic Barcelona Pavilion and Barcelona Chair, but the latter—notable for its curving, scissored frame—carries a facsimile of only Mies's signature, with Reich's absent. Continuing their collaboration, the Brno Chair (right) was designed with Mies for the 1930 Tugendhat House in Brno, now in the Czech Republic, and the fame of the chair—which features an elegant cantilevered profile and tubular steel construction—has arguably surpassed that of the architecture; manufactured by Knoll, it is popular for both home and office environments. Reich went on to teach interior design at the Universität der Künste Berlin and run her own architecture and interior design studio, which also produced textiles and garments.

| Lilly Reich | B. 1885, Berlin. D. 1947, Berlin. | Brno Chair | 1929 |

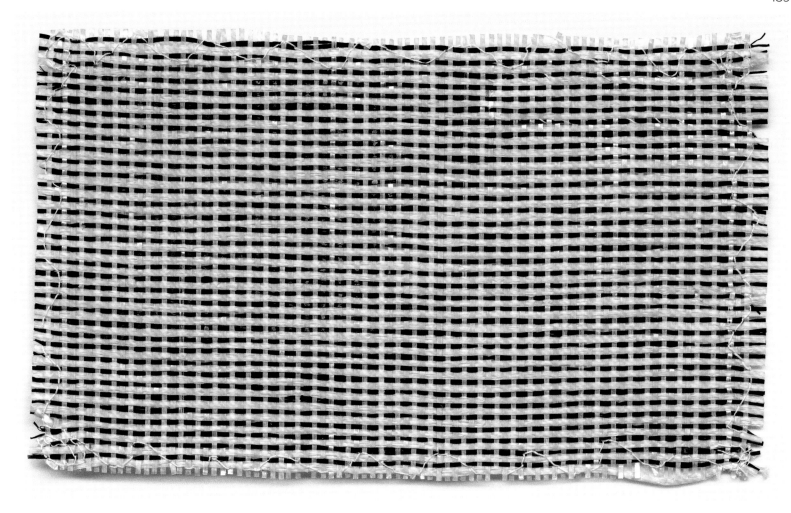

Influential textile designer and weaver Margaretha (Grete) Reichardt studied in Erfurt, Germany at the Kunstgewerbeschule. She joined the Bauhaus Dessau in 1926 where she worked in the weaving workshop under the direction of Gunta Stölzl (see p. 217). While at the Bauhaus, Reichardt invented cellophane weaving (above), cutting the foil by hand into thin strips and experimenting with combinations of other materials, such as cotton, reed, or wooden sticks. She became involved in steel thread weaving, developing a unique polished thread called "iron yarn," which Marcel Breuer incorporated into the construction of his tubular steel furniture. She graduated from the Bauhaus in 1931, and spent time working in a graphic design studio in the Netherlands. By 1933, Reichardt had moved back to Erfurt, founding an eponymous handweaving mill where she produced textiles that garnered widespread recognition over the decade, culminating in her winning the Gold Medal at the Triennale di Milano in 1939. That same year, Reichardt began her own workshop in a house that she built in Erfurt-Bischleben, where for more than fifty years—right up until her death—she trained students on hand looms. At the start of the 1950s, Reichardt was invited to teach at the Hamburg State Art School and she continued to be heavily decorated for her prolific design output.

| 1928 | Weaving Sample | B. 1907, Erfurt, Germany.
D. 1984, Erfurt, Germany. | Margaretha Reichardt |

Sylvia Reid and her husband, John, are perhaps among the least well-known design partnerships of the twentieth century, despite having created some of the most commercially successful furniture ranges ever produced by British designers. Their teak veneer S-range Sideboard for Stag is a modern classic. The metalwork gives the pieces a light, modern look, which Stag advertised using the slogan "[for the] young in heart and in pocket." Reid met her husband while studying at the Regent Street Polytechnic School of Architecture in London at the beginning of World War II. They both went on to work for Robin Day and the manufacturers Hille in the 1950s. The distinctive V-shaped leg seen on the S-Range Sideboard (above) was likely inspired by a Robin Day bench, which was in turn influenced by the work of U.S. designer George Nelson. The Reids built up a recognizable vocabulary of their own with their designs for Stag, and are included in the Council of Industrial Designers' Design Index. The Reids' son reissued his parents' designs in 2018, following his mother's dictum that "good design is always the product of logical thought."

| Sylvia Reid | B. London. | S-Range Sideboard | c. 1960 |

Coco Reynolds established Sydney-based furniture and lighting studio Marz Designs in 2010. After graduating from the University of Canberra where she studied industrial design, Reynolds set out to promote collaboration between craft practice and industry. Designs like the Art Pendant Light (right) are exemplary of this fusion, incorporating five different wood species—including American walnut, smoked ash, rock maple, and American oak—into timber beads, hand-turned on a CNC lathe and threaded onto a fabric cord to form striking vertical compositions. The light's bohemian, mid-century feel was originally inspired by Reynolds's childhood jewelry-making practice of threading beads on string to create colorful necklaces, and was the first piece in what has become her larger Bright Beads series. Each pendant is designed to be adaptable—multiples can be gathered into chandelier-like clusters—and is finished with a naked, dimmable LED lightbulb. Reynolds learned the traditional woodworking techniques that informed this series through her additional studies at craft and design school STURT in Mittagong, New South Wales, where she learned how to shape the pendant lamp elements. She now creates the beads with the woodworking manufacturer Evostyle—third-generation timber turners—who sand and wax each one by hand. Sustainability is at the heart of Reynolds's studio; she contributes a portion of her sales to the reforesting initiative One Tree Planted, an organization dedicated to planting trees in the wake of natural disasters.

| 2010 | Art Pendant Light | B. 1985, Perth, WA, Australia. | Coco Reynolds |

Lucie Rie's early ceramics were made in smooth shades of pale beige, white, and gray, a departure from the contemporaneous English craft ceramics of the postwar period, which were largely roughly textured in earthy, neutral colors. Heavily influenced by her teacher and mentor, the influential architect and Wiener Werkstätte co-founder Josef Hoffmann, Rie believed in the Gesamtkunstwerk, or total work of art. For Rie, this meant handmade items were necessarily artistically contiguous with the interior in which they lived. Her pieces became increasingly bold as her career developed, as seen in her Footed Bowl (below), which features vibrant black and pink glaze and is decorated by

applying deep marks to the surface using the *sgraffito* technique. Alongside Hoffman, Rie was trained as a potter in Vienna under decorative artist and sculptor Michael Powolny at the progressive Vienna Kunstgewerbeschule. She emigrated to England in 1938 to escape Nazi-controlled Austria, as well as a culture hostile to women in the handicrafts. Rie arrived in London, and in her new home she reinstalled the interiors of her Vienna apartment, which she had customized to suit her work. While Rie continued her career as a potter in the UK, she also became an influential teacher at the Camberwell College of Arts, where she taught from 1960 to 1972.

| Lucie Rie | B. 1902, Vienna. D. 1996, London. | Footed Bowl | c. 1980s |

Agnes Studio, established by Estefanía de Ros and Gustavo Quintana, reimagines pre-colonial materials and forms, specifically Mesoamerican objects, into contemporary works. The Guatemala City-based collaboration has worked across a range of mediums, and focuses now on interiors, furniture, and object design. Their revisionist pieces for the Living Stone collection, of which the Altar Console (above) is a part, explore an entirely new design language that unites past and present through objects that serve the rituals of modern daily life and align them with ancient Mayan forms such as corn millstones and sacrificial altars. The Altar Console is the most monumental of the six pieces in the series; hewn from the volcanic rock of Lake Atitlán combined with local black granite, the table's curving stone legs appear to wobble despite their solidity. De Ros grew up surrounded by Guatemalan textiles in her aunt and mother's factory, and as an adult rediscovered her interest in collaborating with artisans while working on a government-funded project aimed at revitalizing the traditional craft industry in the country. Her studio practice with Quintana is guided by the ambition to reinvent design in Central America, giving contemporary meanings and forms to natural, organic, and handcrafted shapes.

| 2018 | Altar Console | B. 1990, Guatemala City. | Estefanía de Ros |

194

Pipsan Saarinen-Swanson studied design at the University of Helsinki before moving to the U.S. with her family in 1923. Born into a family of designers, Saarinen-Swanson has been somewhat overshadowed by her well-known father, Eliel, and brother Eero, as well as her mother, Loja, who heavily influenced her daughter's textile and homeware designs. Saarinen-Swanson's father was a prominent figure at the Cranbrook Academy of Art, where she assisted in designing his architectural projects along with the development of the Flexible Home Arrangements collection of furniture (1939), which has since come to be recognized as one of the first modular systems to be introduced to the consumer market. Over the course of her career, Saarinen-Swanson produced everything from fashion, furniture, and glassware to screen-printed textiles and lighting fixtures. She not only founded her own company, Saarinen-Swanson, with her husband in 1947, but also made designs for a number of others, including the Ficks Reed Company who commissioned the Sol-Air suite of outdoor furniture (below). Produced in wrought iron, with versions made in woven rattan, and stretched canvas, the suite was designed to be unpretentious and bold in color, pitched toward a youthful and stylish consumer.

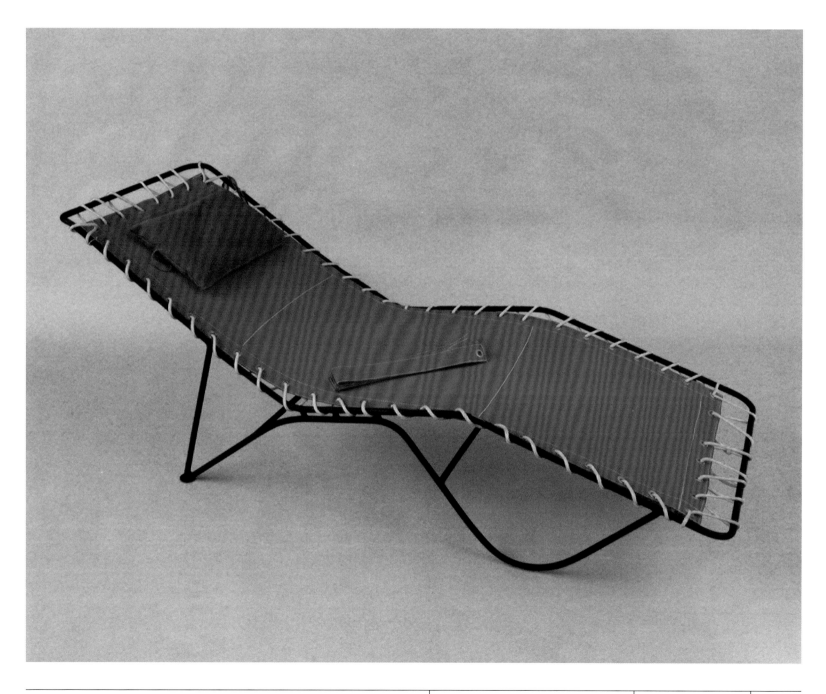

| Pipsan Saarinen-Swanson | B. 1905, Kirkkonummi, Finland. D. 1979, MI, USA. | Sol-Air Lounge Chair | 1950 |

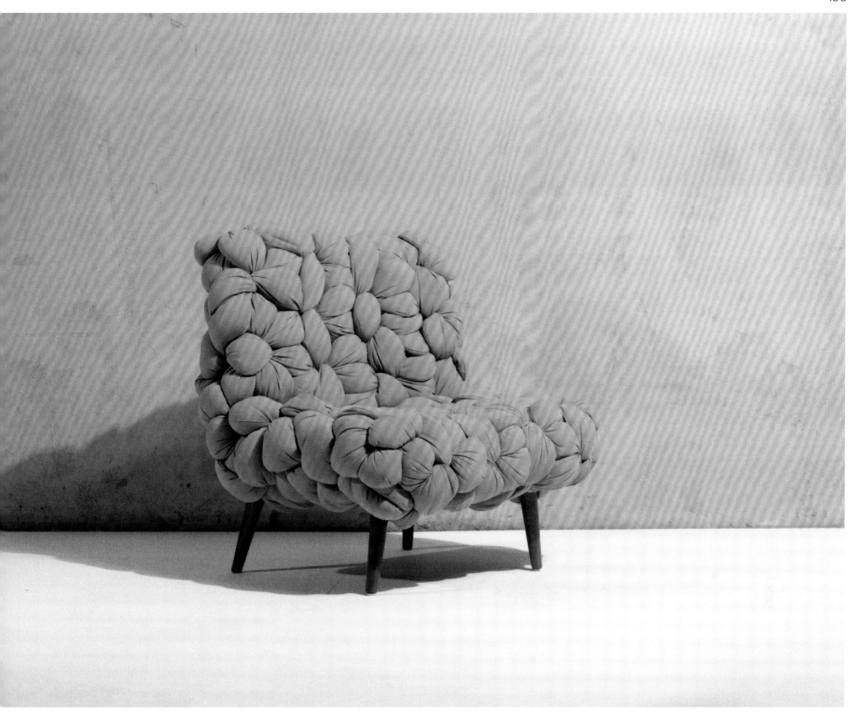

The sculptural, bulbous Braided Chair (above) was inspired by the early childhood hairstyles of Emirati conceptual artist and designer Latifa Saeed. Developing the braiding technique used in the chair's production in her studio then producing the large-scale linen tubes at a local upholstery manufacturer, Saeed designed the braided form to be reminiscent of the typical braids seen in children's hair through her upbringing. Through careful selection of native raw materials and traditional craft techniques, Saeed reflects the distinctive imprint of her milieu through work that explores the capacity of objects to communicate cultural narratives. The Braided Chair was debuted at Design Days in Dubai in 2014. In 2015 Saeed designed a collection of small kinetic sculptures—one taking the form of a crab, for example—woven from palm leaves; the material is ubiquitous in the region, traditionally used for everyday objects such as mats, baskets, and shelter. Saeed's graduation from Zayed University in Dubai coincided with an exciting moment in the UAE for contemporary design, with significant urban and cultural transformations like the establishment of the Louvre Abu Dhabi and numerous large-scale cultural events in the city of Sharjah—including the Sharjah Biennial—paving the way for opportunity within a galvanized design community.

| 2013 | Braided Chair | B. 1985, Dubai, UAE. | Latifa Saeed |

Jumana Taha and Mentalla Said's Hizz Rocking Chair (below) is a twist on the traditional chair; in Arabic "hizz" means "to rock" or "to shake." A special commission for Tashkeel, the chair has an energetic nature that is conveyed through accentuated geometric forms and a suspended, circular back that seems to float between the seat, arms, and base. The playful design is rooted in a sense of childhood nostalgia. Taha and Said worked closely with local artisans to manufacture the handcrafted teak wood spindles and rocker that forms the base of the chair. The angled spokes burst through the upholstered seat, lending a sense of dynamism and movement to the piece whether it is in use or still. Said lived in Egypt and Beirut before moving to Dubai to study interior design, where she met Taha, who was originally from Palestine, and had moved from London to Dubai as a young girl. For both designers, experimenting and working directly with artisans is a refreshing departure from their early career where they worked together in a corporate interior design studio. The duo's mission is to create functional design that preserves the playfulness of childhood—a charm reflected in the name of their studio, MUJU, a reference to both their names—while commemorating the vast craft tradition enabling their designs.

| Mentalla Said & Jumana Taha | Said B. 1989, Alexandria, Egypt. Taha B. 1990, London. | Hizz Rocking Chair | 2016 |

Claudia Moreira Salles was influenced by the emerging Brazilian modernism that surrounded her throughout her upbringing in Rio de Janeiro. She cites pioneering architect Lucio Costa as an inspiration for his simple interpretation of the style tailored to the Brazilian culture and climate. A Carioca (a native of Rio de Janeiro) like Costa, Moreira Salles has been credited for her informal yet refined brand of modernity, arrived at by reducing Brazilian vernacular furniture down to its essentials. For Moreira Salles this means combining seemingly disparate materials, such as stone with wood, to accentuate each material's inherent beauty. Moreira Salles developed her design vocabulary while studying at Latin America's first design school, the Industrial Design College in Rio de Janeiro, from which she graduated in 1978. Her ability to unite traditional Brazilian craftsmanship with technical precision while displaying a keen facility with wood caught the eye of Etel Carmona (see p. 61), a fellow designer and founder of the Brazilian design behemoth ETEL, known for their woodworking expertise. While designing for ETEL, Moreira Salles has also established her own work internationally, having run her own studio in São Paulo for more than thirty years. Designs like her Portuguese Armchair (right), which uses cylindrical wooden battens to form a simple silhouette base around which a straw seat is woven, illustrate her sensitive hybridized approach to intermingling craft and industrial aesthetics.

| 2016 | Portuguese Armchair | B. 1955, Rio de Janeiro. | Claudia Moreira Salles |

One of the few women prominent in the Italian Memphis Group during the 1980s, designer Maria Sanchez began her career in her native Argentina, where, in 1980, she graduated from the National University of Cuyo in Mendoza. Upon finishing, she received a scholarship to attend the University of Applied Arts in Vienna, after which she moved to Milan to immerse herself in Europe's contemporary design hub. She worked as Italian architect and designer Ettore Sottsass's personal assistant, not only managing his clients, but also producing furniture and designing objects of her own. Her signature Squash Ashtray (below) is one of the smallest pieces in the Memphis collection; it combines three vibrant, primary-colored ceramic shapes, and while aesthetically very much of its time, it is still produced today in both original and pastel shades. For fifteen years, Sanchez worked between Italy and the U.S. designing products for large-scale manufacturers while simultaneously launching an industrial design program at the National University of Misiones, Argentina, and at Austral University, Buenos Aires. She has since held numerous academic positions, including at the Politecnico di Milano and at her alma mater, and was a director of the National Fund of the Arts in Argentina.

| Maria Sanchez | B. 1954, Buenos Aires. | Squash Ashtray | 1985 |

In 1950, Cynthia Sargent and her husband Wendell Riggs spent a year in Woodstock, New York developing ideas for woodblock-printed cloth in preparation for their emigration to Mexico, where the couple envisioned deepening their engagement with craft-based production techniques. Sargent's eclectic educational background—she studied dance, painting, block printing, and art history—informed her curiosity as a designer. In Mexico, Sargent and Riggs set up a home workshop, and in 1952 participated in the exhibition *Art in Daily Life: Well-Designed Objects Made in Mexico*—organized by Cuban furniture designer Clara Porset (see p. 182) and hosted at the Palace of Fine Arts in Mexico City. The show was met with an enthusiastic response, establishing a market for the couple's designs. They became regular fixtures of Mexico City's cultural life, forming the Bazaar Sabado, a Saturday crafts market that still exists today. Inspired by Mexican textiles, Sargent began to design hooked rugs that were made by local artisans in the Riggs-Sargent workshop, including the vibrantly colored Bartok Rug (left) in congenial hues. She also created painted, hand-carved furniture but it was her textiles that gained international recognition; Sargent described them as "paintings that you hang on the floor." Following this breakthrough, she largely fulfilled commissions, many for the private clients of architects, and sold through her own galleries in Mexico and, in the U.S., through galleries in Texas, California, Arizona, and Florida.

| 1958 | Bartok Rug | B. 1922, Cambridge, MA, USA. | Cynthia Sargent |

Afra Scarpa, in partnership with her husband Tobia Scarpa, reveled in the success of designs thought to be commercially unviable and impossible to produce. Their approach shaped the evolution of Italian design, embracing new technologies and materials whilst remaining attentive to Italian craftsmanship. Afra met Tobia at a decoration course taught by Franco Albini where together they designed their first chair, the Pigreco Armchair (c. 1950s), featuring a curving half-moon-shaped backrest and fluid legs. Having both studied architecture at the Istituto Universitario di Architettura di Venezia, in 1960 they returned to Montebelluna—Scarpa's hometown—to establish their design office, where they primarily worked on lighting projects for FLOS. The couple also produced innovative work for manufacturers Knoll, B&B Italia, and Cassina, among others, and notably designed every collection for Maxalto from when it was founded in 1975, including the Artona range, of which the Africa Chair (left) was part. Made of natural wood, the grain exposed to decorative effect, the chair was a bold commercial choice in a time when plastic was a more prevalent furniture material. The Scarpas' built work also deployed unexpected materials in ingenious ways, evident in one of their largest architecture commissions—a textile factory (1964) for the clothing company Benetton in Treviso, which comprised a huge zinc-galvanized, steel-clad shed, demonstrating a novel application of ordinary materials.

| Afra Scarpa | B. 1937, Montebelluna, Italy. D. 2011, Trevignano, Italy. | Africa Chair | 1975 |

Furniture designer, interior designer, academic, and gallerist Bertha Schaefer established her first venture, Bertha Schaefer Interiors, in 1924, after studies at New York's Parsons School of Design. At the Bertha Schaefer Gallery of Contemporary Art, the sister company she founded in 1944, she exhibited the works of a number of the twentieth century's most celebrated artists, including Marcel Duchamp, Pablo Picasso, and Jackson Pollock, with whom she conducted a longstanding personal correspondence. A series of exhibitions at the gallery demonstrated her interest not just in art, but also in modern design, made vivid in the exhibition *The Modern House Comes Alive* which she curated in 1947.

A keen advocate of the Bauhaus movement, Schaefer oversaw the production of designs by others, as well as her own, which prioritized economy, craftsmanship, and commercial appeal. She had a longstanding partnership with New York-based furniture maker M. Singer & Sons, who hired Schaefer much later in her career to develop furniture that could be produced for the mass consumer market, exemplified by her 1955 Coffee Table (above). Schaefer was also technically proficient; she used fluorescent lighting decoratively as early as 1939, attempting to eliminate the need for numerous table lamps that she believed made a room "look like a lamp department instead of a home."

| c. 1955 | Coffee Table | B. 1895, Yazoo City, MS, USA. D. 1972, New York. | Bertha Schaefer |

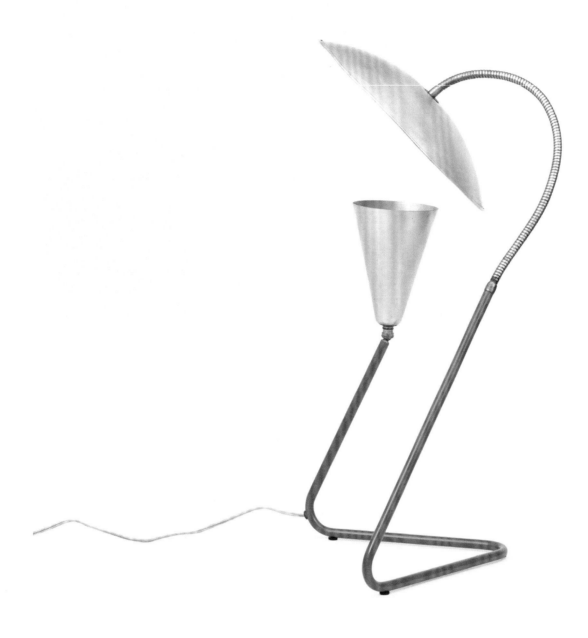

Out of nine winning entries in MoMA's low-cost lighting competition in 1951, Zahara Schatz's was one of only two lamps designed by women—along with Marion Geller's (see p. 103)—awarded an honorable mention. Her lamp (above) was manufactured by Heifetz Lighting Company, and consisted of a single bent tube. Her other products of this period are characterized by a similar economy of form, born from a dearth of raw materials in Israel, inspiring Schatz to elevate inexpensive materials such as sheet metal, to create minimalist sculptures. Schatz studied at the Bezalel Academy of Arts and Design in Jerusalem, founded by her father, but she ultimately rejected his propensity for romantic classicism in favor of her own interest in the abstract modernism of Europe and America. Following her father's death, Schatz, then eighteen, moved to Paris to study at the École Nationale Supérieure des Arts Décoratifs, and in 1938, she emigrated to California to join an artists and writers' colony that had formed in the Big Sur, along with her brother, Bezalel. Upon returning to Israel in 1951, Schatz founded a furniture business, Ya'ad, with her mother and brother, and worked as an industrial design advisor for the Israeli Ministry of Commerce and Industry. She was awarded the Medal of Honor at the 1954 Triennale di Milano.

| Zahara Schatz | B. 1916, Jerusalem. D. 1999, Jerusalem. | Table Lamp | 1951 |

Margarete "Grete" Schütte-Lihotzky conceived the kitchen as a "housewife's laboratory," not quite freeing women from the traditional duties of the era, but still recasting the kitchen as a space of labor, efficiency, and even innovation. Her belief that economic independence for women relied on limiting their housework resulted in her 1926 design for the Frankfurt Kitchen (above). Schütte-Lihotzky admitted that she herself had limited knowledge of kitchen chores, so conducted time-motion studies and undertook interviews with women to understand their workflow as part of the design process, revolutionary not least because she thought to ask women themselves what they thought of their own

homes. Schütte-Lihotzky studied at the Vienna School of Applied Arts, where she was the school's first woman architecture graduate. A period working for the Vienna Housing Office followed, where she worked on modular kitchen design and new housing blocks. Schütte-Lihotzky went on to become part of the "building brigade" sent to the Soviet Union to help shape public housing in new industrial towns. A staunch communist, she spent four years in prison during World War II for her anti-Nazi government campaigning. In exile in Paris and Turkey, Schütte-Lihotzky also traveled to communist countries including China and Cuba, advising on socially oriented design, particularly for children.

| 1926 | Frankfurt Kitchen | B. 1897, Vienna. D. 2000, Vienna. | Margarete Schütte-Lihotzky |

Molded from thermoplastic polymer, the charming Dedalo Umbrella Stand (below) features a dome-shaped form punctured by seven holes that enable multiple umbrellas to be stored at once. Along with the Elisa Umbrella Stand, created a decade later, the Dedalo was designed by Emma Schweinberger, and was available in three sizes and various colorways that responded to seasonal fashion. Its smallest form, the Dedalino, was designed to hold pens and pencils, and the Dedalotto intended for use as a flower vase. Schweinberger initially studied architecture at the Università degli Studi di Milano, following in the footsteps of her brother who was an architect. Later, she studied interior architecture in Switzerland at the Athenaeum of Lausanne, graduating in 1958. She went on to design for Italian furniture company Artemide throughout the 1960s, creating many memorable furnishings and products, including the Giano Vano Nightstand, and a series of three lamps—the Aminta, Chi, and Jota—all now classics of Italian design. Despite her centrality within the milieu of mid-century Italian design, little is known about Schweinberger personally as she eschewed the limelight. Perhaps this is why the Dedalo has often been mis-credited to Italian manufacturer Kartell, also well known for progressive ABS plastic designs of the time.

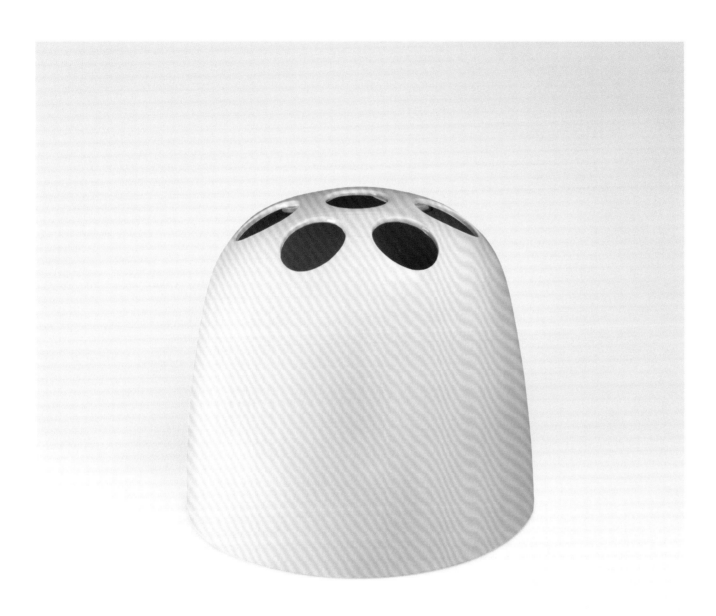

| Emma Schweinberger | B. 1934, Cologna Veneta, Italy. D. 2019, Italy. | Dedalo Umbrella Stand | 1966 |

Denise Scott Brown is best known for her work as an architect, theorist, educator, and writer; her work designing furniture is far less known. Despite this, the Queen Anne Side Chair (left) she designed for Knoll encapsulates some of the major threads of design thinking that have defined Scott Brown's career across a range of mediums and scales. Scott Brown flattens the Queen Anne style, reducing a historical icon to an easily recognizable symbol of the era, but also a wholly contemporary invocation of a familiar design trope; it was produced in a number of different prints, including the Grandmother pattern seen here. While teaching at Yale, Scott Brown and her partner Robert Venturi analyzed Las Vegas in much the same way, resulting in *Learning from Las Vegas* (1972), a publication which communicated a view of the world read entirely through its symbols, pre-empting—if not defining—Postmodernism in design. Scott Brown studied at the Architectural Association School of Architecture in London before studying under Louis Kahn at the University of Pennsylvania's School of Design, where she later became Associate Professor. She published frequently, and with impact. Her 1989 essay "Room at the Top? Sexism and the Star System in Architecture" undoubtedly rattled some cages; the Pritzker Prize jury chose only to bestow Venturi with the accolade in 1991, despite their joint professional partnership. Scott Brown has since been recognized through a number of awards, including the American Institute of Architects' Gold Medal in 2016.

| 1983 | Queen Anne Side Chair | B. 1932, Nkana, Zambia. | Denise Scott Brown |

Kazuyo Sejima studied architecture at the Japan Women's University in Tokyo, and subsequently trained under architect Toyo Ito before founding her own practice, SANAA, in 1987. She has become one of Japan's most prominent architects, and is perhaps better known for her delicate buildings that commune effortlessly with her surroundings than for her furniture designs. SANAA's Armless Chair (right), is one of the practice's most recognizable pieces of furniture, and is a seamless extensions of Sejima's architecture. With its rabbit-ear-like shape delineating a charming silhouette, the chair was designed for the Japanese furniture maker Maruni Wood Industry, for whom the design, manufactured in three different sizes, has been a big commercial success. While Maruni produced the chair as part of a series exploring a "Japanese aesthetic," Sejima has refuted this characterization, as an architect and designer known for innovating on an international scale. Emerging designers aspire to Sejima's organizational clarity and methodical approach; her drawings and publications have become key references for a next generation keen to reproduce the simplicity and structural delicacy of her architecture, the result of a mix of intuition and logic that she brings to her understanding of building.

| 2011 | Armless Chair | B. 1956, Hitachi, Japan. | Kazuyo Sejima |

One of the most well-known names in contemporary French design, Inga Sempé had an eye for design from a young age, inspired by the utility of household items she saw at flea markets. Her designs go beyond pure function, characterized by offbeat colors and playful forms. Sempé's knowledge of manufacturing processes has come to influence her design process as one that honors the constraints of the manufacturers rather than purely privileging her aesthetic or material choices. This attentive approach to fabrication is influenced by her time spent in workshops while she trained as an industrial designer, where she learned the possibilities, and also limits, of production. As a result she often chooses to work with family-owned manufacturers, producing designs created in her home studio in Paris. Her range of lamps (above) made for the Swedish lighting brand Wästberg can be assembled from flat-packed components, and their lampshades attach with a simple magnet, which can be adjusted to control illumination direction. A small clamp means that the lamp can be placed on the edge of a desk or other flat surface, or mounted on the wall. The lamp reflects Sempé's interest in adaptability, as many of her products are designed to be used in different configurations, an approach she hopes achieves "simple, useful, happy design."

| Inga Sempé | B. 1968, Paris. | w153 île | 2015 |

Under the moniker of her Cape Town-based studio, murrmurr, designer Mia Senekal creates elegant, simple furnishings influenced by the contours, textures, and shapes found in nature. Murrmurr's name is drawn from "murmuration," the phenomenon of synchronous flying swallows whose formations create a range of complex, undulating patterns in the sky. Senekal describes murmuration as a metaphor for her design process, where she seeks "natural harmony" through her work's flowing forms and botanical patterning. Senekal's hands-on approach to making was nurtured from a young age through woodworking with her father and dressmaking with her mother, which developed conceptually in her interior design studies at the BHC School of Design in Cape Town. Her Quarter Coffee Table (below), for example, is part of her first collection, Moon, in which the form of each piece—including a sofa, a side table, and two chairs—references a different phase of the lunar cycle. The graphic marble table features a half-circle cutout and curved top inspired by the quarter moon phase, when half of the moon's disc is illuminated; in contrast, the Full Moon Armchair, upholstered in blue velvet, is deep and rounded. In 2020, Senekal was selected as part of Design Indaba's Emerging Creatives program, mentoring young designers in South Africa.

| 2019 | Quarter Coffee Table | B. 1989, Cape Town. | Mia Senekal |

The fluid Dip Lounger (below) was one of British-Nigerian designer Mimi Shodeinde's first furniture pieces, created soon after she graduated from Heriot-Watt University in Edinburgh, where she studied interior design. The Dip Lounger's undulating form is crafted from strips of wood shaped and rounded using steam, and exemplifies Shodeinde's sophisticated take on traditional craft aesthetics that plays with line and symmetry. In the same way, her series of ICE sconces merges circular marble frames with dramatically intersecting, opalescent tubular bulbs to create surprising, minimal forms. Shodeinde's fluid way of working translates her design ideas quickly through hand sketching onto Computer-Aided Design (CAD) software to rapidly model physical prototypes. As a result, Shodeinde's designs have clarity in their conceptual form, which is later realized in materials selected by artistic intuition rather than because of their function. This expressive approach is derived from her fine arts background; and she inherited her love of sketching from her architect father, which led her to naturally think about the design of objects in a spatial capacity (rather than individual contextless objects). Her design practice, called Minimat, also encompasses interior architecture, realizing sleek projects internationally in cities including London and Lagos, as well as in the Middle East.

| Mimi Shodeinde | B. 1994, London. | Dip Lounger | 2016 |

Designing for children is a lesser-known part of the Bauhaus output, which included toy designs that sold in the local Weimar market and children's furniture manufactured in the Bauhaus workshops by students, among them Alma Siedhoff-Buscher and Friedl Dicker-Brandeis (see p. 211). In 1923, Siedhoff-Buscher created the Bauhaus Bauspiel (above), still in production today, consisting of twenty-two brightly colored wooden pieces that when pieced together can resemble the abstracted form of boats. The design was was one of many flexible building block games designed at the Bauhaus such as the chess set (1924) designed by Siedhoff-Buscher's tutor Josef Hartwig. Hartwig had encouraged

Siedhoff-Buscher to transfer from the weaving workshop to wood carving, which better suited her vocational training in the applied arts. Siedhoff-Buscher continued to make wooden toys for mass production as well as furnishings, including the nursery furniture for the children's room of the Haus am Horn, a model dwelling designed by her tutor Georg Muche. A toy cupboard she designed was subsequently put into production and a set bought by architecture critic Nikolaus Pevsner. In 1925, she followed the Bauhaus when it moved to Dessau, joining the teaching staff and designing coloring books for the publisher Ravensburger. Siedhoff-Buscher died during World War II in an Allied bombing raid.

| 1923 | Bauhaus Bauspiel | B. 1899, Kreuztal, Germany. D. 1944, Frankfurt. | Alma Siedhoff-Buscher |

Jutta Sika was one of a number of women who radically rethought the relationship between design and production at the turn of the twentieth century. She studied at Vienna's Graphische Lehr- und Versuchsanstalt and later the Kunstgewerbeschule. Sika was a founding member of the group Wiener Kunst im Hause (Viennese Art at Home), made up of five men and five women who had studied together at the Kunstgewerbeschule. With an emphasis on creating unified interiors embodying the idea of the Gesamtkunstwerk, or total work of art, the group is credited as the precursor to the formation—by Sika's famed tutors Josef Hoffmann and Koloman Moser—of the Wiener Werkstätte. The

women of Kunst im Hause took responsibility for designing women's fashion alongside the ceramics and glasswares for which Sika is best known. Overshadowed by the success of their elder male counterparts, women designers like Sika and Hilda Jesser-Schmid (see p. 130) are only now becoming the focus of larger revisionist studies recuperating the role of women in the foundation of the Wiener Werkstätte. Her Coffee Set (above) for porcelain manufacturer Josef Böck shows her characteristic patterns invoking traditional Austrian folk art, motifs she would apply to her work with commercial products, including graphics for postcards and Christmas tree decorations.

| Jutta Sika | B. 1877, Linz, Austria. D. 1964, Vienna. | Coffee Set | c. 1902 |

Trudi Sitterle studied at the Art Institute of Chicago, after which she founded Sitterle Ceramics with her husband Harold Sitterle, a graphic designer, in 1949. Simultaneously with running the pottery studio, Sitterle was director of art in department stores and advertising agencies in Chicago, New Orleans, and Washington, D.C. She became known for her white-glazed porcelain range, which included the hourglass-shaped Pepper Mill and its accompanying Salt Dish and Spoon (below). The collection was exhibited at the Museum of Modern Art in New York, where it won a Good Design Award in 1950. The Pepper Mill would be Sitterle Ceramics' best-selling product. In a 1965 *New York Times* article,

Sitterle described herself as "awfully conservative," maintaining her role as both housewife and ceramicist, while Harold Sitterle was art director of *Woman's Day* magazine. They manufactured their products at home in upstate New York, with their kiln housed in a basement below their kitchen. At times, they involved their teenaged daughters in production for their range, which grew to include nearly thirty-five different porcelain products. The functional, elegant ceramics designed for the Sitterle company contrasted with the family's hobby to create "Useless Things," abstract porcelain objects made intentionally to resemble nothing, which they used to decorate their home.

| c. 1949–50 | Pepper Mill, Salt Dish, and Spoon | B. 1921, Joliet, IL, USA. D. 2001, Tarrytown, NY, USA. | Trudi Sitterle |

Alison Smithson was one of the UK's most prominent postwar architects. Alongside her husband, Peter Smithson, she participated in exhibitions jointly organized with the artists Eduardo Paolozzi and Nigel Henderson, whose focus was to explore avant-garde approaches to modern living. The Smithsons were known as provocateurs within their European architectural circles, and not only took part in several Congrès Internationale d'Architecture Moderne (CIAM) conferences, but were also instrumental in disbanding the organization entirely, establishing Team 10—formed of a younger generation of architects—in its place. The Smithsons' D38 Trundling Turk I Armchair (above) was assembled from a number of upholstered cushions on casters. Designed for TECTA, the chair would be used in the interiors of the Smithsons' Economist Buildings (1964) in London, and was designed to be wheeled about and appropriated for use when needed. Though her work was predominantly architectural, Smithson contributed to various magazines advancing everyday objects and their use as primary decorative elements for interiors. In her piece titled "Beatrix Potter's Places," published in a 1967 issue of *Architectural Design*, she describes the home of the character Peter Rabbit as the ideal domestic setting because every utensil, hung on the wall, has a use.

| Alison Smithson | B. 1928, Stockton-on-Tees, England, UK. D. London, 1993. | D38 Trundling Turk I Armchair | 1953 |

By the age of thirty-one, Sylvia Stave
had had a successful career designing silverware for the Swedish
manufacturer C.G. Hallberg, exhibited her work internationally, and
retired from it all following her marriage. Stave first worked as a silversmith in Stockholm, where she
studied at the Royal Academy of Fine
Arts. The Nationalmuseum immediately acquired her early design for an
enameled silver box for the Stockholm
Exhibition, and at twenty-three she
became the director at C.G. Hallberg
where she had begun her career.
Working almost exclusively in silver,
Stave's designs attracted the attention of Crown Prince Gustav Adolf,
who purchased an inkwell from one
of the many exhibitions that she organized, helping to establish her internationally as an avant-garde and wildly
innovative designer. She did not seek
to mass-produce her work, favoring unadorned designs, although
these were less successful among
Hallberg's consumers. Ornament was
however occasionally added as a selling point, against Stave's own wishes.
The simple geometry of her designs
has meant that Stave is often linked
to the Bauhaus, which was likely an
inspiration, although Stave denied
this. Indeed, Alessi revived Stave's
design for a spherical seamless metal
Cocktail Shaker (left) in 1989, mis-
attributing it to Bauhaus designer
Marianne Brandt (see p. 52). After
much research by Peter Hahn, former director of the Bauhaus Archiv, it
is now properly attributed to Stave.

| 1930–34 | Cocktail Shaker | B. 1908, Växjö, Sweden. D. 1994, Paris. | Sylvia Stave |

Nanny Still initially intended to work in silversmithing after graduating from the Department of Metal Art at the Central School of Arts and Design in 1949. Due to the shortage of materials in the early postwar period, she instead submitted designs for a competition organized by Riihimäki Glassworks, and despite her inexperience she was offered a job. Along with Helena Tynell (see p. 227), she became a chief designer at the company for over thirty years until its closure in 1976. Her early pieces took advantage of the plasticity of glass, demonstrating an organic modernism characteristic of Scandinavian design of this period. After her marriage in 1959, Still relocated to Brussels, where she continued to design for Riihimäki. In 1965 she won the International Design Award of the American Institute of Interior Designers for her geometrically patterned Flindari series. Her Grapponia series of bottle vases (above) used similar geometric motifs, and was produced in various hues using glass that changed in appearance throughout the day as lighting conditions shifted, resulting in hazy ombré effects. The prolific Still was accomplished in other media, including ceramics, wood, steel, and aluminum. Her Mango Cutlery Set (1973), for example, whose rounded form was inspired by her first sighting of the fruit on a trip to India in the early 1970s, is still in production by Iittala today.

| Nanny Still | B. 1926, Helsinki. D. 2009, Brussels. | Grapponia Vase | c. 1970s |

Gunta Stölzl is best known for her role as master—the only female one—of the Bauhaus weaving workshop, the most commercially successful of the school's workshops. Stölzl first studied at the Kunstgewerbeschule in Munich, where she explored a range of media, including painting and ceramics. Stölzl joined the Bauhaus in 1919, initially studying under Johannes Itten. She drove innovations in textile design, introducing new fibers such as rayon, as seen in her Curtain Fabric (right). She intermittently explored opportunities outside the school, one such at Itten's invitation to set up and direct his Ontos Weaving Workshops in Herrliberg, Switzerland. In 1929, Stölzl married architect Arieh Sharon; she was subsequently stripped of her German citizenship because of his identity as Jewish, not long after which she was forced by Bauhaus members with Nazi sympathies to resign from her position as head of the weaving workshop. Stölzl moved to Switzerland, where she pursued a number of textile-based ventures, notably technical innovation with Jacquard looms. Much of Stölzl's life is known from her prolific diary writing; the accounts are so vivid that her second husband, Willy Stadler, supressed their publication upon her death, fearing that her love for life, particularly at the Bauhaus, might prove too scandalous.

| c. 1926–27 | Curtain Fabric | B. 1897, Munich.
D. 1983, Zürich. | Gunta Stölzl |

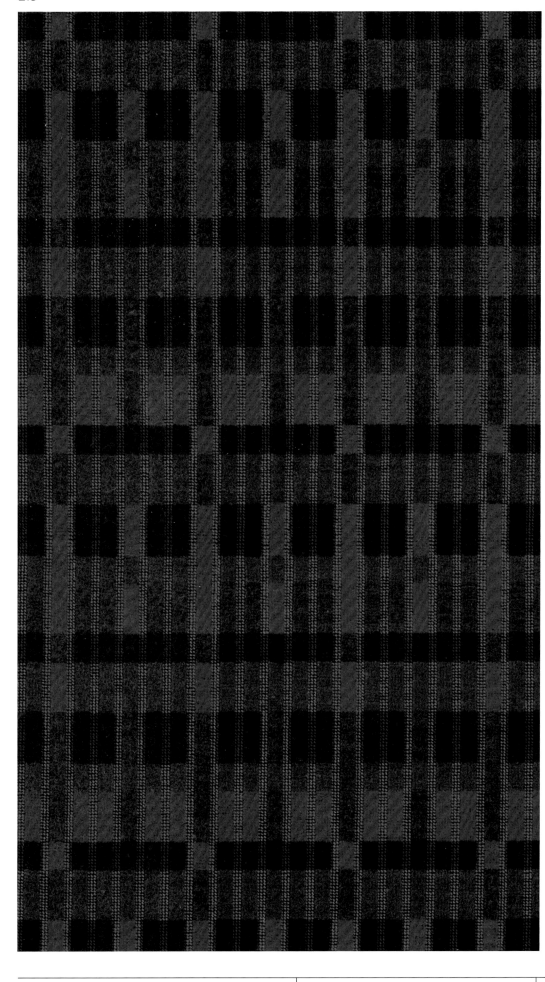

Commercial textile designer Marianne Straub was born in Switzerland to a family involved in the textiles trade. She studied weaving at the Zürich Kunstgewerbeschule under the former Bauhaus student Heinz Otto Hürlimann before coming to the UK to study at Bradford Technical College, as Swiss technical colleges at the time did not admit women. Throughout her career, Straub wove her industrial test samples by hand, a practice adopted from her work at Ditchling under the mentorship of Ethel Mairet, earning Straub her reputation as a "weaver's weaver." Straub worked for the Rural Industries Bureau as a consultant to the Welsh milling industry where she created more than one hundred textile designs per year before joining Helios as managing director. While she was a designer at Helios, Professor Misha Black, one of the coordinating architects for a section of the Festival of Britain (1951), invited Straub to design fabrics for London Transport, including this moquette, which features a geometric block motif rendered in navy, bright green, sea green, and blue (left). When Helios was taken over by Warner & Sons, Straub moved to Great Bardfield to be nearer to the company, and she joined the creative community there, which included another prolific textile designer Enid Marx, who also developed numerous fabrics for the London Underground. In later life, Straub pursued a career in teaching, including at the Royal College of Art in London, and traveled internationally to lecture.

Marianne Straub

B. 1909, Amriswil, Switzerland.
D. 1994, Berlingen, Switzerland.

London Transport
Moquette

1965

After graduating from the Central School of Industrial Art in Helsinki in 1929, Marianne Strengell spent her early career working as a freelance textile designer. In 1937, she moved to America at the invitation of architect Eliel Saarinen to teach at the Cranbrook Academy of Art in Michigan, where she eventually became the Head of Department of Weaving and Textile Design through 1961. Her tenure defined a period of textile production that was practical, functional, and cost-effective. She celebrated the integrity of materials used in weaving, and discouraged pictorial designs, even prohibiting her students—one of whom was Ray Eames (see p. 93)—from visiting the school library. While at Cranbrook, her handcrafted approach to industrial weaving caught the attention of Florence Knoll (see p. 138) who enlisted Strengell in the company's growing textile division. Alongside her work with Knoll, she maintained a number of successful commercial relationships with companies including General Motors and United Airlines, who brought her designs to the mass market. In her household fabrics Strengell often integrated synthetic fibers, as in the Throw Blanket (above), which weaves mohair with Mylar (a form of polyester resin). Strengell was also attentive to smaller-scale handicrafts, travelling to Asia and the Caribbean to look at textiles produced both artistically and economically.

| c. 1950s | Throw Blanket | B. 1909, Helsinki. D. 1998, Wellfleet, MA, USA. | Marianne Strengell |

Saša Štucin cofounded the design studio Soft Baroque with Australian-born Nicholas Gardner in 2013. Through her practice, she conceives of the Baroque period's integration of aesthetics across entire environments as strikingly modern. Works such as the zebrano wood Hard Round Armchair (above), with its striped zebra-like finish, challenge traditional furniture typologies, reducing them to sculptural gestures, in this case derived from Adobe Photoshop's "hard round" brush tool. As functional as they are fantastical, the pair's objects play with the basic notions of value underpinning much of the consumer market. Štucin met Gardner while studying visual communication and furniture design at the Royal College of Art in London. Their first collaboration was the oval Lenticularis mirror, which obscures its reflective properties by emitting a scented cloud; like many of Soft Baroque's projects, the Lenticularis plays conceptually with natural phenomena. Štucin describes their work as "future practical," introducing uncanny elements that intimate toward how certain objects might serve a new purpose in the future if traditional functions are reevaluated—a mirror that no longer reveals a reflection for example. Their work has been exhibited internationally, including at the Museum für Gestaltung in Zürich and Etage Projects in Copenhagen.

| Saša Štucin | B. 1984, Kranj, Slovenia. | Hard Round Armchair | 2019 |

Claudia Suárez Ahedo always wanted to be an architect, having spent her childhood constantly experimenting with the decoration of her own room, in search of improvement and beauty inspired by images in the design sections of her mother's magazines. Suárez Ahedo later moved to Spain to study for a master's degree in interior design at the Istituto Europeo di Design Madrid. Her work draws inspiration from a variety of disciplines, which she states includes music, history, and engineering, to develop designs in search of a balance between functionality and poetry. Women from Suárez Ahedo's home country of Mexico inspired the Ch'up Chair (right)—with its elegant curved shape, formed from layered sheets of terra-cotta pink powdercoated aluminum—representing their strong identity. Inaugurated at Mexico Design Week in 2018, the Ch'up, which means "woman" in the indigenous Mayan language, is fabricated from aluminum. Suárez Ahedo chose the material because it can be easily bent, allowing her to manipulate the shape in order to achieve a sculptural form without compromising the chair's structural integrity. Now based in Milan, Suárez Ahedo works across a range of scales, from designing furniture to architecture.

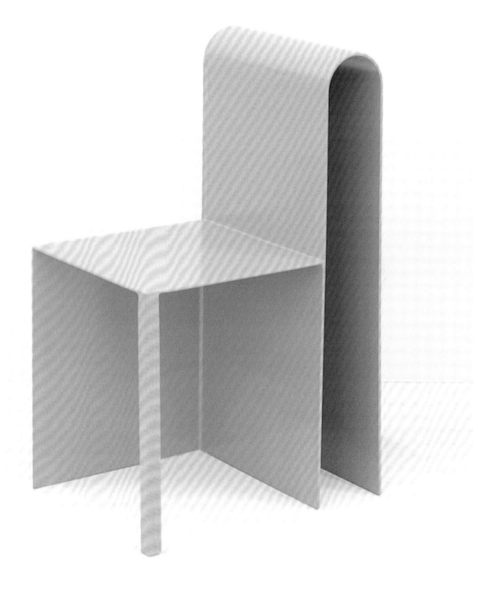

| 2018 | Ch'up Chair | B. 1985, Mexico City. | Claudia Suárez Ahedo |

After graduating from the Tokyo Academy in the 1960s, Hiroko Takeda began her career by designing furniture for various companies in Japan. In 1972, she traveled to Milan in search of work experience, enquiring at the studio of Dutch designer Andries van Onck. The pair formed a partnership and over the course of their shared career have created numerous inventive products, including household appliances, furniture, and electronic equipment, notably winning the 1979 Compasso d'Oro prize by the Italian Design Association for their Habitat family of light switches and outlets manufactured by Ave Interruttori. While Takeda had been impressed by van Onck's technological focus when she first joined his studio, she was keen for them to try furniture design, as she believed it the only way to build a reputation as a designer in Milan. The design for the Lem Adjustable Table (below) created for Magis originated during a conversation over dinner with the Magis company director, who expressed the desire for a table that could change heights. Takeda was encouraged to experiment, working with craftspeople to develop a sophisticated three-legged mechanism. The steel-framed table inspired a plethora of adjustable designs—a signature of their work—with the Lem still in production today.

| Hiroko Takeda | B. 1945, Japan. | Lem Adjustable Table | 1984 |

Although the Murai Stool is still in production today, little is publicly known about its designer Reiko Tanabe. Born in Tokyo, Tanabe studied design at the Joshibi University of Art and Design. She used her maiden name, Murai, for the stool (above), which was her entry to the inaugural design competition held by Japanese plywood furniture manufacturer Tendo Mokko. The design was inspired by a large, polyhedral ashtray that Tanabe had seen on a table at a cafe, which she scaled up and recreated in teak-veneered plywood; the three repeated pieces were attached using traditional Japanese joinery methods. Now internationally recognized as an icon of Japanese design, it was the only piece from the competition that was put into production, and quickly became a best-selling item for Tendo. Its advertisement in foreign publications even drew the attention of a curator of the Museum of Modern Art in New York, who in 1967 acquired the stool for their permanent collection. After her graduation, Tanabe worked at Kenji Fujimori design office and MHS Planners, Architects and Engineers as an interior designer. She also taught at Joshibi University for more than thirty-five years. Her own studio, called Tanabe Reiko Design, later focused on furniture and interior design projects, where she continued to create works that combined craft and technology.

| 1961 | Murai Stool | B. 1934, Tokyo.
D. 2017, Tokyo. | Reiko Tanabe |

Jacqueline Terpins moved to Rio de Janeiro as a child, and studied there with renowned Brazilian artists Lygia Pape and Frederico Morais. Terpins identifies primarily as an artist, grounding her work in her interest in the way people and objects interact, and the way emotions are conveyed through tactility and form. Drawn toward design after the death of her husband in 1988, Terpins turned to the commercial market, producing what she calls "art for everyday situations." Terpins' time studying under the tutelage of painter Ivan Serpa at the Museum of Modern Art in Rio de Janeiro introduced her to glass making, and inspired her to move first to the UK, and then to the U.S., to deepen her knowledge of blown glass, which would become her specialty. Describing heat as her main tool, she evocatively describes glass as being like "lava from a volcano." Terpins established her own design studio in São Paulo in 2001. Although she is best known for her glassware, Terpins' ability to transform materials through heat is present in her furniture designs, whose raw wood and metal materials form a fluid aesthetic. More recent works such as her Console Table Cello (right) demonstrate Terpins' interest in the organic qualities of wood, and how sculpting using both machinery and handcraft techniques has transformative effects.

| 2014 | Console Table Cello | B. Campina Grande, Brazil. | Jacqueline Terpins |

British artist Faye Toogood runs an interdisciplinary practice working across sculpture, furniture, and fashion design. Her career path was unconventional; she first studied art history at Bristol University, after which she worked as a stylist for *World of Interiors*. With no formal design training, Toogood's work does not play by industry rules—it is playful, yet deeply serious. Brought up in the English countryside, Toogood would forage bits of nature from her surrounding landscape, cultivating what she describes as her "cut and paste" style, reflecting an early interest in juxtaposition and contrast. This approach resonates throughout her design work, which uses both precious and raw materials.

Her furniture, for example, embraces heavy industrial materials such as fiberglass and metal, while natural fabrics like raw denim, linen, or silk are prominent in her clothing. Toogood describes her studio's designs as "deeply human," which can be felt in the Roly-Poly Chair (below), whose smooth, dish-shaped seat supported by chunky legs gives the chair a sense of refined childishness. Toogood channels this playful yet elegant register into larger-scale commissions, with her practice extending into interior design for residential and retail projects for clients including Mulberry, Carhartt, Hermès, and Comme des Garçons.

| Faye Toogood | B. 1977, Rutland, England, UK. | Roly-Poly Chair | 2014 |

Helena Tynell was a chief designer at the Finnish glass manufacturer Riihimaki Glassworks, where she worked for thirty years along with three other women including the designer Nanny Still (see p. 216). Tynell's prolific career produced a number of iconic Finnish works in glass, including the Sun Bottle (above) series, which remained in production for ten years cycling through a multitude of shades. The bottle's rounded body, slender neck, and joyous decorative sun relief impart Tynell's aesthetic impression of the 1960s into glass, made vivid through what she referred to as the new colors of the era, notably lime greens, golden browns, and oranges. Educated at the Central School of Arts and Crafts in Helsinki, Tynell started out designing lamps for Finnish lighting company Taito and ceramics for Arabia pottery. It was while working at Taito as a junior designer that she met the company's co-founder Paavo Tynell while creating drawings for his light fixtures. Known as the "man who illuminated Finland," he eventually became her husband, and his fame overshadowed Tynell's work, particularly her lighting designs. Despite her glassware's simplicity, Tynell's lamps were often ornate. From 1976, after the closure of Riihimaki Glassworks, she worked in Germany for a number of other companies, including lighting firm BEGA, before returning to Finland in 1986.

| 1964 | Sun Bottle | B. 1918, Äänekoski, Finland.
D. 2016, Tuusula, Finland. | Helena Tynell |

Spanish-born, Milan-based Patricia Urquiola studied under the designer Achille Castiglioni at the Politecnico di Milano—she credits her interest in designing for the everyday to Castiglioni's own concept of "tools for living," where objects should stand the test of time, used until they wear out. Her first job was in the technical office of Italian furniture company De Padova in Milan, where she worked alongside the likes of Vico Magistretti. Her fusion of the artisanal and the industrial can be seen in her tubular steel-framed Tropicalia Chair (above) for Italian manufacturer Moroso, where woven threads of thermoplastic polymer, polyester, or artificial leather create both pattern and structure. After graduating in 1989, Urquiola taught and designed for others before founding her eponymous studio in 2001, which was one of few woman-led studios at the time. Urquiola speaks of challenging gender-based prejudice throughout her career, not just as a designer in her own right, but also as art director of Cassina, a position she has held since 2015. Having dreamed of becoming a designer from the age of twelve, Urquiola moves with ease across scales from product design to architectural commissions. She was awarded the Gold Medal for the Arts in the Order of Isabella the Catholic by Spain's King Juan Carlos I for her services to the arts.

| Patricia Urquiola | B. 1961, Oviedo, Spain. | Tropicalia Chair | 2008 |

Metallurgical engineer turned furniture designer Mpho Vackler studied design at Inscape Design School in Pretoria, South Africa. She first worked as an interior designer while she was developing her own products, and in 2016 launched her brand, TheUrbanative. Vackier's work uses a range of materials including sustainable woods, with an emphasis on manufacturing locally in South Africa. Through her work, she not only advances her own designs in her showroom, but also displays other designers' work, building a community around her practice. Vackier's initial work merged minimalist silhouettes influenced by European modernism with vibrant geometric African prints. Other pieces are rooted in African stories and culture. The Oromo Dining Chair (left) is inspired by the Oromo tribe's hairstyle popular in Jimma, Ethiopia in the late 1800s. The chair's use of weaving and texture celebrates the sculptural forms of braiding, while elsewhere a graphic sideboard pays homage to the bold patterned artworks of South African Ndebele peoples. Vackier's modern cultural hybrids gained her recognition as an emerging designer of note by the Design Indaba, an organization promoting African creativity on a global stage.

| 2019 | Oromo Dining Chair | B. 1982, Soweto, South Africa. | Mpho Vackier |

From a young age, the artist, architect, and designer Garance Vallée's influences have been eclectic. Her mother was an art historian and her father, the painter known as Kriki, made bright geometric works; she credits her parents for introducing her to the 1980s Parisian underground art scene. Her playful, Escher-like illustrations depicting furniture, objects, and Modernist-inspired shapes in stage-set-like compositions are starting points for her works in design, which explore the relationship between objects and their wider environment. In 2017, after completing her studies at the École Nationale Supérieure d'Architecture de Paris-La Villette, Vallée relocated to New York to work for the architecture firm LOT-EK. She describes her time there as pivotal to her experimental approach and unique methodology, working with materials in a hands-on way. Returning to Paris in 2019, Vallée established her eponymous studio. Her objects are sculptural yet functional, as in the Puddle Table (below) for SWING Design Gallery, which combines two organically carved solid wood legs with a curved, puddle-shaped smoky glass top. Vallée's sculptural forms appear in other projects, including the throne-like powder-coated steel Triangle Chair (2020), which was exhibited at the Asia Now art fair.

| Garance Vallée | B. 1993, Paris. | Puddle Table | 2020 |

Ionna Vautrin makes everything from small utilitarian objects to furniture—all suffused with a sense of mischief and play. Growing up, Vautrin was torn between her ambition to become a cook and her desire to pursue a career in design, seeing both as a way of bringing people together. She chose making through study of industrial design at L'École de Design Nantes Atlantique, a design school in Nantes, France. Vautrin was working in Paris with designers Ronan and Erwan Bouroullec when she won the Grand Prix de la Création de la Ville de Paris for her design of the Binic Table Lamp (2010). The piece was produced by Italian light company Foscarini, who chose the design from a number of her sketches. Its spotlight form was inspired by the ventilation funnels seen on boats in her upbringing in Brittany. In 2011, Vautrin left the Bouroullecs to set up her own studio, and she was subsequently approached by the French national railway, SNCF, who had used the Binic to illustrate plans for the interiors of new train carriages. Invited to develop a bespoke lamp to be used throughout the rail system, Vautrin created the Art Deco-like Lamp TGV (above), named for the country's high-speed rail service. With two shades and a rounded shape, the object perfectly synthesizes Vautrin's belief in design as a meeting between industry and poetry.

| 2017 | Lamp TGV | B. 1979, Hennebont, France. | Ionna Vautrin |

Lella Vignelli, in partnership with Massimo Vignelli, believed the purpose of design was to fight ugliness, against which they levied numerous and varied designs now considered classics. From Bloomingdale's iconic brown paper bag to the American Airlines logo, a plastic stacking dinnerware set for Heller (one of their most successful product designs), and the New York City subway map and signage system, their synthesis of industrial, graphic, and furniture design led to their wide influence. The couple established several different companies between Italy and the United States, consciously building their joint identity as a brand so as to receive equal credit. Born into a family of architects, Lella studied

architecture in Venice and then at MIT, gaining further experience while working at Skidmore, Owings & Merrill (SOM). The Vignellis' work is famous for its minimalism and emphasis on function; Lella described herself as the realist, while Massimo was the dreamer. These complementary attributes are keenly felt in their design for the Metafora Coffee Table #1 (above), produced originally for Casigliani, which introduced four marble shapes referencing the four forms of Euclidean geometry playfully united under a single piece of glass to provide structure; the "legs" can be detached from the glass and placed anywhere needed to stabilize the table.

| Lella Vignelli | B. 1934, Udine, Italy. D. 2016, New York. | Metafora Coffee Table #1 | 1979 |

The Due Più Chair (right)—made for Coconi—has a whimsical, comfortable appearance imparted by its shaggy fur upholstery, the maximalism of which belies the chair's dramatic use of negative space that seemingly undermines a seat's typical function. This unexpected combination evinces Nanda Vigo's ability to blur architecture, art, and furniture design. Seeing architect Giuseppe Terragni's Casa del Fascio (1932) in Como, Italy as a child, with its iconic glass blocks, inspired Vigo to train as an architect in Switzerland, and informed her interest in light and translucency as key design elements. After a brief period spent working for Frank Lloyd Wright at Taliesin, where she became disillusioned by the vision behind his architecture, Vigo eventually returned to Italy, establishing her own design studio in 1959. She would organize the first group show of Gruppo Zero, their interest in light and motion to alter perception influencing Vigo's own approach to sculpture—notably often illuminated by diffused neon light—and interiors, seen in works such as the monochromatic Casa Sotto una Foglia (House Under a Leaf), which she designed with Gio Ponti. Ponti's belief in the total integration of art and architecture further encouraged Vigo to work across disciplinary limits, including programming what is considered the first "happening" at the Triennale di Milano in 1973, in which musicians and artists comingled and performed organically.

| 1971 | Due Più Chair | B. 1936, Milan. D. 2020, Milan. | Nanda Vigo |

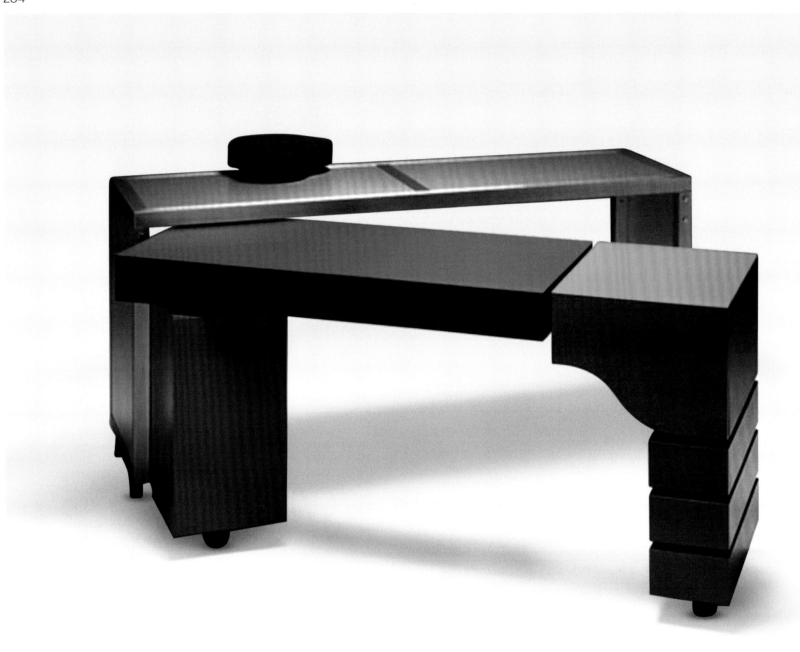

Designer Hisako Watanabe graduated from the Department of Stage and Display Design at Musashino Art University in Tokyo before moving to France, where she worked with the design group ENFI. Returning to Japan in 1979, Watanabe established Air Design Studio with designer Kenji Oki, and began teaching at the Tokyo Design Academy. Watanabe and Oki used design to explore the dual effects of technology and countercultural movements of the 1960s on modern society. Their furniture brought the pop pacifism of the anti-war flower power slogan together with the futuristic promises of the space age; as Watanabe stated, "it is a fusion of the speed mania of technologists and the countermeasures of the ecologists." Pieces like the Papillon Sofa (1988)—whose backrest emulates the shape of butterfly wings and whose coiled spring base allows bouncy movement—for example, functioned like a speculative dream object. These themes played out through playful lines and bright colors, which were intended to stimulate the mind and the senses. The aluminum Analogon Desk (above), manufactured by Ishimaru, was designed for a furniture exhibition in France. Its different elements were conceived as an analogy for the human body. Both conceptual and practical, the "body" of the desk pivots apart to provide additional workspace.

| Hisako Watanabe | B. 1951, Osaka, Japan. | Analogon Desk | 1984 |

Taipei-born, Stockholm-based Chen-Yen Wei describes the philosophy of Afteroom—a design studio established with her partner Hung-Ming Chen—as the desire to create objects that are simple, sophisticated, and honest. As a fledgling studio, the pair were hoping to get noticed with their eponymous chair, a refined, slender piece first shown in 2013 at the Greenhouse Exhibition at the Stockholm Design Fair. The Afteroom Chair (right) was designed in homage to functionalism, inherited from the philosophy of the Bauhaus where materials—in this instance powder-coated steel and wood—are carefully used to create something minimal without compromising on comfort. It was at the fair that Wei and Chen were introduced to Danish brand MENU, who decided to manufacture the piece. Although she was raised in the city, Wei was in close contact with nature throughout her upbringing as a result of her parents' efforts, a fact that Wei says influences her design practice today. She was struck by the natural beauty she saw, inspiring her to foster refined environments within her work. She attended the National Taipei College of Business before discovering design, first through her perennial fascination with fashion. She took courses in fashion design, and later worked as a fashion assistant in Taipei, honing her stylish, signature approach to color, favoring a muted palette of rich, earthy tones which can be seen throughout Afteroom's work.

| 2013 | Afteroom Chair | B. 1980, Taipei. | Chen-Yen Wei |

The colorful world of textile designer Donna Wilson is inhabited by her knitted Creatures (above), a handmade collection of soft, spirited animals whose unusual forms—inspired by textbook illustrations of medical oddities like conjoined twins and gigantism—have become a signature product in a career spanning nearly two decades. Wilson describes her aesthetic as a "woolly wonderland" where pattern, texture, color, and imagination collide. Her practice revolves around a love for wildlife and the natural landscape; for inspiration she often returns to rural Aberdeenshire, Scotland, where she grew up playing on her parents' farm, creating sculptures from mud, branches, and twigs.

Formalizing her artistic practice, Wilson attended Gray's School of Art in Aberdeen to study textiles, and then went on to study Mixed Media and Constructed Textiles at the Royal College of Art in London. Based in East London, Wilson now helms a global brand. She designed her first piece of furniture, a multi-hued Chesterfield-inspired ottoman named Motley, for London-based retailer SCP in 2007; since then, collaborations like that one have allowed her to expand her product range to include furniture, homewares, and clothing, all while retaining a charming, playful, and handcrafted aesthetic.

| Donna Wilson | B. 1977, Banff, Scotland. | Creatures | 2003 |

Esther Wood and her husband Gross were a self-taught duo who became interested in lighting after working together in commercial photography. When they set up a design company in San Francisco, Gross Wood & Co., the couple focused on affordable, mass-produced items. Many of their designs included interchangeable components that could be purchased separately and fitted together to create multiple designs. For example, in one year they made 653 sketches based on only 16 basic modular pieces, with the idea to provide accessible mass-market lighting fittings that had the adaptability of custom design. Starting with a lamp in 1939, the Woods moved into designing bowls, waste paper baskets, and candleholders. At one point, using their design components, one would have been able to create more than 70,000 products through various combinations. The advertising and print marketing materials that accompanied their products were witty and humorous, as can be seen in the description of their Tripod Ashtray (below) as having two sets of legs to be used as a "bowl for fruit, flowers or mammoth ashtray." Fabricated in wrought iron with a matte black, baked-enamel finish, the ashtray came with a partial perforated steel mesh lid that had a wire cigarette holder attached, bent in a tight wave formation.

| c. 1950s | Tripod Ashtray | B. 1921, CA, USA. | Esther Wood |

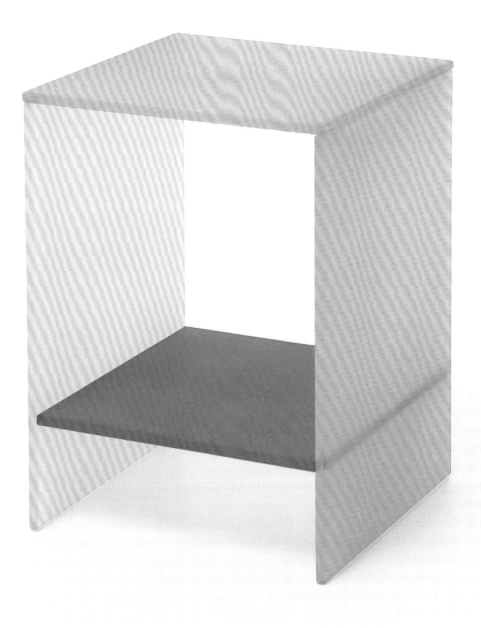

With a background in industrial design as well as fine art and graphics, Sohyun Yun deploys her varied skills to create objects that are both functional furniture pieces and also works of art. Yun graduated from Seoul National University of Science and Technology, spending time as an exchange student at the School of Visual Arts in New York and Istanbul Technical University in Turkey. Upon graduation, she made work that put a contemporary twist on traditional Korean design, using materials such as acrylic to make simple pieces that are at once vibrant and playful. Yun invites consumers to participate through modifying her furniture designs; she believes this collaboration forges a long-term sense of ownership. Yun's work is often highly customizable, as in the Layer Chair (2015), where intersecting pieces of acrylic allow for different materials—wood or glass, for example—to be slotted into the seat to suit the user's desire. Her TONE Table (above) uses vivid hues inspired by the centuries-old form of Korean clothes known as *hanbok*. The smooth form of the table—which can also be turned on its side to make a small bookshelf—draws inspiration from the *hanbok* garments' inherent flowing lines. The series' items can be ordered in more than twenty custom-dyed tones, based on traditional Korean colors that when combined in different compositions convey a range of moods.

| Sohyun Yun | B. 1989, Seoul. | TONE Table | 2019 |

Softness is used both metaphorically and literally in the work of emerging Indian design studio Soft Geometry in their playful, often humorous pieces that explore connections between how an object looks and the way that it feels, seeking an understanding of what makes an object "soft." Originally from Kochi in southern India, cofounder Utharaa Zacharias grew up absorbing the passionate work ethic of her architect parents. Zacharias moved to New Delhi to study product design at the National Institute of Fashion Technology, where she met cofounder of Soft Geometry, Palaash Chaudhary. Describing New Delhi as "ripe with inspiration, materials, tools, and ingenuity," Zacharias collaborated with Chaudhary for a time in the city before later studying furniture design at the Savannah College of Art and Design in the U.S. While they were students, Zacharias taught her how to weld, which Chaudhary credits as a starting point for their first collection. Through what Zacharias calls "oversimplified line drawings of basic forms that grow in complexity," the studio develops products that align with their concept of the soft as a manifestation of material, color, and texture. The Elio Lamp (right) was inspired by a photo series capturing the interplay between light and transparency on glass, water, skin, and even dust. Made from textured, hand-cast resin, the lamp's tubular form is a nod to Eileen Gray's Bibendum Chair (see p. 109).

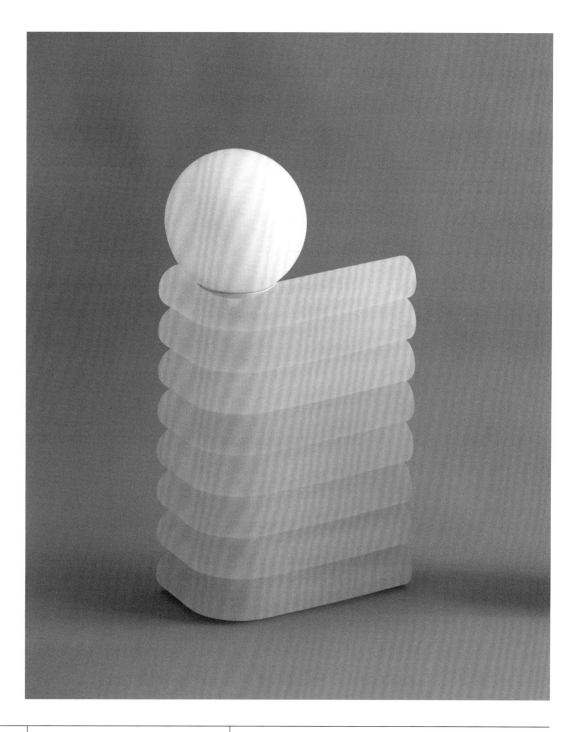

| 2020 | Elio Lamp | B. 1992, Kochi, India. | Utharaa Zacharias |

Studying painting at the Hungarian Royal Academy of Fine Arts, Eva Zeisel changed to ceramics at the behest of her mother, who deemed it a practical way to support herself. Self-declared "maker of useful things," Zeisel worked across furniture and ceramics, coordinating the production of her designs in factories globally. In 1936, while working as artistic director for the Russian Glass and Porcelain Trust in the Soviet Union, she was falsely accused of plotting against Stalin and imprisoned. Briefly settling in Vienna upon her release she moved to the U.S. at the outbreak of World War II. Zeisel taught Ceramics for Industry—a course she invented—at New York's Pratt Institute for nearly fifteen years. In

1946 she was invited to exhibit at the Museum of Modern Art, where her show *Modern China* not only introduced her work to the American consumer market, but was also the first exhibition at the museum dedicated to a woman. This led to many commissions, including a collaboration with Red Wing Potteries, for whom she created her now famous embracing salt and pepper shakers. While Zeisel is best known for her ceramics, her bold orange cotton and tubular steel Resilient Chair (above) is an evocative image of the organic yet elegant forms she applied to all her designs. She received a patent for its unique construction, which works like a spring.

| Eva Zeisel | B. 1906, Budapest. D. 2001, New York. | Resilient Chair | 1948–49 |

Designer Sandrine Ébène de Zorzi works between Paris, Kinshasa, and Porto, where her extensive range of wooden furniture is fabricated. De Zorzi's fascination with wood, a plentiful resource of Congo, began while working in the conservation workshops of the Musée du Louvre. After training at the prestigious École Boulle in Paris, in 2013 she founded a workshop in Kinshasa, Congo to explore the absence of African artisanal techniques in Western design. The wood Kiti Makasi Chair (right) was made in collaboration with cabinetmaker Michel Vamba Tiwete; with its gentle bucketlike seat, the pair considered and rethought Ray and Charles Eames's (see p. 93) DSW Chair (1950), an icon of Western design, using what de Zorzi describes as Tiwete's "traditional know-how," such as a lamination technique. As a result, tool marks could be observed on early editions of the chair, making each one of them unique. She works in collaboration with a network of craftspeople, cabinetmakers, millworkers, varnishers, metalworkers, and upholsterers to iterate her designs during the process of making. When working in the Congo, de Zorzi would often do this without drawings as a form of "no design." De Zorzi also has a cabinetmaking and furniture workshop in Paris called ÉbéneSand.

| 2013 | Kiti Makasi Chair | B. 1977, Kinshasa, Democratic Republic of Congo. | Sandrine Ébène de Zorzi |

1877–1964 Jutta Sika

○ Carafe with Stopper and Four Liquer Glasses, 1901
  ○ Plate with Koloman Moser, c. 1901–02
    ○ Sugar Bowl with Lid for Wiener Werkstätte, 1902
      ⬢ Coffee Set for Josef Böck, 1902 (p. 212)
        ○ Teapot, 1914

1878–1976 Eileen Gray

○ Day Bed, 1925
  ⬢ Bibendum Chair, 1926 (p. 108)
    ○ Adjustable Table, 1927
      ⌂ E-1027 Villa, Roquebrune-Cap-Martin (FR), 1929
        ○ Coubre Sofa, 1929
          ⌂ Tempe à Pailla Villa, Menton (FR), 1931
            ⌂ House at Castellar, Alpes Maritimes, France, c. 1932-34
              ○ Chair for the Villa Tempe à Pailla, 1935
                ⌂ S-bend Chair, 1938

1882–1972 Helen Dryden

○ Americana Print: Accessories Textile, 1925
  ○ Studebaker President Automobile, 1936
    ⬢ Candlesphere Candleholder, 1937 (p. 88)
      ○ Masque Lamps for Revere, 1937

1885–1968 Helen Hughes Dulany

○ Caviar Server, 1930
  ⬢ Coffee Service, 1934 (p. 89)
    ○ Dining Ware for Burlington Zephyr Trainset, 1934
      ○ Candelabrum, c. 1935

1885–1947 Lilly Reich

⬢ Brno Chair, 1929 (p. 188)
  ○ Barcelona Chair with Ludwig Mies van der Rohe, 1929
    ⌂ Barcelona Pavillion with Ludwig Mies van der Rohe, Barcelona (ES), 1929
      ○ Garden Table LR500, 1931
        ○ Tubular-Steel Chair LR 36/103, 1936–38

1889–1990 Noémi Raymond

⌂ Golconda Ashram with George Nakashima, Pondicherry (IN), 1936
  ○ Blobs, Leaf Textile Pattern, 1940
    ⬢ Circles Textile Pattern, 1941 (p. 187)
      ○ Chinese Coins Fabric, 1948
        ⌂ Readers Digest Office Building, Tokyo (JP), 1951

1893–1993 Marianne Brandt

○ Ashtray, 1924
  ⬢ Kettle, 1925–26 (p. 52)
    ○ Napkin Holder, 1930
      ○ Desk Set, 1930–31
        ○ Paper Tray, c. 1931
          ○ Table Clock, c. 1932

1894–1949 Aino Aalto

○ Child's Chair with Alvar Aalto for Artek, 1929
  ⬢ Pressed Glass 4644 for Iittala, 1932 (p. 14)
    ○ Savoy Vase for Iittala, 1936
      ⊡ Riihitie House with Alvar Aalto, Helsinki (FI), 1936

1894–1975 Ruth Hildegard Geyer-Raack

○ Panel (Dress or Furnishing Fabric), c. 1920s
  ○ Floral Textile, 1928
    ⬢ Adjustable Floor Lamp, 1952 (p. 104)

1894–1985 Hilda Jesser-Schmid

○ Tower-Shaped Lidded Vessel, 1917
  ○ Tulle Blanket for Wiener Werkstätte, 1920
    ○ Vase, 1921
      ⬢ Bowl, 1928 (p. 130)

1894–1996 Elizabeth Eyre de Lanux

○ L'attrapeur de Rêve Rug with Evelyn Wyld, 1927
  ○ Swing Chair, 1929
    ○ Quatre Armchairs, 1929
      ⬢ Dressing Table, 1930 (p. 147)
        ○ Side Table, 1935

1895–1982 Clara Porset

⬢ Butaque Chair, c. 1952 (p. 182)
  ○ Rattan Beach Chairs, 1957
    ○ School Furniture for the Camilo Cienfuegos Military Schools System (CU), 1959
      ○ Chaise Lounge CP-403 for IRGSA, c. 1950s

1895–1972 Bertha Schaefer

○ Asymmetrical Cabinets, 1950
  ○ Nesting Tables, 1950
    ○ Armchair for M. Singer & Sons, 1952
      ⊡ Temple Washington Hebrew Congregation, Washington, D.C. (US), 1954
        ○ Desk, 1955
          ⬢ Coffee Table, c. 1955 (p. 201)

1896–1981 Ilonka Karasz

○ Coffee Pot with Lid, 1928
  ○ Candlestick, 1928
    ○ Oak Leaf Textile, 1928
      ⬢ Armchair, 1930 (p. 135)
        ○ Rug, 1930
          ○ Rougeware Plate, 1935
            ○ Calico Cow Textile, 1952

1897–2000 Margarete Schütte-Lihotzky

⬢ Frankfurt Kitchen, 1926 (p. 203)
  ⌂ Werkbund Housing, Vienna (AT), 1930–33
    ⌂ Fröbel Kindergarten, Vienna (AT), 1950–52

1897–1983 Gunta Stölzl

○ Knotted Floor Carpet, 1923
  ⬢ Curtain Fabric, c. 1926–27 (p. 217)
    ○ Dress Fabric, c. 1940s
      ○ Decorative Mohair Fabric, 1964
        ○ Geometrisch II Wall Carpet, 1979

1898–1944 Otti Berger

⬢ Rug, c. 1929 (p. 39)
  ○ Bauhaus Curtain Fabric, 1933
    ○ Excella Pattern Fabric, c. 1932–37
      ○ Curvo Pattern Upholstery Fabric, c. 1935–36

1898–1944 Friedl Dicker-Brandeis

○ Costume of Portia, The Merchant of Venice for the Deutsches Theater, Berlin (DE), c. 1924–25
  ⊡ Montessori Kindergarten, Vienna (AT), 1932
    ⬢ Chair, 1930 (p. 84)

1898–1980 Virginia Hamill

⬢ Dinette Tea Set co-designed with Jean Theobald, 1928 (p. 114)

1898–1975 Greta von Nessen

○ Coronet Coffee Maker, c. 1938–42
  ⬢ Anywhere Lamp for Nessen Studios, 1952 (p. 168)

1899–1994 Anni Albers

○ Wallhanging, 1927
 ○ Bauhaus Textile Sample, c. 1930
  ○ Wall-covering Material for the School of the General
   German Trade Union Federation (ADGB), Bernau, 1929
    ○ Necklace with Alexander Reed, c. 1940
     ○ Drapery Material for Rockefeller
      Guest House (Philip Johnson), 1944
       ⬢ Free-Hanging Room Divider for
        Harvard Graduate Center, c. 1949 (p. 20)
         ○ Eclat for Knoll Textiles, 1975–76
          ○ Monarch Fabric for Sunar Textiles, 1982

1899–1990 Margarete Heymann-Löbenstein

○ Moccha Set, 1926
 ○ Bowl, 1930
  ⬢ Tea Service for Haël-Werkstätten,
   1930 (p. 121)
    ○ Wall Clock, 1930

1899–1944 Alma Siedhoff-Buscher

⬢ Bauhaus Bauspiel, 1923 (p. 211)
 ○ Nursery Furniture for Haus am Horn,
  c. 1923–24
   ○ Kugelspiel (Ball Game), 1924
    ○ Throw Dolls, 1924

1902–2000 Belle Kogan

⬢ Serving Dish, c. 1930 (p. 139)
 ○ Bakelite Bracelet, 1930s
  ○ Duck Clock for Telechron, 1934
   ○ Lighter for Zippo, 1938
    ○ Prismatic Compote, 1962

1902–1996 Lucie Rie

○ Stoneware Lettuce Button, c. 1940–45
 ○ Stoneware Bottle, 1967
  ○ Vase with Flaring Lip, c. 1970s
   ○ Porcelain Bowl, c 1980–81
    ⬢ Footed Bowl, c. 1980s (p. 192)

1903–1999 Charlotte Perriand

○ LC7 Revolving Armchair with Le Corbusier and
 Pierre Jeanneret, 1928
  ○ LC4 Chaise Longue with Le Corbusier and
   Pierre Jeanneret, 1928
    ○ Méribel Chair, c. 1950
     ⬢ Ombre Chair, 1954 (p. 181)
      ○ Les Arcs Dining Chair, c. 1960s
       ⌂ Arc 1600, Les Arcs Ski Resort,
        Savoie (FR), 1968

1905–1998 Freda Diamond

○ Classic Crystal Glasses for Libbey Glass
 Company, 1949
  ○ Kitchenware for Sears & Roebuck, 1951
   ⬢ Shelving for Baumritter, 1954 (p. 83)
    ○ Urethane Foam Furniture for Mobay, 1959
     ○ Wine Goblet for Libbey Glass Company, c. 1960s
      ○ Toilet Seat Covers for Magnolia Products, 1964

1905–1979 Pipsan Saarinen-Swanson

○ Dress, c. 1933–35
 ○ Sherbet Glass, 1946
  ○ Candelabrum, 1947
   ○ Flower Floater and Fawn, c. 1948–50
    ⬢ Sol-Air Lounge Chair, 1950 (p. 194)
     ○ Spelunking Textile, 1952

1906–1999 Greta Grossman

○ Coffee Table, 1930s
 ⬢ Gräshoppa Floor Lamp for Gubi, c. 1947 (p. 111)
  ○ Cobra Lighting Fixture, 1948
   ○ Glenn Chair for Glenn of California, 1952
    ⌂ Hurley House, Los Angeles, CA (US),
     1958

1906–2001 Eva Zeisel

○ Stratoware for Sears, Roebuck & Co., 1942
 ○ Museum Shape Dinnerware for
  Castleton China and MoMA, 1946
   ○ Town and Country Dinnerware for
    Red Wing Potteries, 1947
     ⬢ Resilient Chair, c. 1948–49 (p. 240)
      ○ Dinnerware for Noritake China, 1963
       ○ Closet Furniture, c. 1978–82
        ○ Office Furniture for Brownstone Publishers, 1996

1907–2001 Hedwig Bollhagen

○ Tea Service 501, 1934
 ○ Carafe, 1934
  ○ Cheese Bell, 1937
   ○ Butter Dish, 1937
    ⬢ 766 Watering Can, 1955 (p. 51)
     ○ Vases, c. 1960s

1907–1989 Lisa Johansson-Pape

⬢ Pendant Lamp, 1947 (p. 131)
 ○ Floor Lamp, 1947
  ○ Pendant for Orno, 1953
   ○ Arc Wall Lamp, 1954
    ○ Frosted Table Lamps for Iitala, 1954
     ○ Apila Stool for Oy Stockmann Ab,
      c. 1960s

1907–1984 Margaretha Reichardt

○ Jumping Jack Toy for Naef Toy Company, 1926
 ○ Eisengarn Fabric, 1927
  ⬢ Bauhaus Weaving Sample, 1928 (p. 189)
   ○ Skirt Fabric, 1930

1908–1994 Sylvia Stave

⬢ Cocktail Shaker for Alessi, 1930–34 (p. 215)
 ○ Jug with Side Handle for C.G. Hallberg, 1930–33
  ○ Pewter Vase for C.G. Hallberg, c. 1930s
   ○ Cocktail Shaker for C.G. Hallberg, c. 1930s
    ○ Vodka Cooler for C.G. Hallberg, c. 1930s

1909–1948 Gunnel Nyman

○ Drinking Glass, 1946
 ⬢ Munankuori Bowl for Iittala, 1947 (p. 174)
  ○ Pore Pitcher and Glasses, 1947
   ○ Serpentine Vase, 1947
    ○ Bowl, 1948

1909–1994 Marianne Straub

○ Furnishing Fabric, 1928
 ○ Cockermouth Furnishing Fabric for Helios, 1949
  ○ Helmsley Fabric for Warner & Sons, 1951
   ○ Aleppo Fabric for Liberty & Co., 1954
    ⬢ Moquette Sample for London Transport,
     1965 (p. 218)

1909–1998 Marianne Strengell

○ Casement Cloth, 1940
 ○ Shooting Stars for Knoll Textiles, c. 1947–52
  ○ Propellers for Knoll Textiles, c. 1947–50
   ⬢ Throw Blanket, c. 1950s (p. 219)

1911–2005 Edith Heath

○ Coupe Collection for Heath Ceramics, c. 1940–49
 ○ Dinnerware for Gump's, 1945
  ⬢ Tea Pot for Heath Ceramics, 1947 (p. 119)
   ○ Architectural Tiles for the Pasadena
    Art Museum, CA (US), 1967
     ○ Rim Collection for Heath Ceramics,
      c. 1970s

1912–1988 Ray Eames

○ Eames Elephant with Charles Eames, 1945
  ○ LCW Chair with Charles Eames, 1945
    ⌂ Eames House, Pacific Palisades, CA (US), 1949
      ○ Wire Chair (DKR) with Charles Eames, 1951
        ○ Hang-It-All with Charles Eames, 1953
          ○ ESU 426-C Storage Unit with Charles
            Eames, 1954
            ● Lounge Chair with Charles Eames, 1956 (p. 93)
              ○ Aluminum Chair with Charles Eames, 1958

1914–1992 Lina Bo Bardi

○ MASP 7 de Abril Chair, 1947
  ○ Metal Tripod Chair, 1949
    ● Bowl Chair, 1951 (p. 49)
      ⌂ Casa de Vidro, São Paulo (BR), 1951
        ⌂ São Paulo Museum of Art,
          São Paulo (BR), 1968
          ⌂ SESC Pompéia, São Paulo (BR), 1982
            ⌂ Teatro Oficina, São Paulo (BR), 1984
              ○ Giraffe Chair and Table, c. 1986

1914–1990 Luisa Parisi

● Desk with Ico Parisi, c. 1950s (p. 178)
  ○ Rosewood Dining Table with Ico Parisi for
    Mobili Italiani Moderni, c. 1950s
    ○ Egg Chair with Ico Parisi for Cassina, 1951
      ○ Telephone Table with Ico Parisi for
        Angelo De Baggis, 1954
        ○ Open Arm Chair with Ico Parisi for
          Cassina, c. 1962
            ○ Iride Standing Lamp with
              Ico Parisi, 1970

1915–1999 Marion Geller

● F-2-G Floor Lamp, 1951 (p. 103)

1915–1997 Estelle Laverne

○ Fun to Run Textile, c. 1947–48
  ○ Calder #1 Textile with Alexander Calder for Laverne Originals, 1949
    ○ Champagne Chair with Erwine Laverne, 1957
      ● Daffodil Chair with Erwine Laverne, 1957 (p. 149)
        ○ Lotus Chair with Erwine Laverne, 1958
          ○ Tulip Chair with Erwine Laverne, 1960

1916–1999 Zahara Schatz

○ Pendant, c. 1950s
  ○ Plexiglas Screen, c. 1950
    ● Table Lamp, 1951 (p. 202)
      ○ Six-branch Candelabrum for
        Yad Vashem, Jerusalem (IL), 1960

1917–2001 Karen Clemmensen

⌂ Clemmensen House with Ebbe Clemmensen,
  Gentofte (DK), 1953
    ● Safari Lounge Chair with Ebbe Clemmensen
      for Fritz Hansen, 1958 (p. 67)
      ○ Atrium Wallpaper with Ebbe Clemmensen, 1959
        ○ Blågård Pendant Lamp with Ebbe Clemmensen
          for Fog & Mørup, c. 1960s
          ⌂ Kildeskovshallen public baths with
            Ebbe Clemmensen, Copenhagen (DK), 1969

1917–2003 Muriel Coleman

○ Pacifica Bookshelf for
  California Contemporary, c. 1950s
  ○ Stools with Cowhide for
    Pacifica Iron Works, c. 1950
    ● Coatrack, c. 1952 (p. 68)
      ○ Student Desk for California
        Contemporary, 1952

1917–2010 Lucienne Day

○ Fluellin Furnishing Fabric, 1950
  ● Calyx Textile for Heal's Fabrics, 1951 (p. 77)
    ○ Herb Antony Furnishing Fabric for Heal's Fabrics, 1956
      ○ Pattern for Ilias Tableware for Rosenthal, 1962
        ○ Sunrise Furnishing Fabric for Heal's Fabrics, 1969
          ○ Halloween Furnishing Fabric, 1975
            ▭ Decoy and Pond Silk Mosaic for
              John Lewis, 1983
              ▭ Aspects of the Sun Silk Mosaic for
                John Lewis, 1990

1917–2019 Florence Knoll

○ Hairpin Stacking Table for Knoll, 1948
  ○ Coffee Table for Knoll, 1954
    ● Sofa 1206 for Knoll, 1954 (p. 138)
      ○ Oval Table Desk for Knoll, 1961
        ○ Executive Desk for Knoll, 1961

1918–2006 Anna Castelli Ferrieri

⌂ Kartell Headquarters with Giulio Castelli,
  Noviglio (IT), 1949
  ○ Round Dining Table for Kartell, 1964
    ● Componibili Modular Storage System,
      1967 (p. 63)
      ○ Cylincrical Storage for Kartell, 1969
        ○ 4870 Side Chair for Kartell, 1986
          ○ 4814 Armchair for Kartell, 1988
            ○ Sambonet Hannah Flatware, 1992

1918–2008 Grethe Meyer

○ Home Construction Cabinets with
  Børge Mogensen, c. 1954–59
  ○ Blue Line Fajance Tea Set for Royal
    Copenhagen Porcelain Factory, 1965
    ● Firepot Series for the Royal Copenhagen
      Porcelain Factory, 1976 (p. 162)
      ○ GM 15 Pendant Lamp for Menu, 1984
        ○ Copenhagen Cutlery for Georg Jensen,
          1991

1918–2016 Helena Tynell

○ Bubble Glass Pendant Lamp for
  Glashütte Limburg, c. 1960s
  ● Sun Bottle for Riihaimäki Glassworks, 1964 (p. 227)
    ○ Ahkeraliisa Vase for Riihaimäki Glassworks, 1968

1920–1976 Gegia Bronzini

○ Le Trottole Fabric, 1942
  ○ Tessuto 40 Fabric, 1952
    ○ Diagonale Fabric, 1954
      ● Striped Fabric, 1964 (p. 54)
        ○ Roller Chair, 1973
          ○ Upholstery for Zagato, c. 1970s

1920–1994 Eszter Haraszty

○ Cinders for Knoll Textiles, 1950–52
  ○ Tracy for Knoll Textiles, 1952
    ○ Fibra for Knoll Textiles, 1953
      ● Triad for Knoll Textiles, c. 1954 (p. 116)

1920–1989 Franca Helg

● Primavera Armchair, 1967 (p. 120)
  ⌂ La Rinascente with Franco Albini, Rome (IT), 1957
    ▭ Olivetti Showroom with Franco Albini, Paris (FR), 1958
      ○ Chairs for Poggi, 1958
        ▭ Station Design for the Metropolitana di Milano (IT), 1964
          ○ Interior/Exterior Sconces for Arteluce, 1970

1920–2006 Franziska Hosken

● Bar Cart, 1947 (p. 122)
  ○ Stacking Stools, 1947
    ○ Ash Table, 1950

1920–2006 Grete Jalk

○ Furniture Set for the Modern Professional Woman, 1947
  ○ Sofa for for Poul Jeppesen, c. 1960s
    ● GJ Chair for Poul Jeppesen, 1963 (p. 127)
      ○ She & He Chairs, 1963
        ○ Watch and Listen Living Room Unit, 1963

1921–2001 Trudi Sitterle

● Pepper Mill, Salt Dish, and Spoon, c. 1949–50 (p. 213)
○ Ashtray, 1951
○ Ladle, 1951

1921– Esther Wood

○ Lamp with Gross Wood, 1939
○ Ceiling Lamp with Gross Wood, 1946
● Tripod Ashtray with Gross Wood, c. 1950s (p. 237)
○ Minimesh Wastebasket with Gross Wood, 1952

1922–2017 Gabriella Crespi

○ Lune Lamp, 1969
○ Yang Ying Desk, 1970
● Scultura Coffee Table, 1970 (p. 74)
○ Z-Desk, 1974
○ Gothic Mirror with Drawer, 1977

1922– Cynthia Sargent

● Bartok Rug, 1958 (p. 199)
○ Scarlatti Rug, c. 1960s

1923–2014 Joyce Anderson

○ Dictionary Stand with Edgar Anderson, 1960-61
● Chair with Edgar Anderson, c. 1970 (p. 24)
○ Stool with Edgar Anderson, 1985

1923–2005 Nanna Ditzel

○ Jewelry for Georg Jensen, 1956
● Hanging Egg Chair with Jørgen Ditzel, 1959 (p. 87)
○ Hallingdal Textile for Kvadrat, 1965
○ Fiberglass Furniture for Domus Danica, 1969
○ Bench for Two for Fredericia, 1989
○ Trinidad Chair for Fredericia, 1993

1923– Ruth Adler Schnee

○ Batik Furnishing Fabric, 1945–49
● Construction Furnishing Fabric, c. 1950 (p. 19)
○ Seedy Weeds Furnishing Fabric, c. 1953
○ Wireworks Textile, 1961–63
○ Bells Furnishing Fabric for Anzea, 1995
○ Fission Chips for Knoll Textiles, 2012

1924–2004 Liisi Beckmann

○ Naranza Pendant Lamp for Vistosi, 1960
● Karelia Easy Chair for Zanotta, 1966 (p. 35)
○ Pair of Candleholders for Gabbianelli, 1967

1924–2020 Cini Boeri

⌂ La Rotonda, Sassari (IT), 1966
○ Partner Suitcase for Franzi, 1967
○ Mod.602 Table Light, 1968
⌂ Wood House, Osmate (IT), 1969
○ Lunario Table for Gavina, 1970
○ Strips Seating System for Arflex, 1972
● Ghost Chair for FIAM, 1987 (p. 50)
⌂ Villa su Tre Livelli, Vigolzone (IT), c. 1992–93
○ Ben Ben Sofa System, 2009

1924–2013 Maria Chomentowska

● Chair Model 200-102, c. 1950s (p. 66)
○ Armchair manufactured by the Warsaw Industrial Design Institute, 1957
○ Chair manufactured by the Elbląg Furniture Factory, 1960
○ School Tables and Chairs manufactured by the Warsaw Industrial Design Institute, 1963

1924–2019 Claude Lalanne

○ Iolas Flatware, 1966
○ Bouche Necklace and Bracelet, 1972
○ Gingko Chair, 1996
○ Singerie Bed, 1999
● Table Lotus et Singe Carrée, 2013 (p. 145)

1924–2014 Olga Lee

● Olga Lee Lamp, 1952 (p. 151)
○ Elements Furnishing Fabric, 1954

1924–2020 Althea McNish

○ Cascade Fabric for Liberty, 1959
● Golden Harvest Textile for Hull Traders, 1959 (p. 156)
○ Tropic Dress Fabric for Zika Ascher, 1959
○ Trinidad Furnishing Fabric for Heals, 1960
○ Gilia Furnishing Fabric for Hull Traders, 1961
○ Zircon Wallpaper for Sanderson-Rigg, 1968

1925–2013 Andrée Putman

⊡ Morgans Hotel, New York, NY (US), 1984
⊡ Balenciaga Store, Paris (FR), 1989
⊡ CAPC musée d'art contemporain de Bordeaux, Bordeaux (FR), 1990
⊡ Interior of the Air France Concorde, 1994
○ Vertigo Tableware Set with Christofle, 2000
⊡ Pagoda House, Tel Aviv (IL), 2003
● Crescent Moon Sofa, 2007 (p. 183)

1926–2009 Nanny Still

○ Wooden Salad Servers, 1954
○ Siren Vase for Riihimäki Glassworks, 1955
○ Sulttaani Decanter and Glasses for Riihimäki Glassworks, 1967
● Grapponia Vase, c. 1970s (p. 216)
○ Mango Cutlery Service for Hackman, 1973
○ Cast Iron Pots for Hackman, 1990s

1927–2012 Gae Aulenti

○ Locus Solus Sun Lounger for Centro Studi Poltronova, 1964
○ Giova Lamp for FontanaArte, 1964
⊡ Olivetti Showroom, Paris (FR), c. 1966–67
○ King Sun Lamp, 1967
○ No. 4794 Chair for Kartell, 1968
● Tavolo con Ruote for FontanaArte, 1980 (p. 29)
○ Parola Lamp for FontanaArte, 1980
⌂ Musée d'Orsay, Paris (FR), 1981

1927–2014 Cleo Baldon

○ Occasional Table, c. 1950s
○ Armchairs for Terra, 1966
⌂ Lap Pools for Galper-Baldon Associates, c. 1970s
⬡ Counter Stool, c. 1970s (p. 31)

1927–2014 Teresa Kruszewska

● Scallop Chair for the Ład Artists' Cooperative, 1956 (p. 142)
○ Reversible Child's Armchair for the Mebloartyzm Cooperative in Wojnicz, 1966
○ Tulip Armchair for the People's Guard Furniture Factory in Radomsko, 1973
○ Furnituretoy for Warsaw Industrial Design Institute, 1974
○ Rim Collection for Heath Ceramics, c. 1970s

1928–1993 Alison Smithson

⬢ D38 Trundling Turk I Lounge Chair for TECTA, 1953 (p. 214)
  ⌂ School at Hunstanton, Norfolk, England (UK), 1954
    ⌂ Economist Building, London, England (UK), 1965
      ⌂ Robin Hood Gardens Housing Complex, London, England (UK), 1972

1928– Marisa Forlani

○ Hanging Drawers with Luciano Grassi and Sergio Conti, 1954
  ⬢ Handicraft Monofilo Armchair with Luciano Grassi and Sergio Conti, c. 1953–55 (p. 100)

1929–2019 Mercedes "Ched" Berenguer-Topacio

⬢ Metal Klismos Chair, c. 1990 (p. 38)

1929–2016 Aída Boal

○ Augusta Chair, c. 1960s
  ⌂ Restoration of Convento do Carmo, Rio de Janeiro (BR), c. 1960s
    ○ Ipanema Armchair, c. 1970s
      ⌂ Hospitals for the State of Amazonas, Amazonas (BR), 1968
        ⬢ Angela Chair, 1995 (p. 47)

1929–2011 Raffaella Crespi

⬢ Lounge Chair for Mobilia, c. 1960s (p. 75)
  ○ Cristina Armchair for Elam, c. 1962
  ○ System Bookcase, c. 1960s

1929–2012 Anna Maria Niemeyer

○ Alta Lounge Chair with Oscar Niemeyer, 1971
  ○ Marquesa Bench with Oscar Niemeyer, 1974
    ⬢ Rio Chaise Longue with Oscar Niemeyer, 1978 (p. 171)
      ○ Furniture Design for Niterói Contemporary Art Museum (BR), 1996

1930– Maria Pergay

○ Coffee Table, 1957
  ○ Ring Chair, 1968
    ○ Flying Carpet Daybed, 1968
      ⬢ Wave Bench, 1968 (p. 180)
        ⊡ Residences of the Saudi Arabia Royal Family, Riyadh (SA), 1970s
          ○ Turtle Sofa for Pierre Cardin, 1977
            ○ Ruban Chair and Pouf, 2007
              ○ Marronnier Table, 2015

1931– Susi Aczel

○ Coca Chair, 1953
  ○ Curves Sofa, 1954
    ⬢ Round Coffee Table for Forma, 1955 (p. 16)

1931– Gloria Caranica

⬢ Rocking Beauty Hobby Horse, 1964–66 (p. 60)

1931– Francesca Lindh

⬢ Double Tea Pot with Richard Lindh, 1956 (p. 154)
  ○ Stoneware for Arabia, c. 1960s–80s

1932–2008 Janete Costa

⬢ Borsoi Table for Vermeil, c. 1960s (p. 70)
  ⊡ Hotel Pergamon, São Paulo (BR), 1997
    ⊡ Apartment by the Sea, Fortaleza (BR), 2002
      ⊡ Praia de Toquinho Residence, Toquinho Beach (BR), 2005

1932– Barbara Brown

○ Sweet Corn Textile for Heal's, 1958
  ○ Coffee Set for Midwinter Pottery, 1960
    ○ Reciprocation Textile for Heal's, 1962
      ⬢ Frequency Textile for Heal's, 1969 (p. 55)
        ○ Ikebana Textile for Heal's, 1971
          ○ Scherzo Textile for Heal's, 1974

1932– Bodil Kjær

⬢ Office Desk (Elements of Architecture series), 1959 (p. 137)
  ○ Indoor-Outdoor Series, 1959
    ⊡ Workplace Design for Arup, 1967–69
      ○ Crosses Vase, 1961
        ○ Cross-Plex Lamp, 1961
          ○ Serving Cart for E. Pedersen & Son, 1963
            ○ Headboards for Hotel Alexandra, Copenhagen (DK), 2016

1932– Denise Scott Brown

⌂ Franklin Court with Robert Venturi, Philadelphia, Pennsylvania (US), 1976
  ⬢ Queen Anne Side Chair for Knoll, 1983 (p. 205)
    ⌂ Gordon Wu Hall with Robert Venturi, Princeton, New Jersey (US), 1983
      ⌂ Provincial Capitol Building with Robert Venturi, Toulouse (FR), 1999

1933– Trix Haussmann

⊡ Boutique Courrèges with Robert Haussmann, Zürich (CH), 1961
  ⊡ Kronenhalle Bar with Robert Haussmann, Zürich (CH), 1965
    ○ Chair-Fun: Neon Chair with Robert Haussmann, 1967
      ⬢ Lehrstück II with Robert Haussmann, 1978 (p. 117)
        ⊡ Galleria Hamburg with Robert Haussmann, Hamburg (DE), 1978–83
          ⊡ Da Capo Bar with Robert Haussmann, Zürich Hauptbahnhof (CH), 1981
            ○ Intarsia Sideboard with Robert Haussmann, 1992

1934–1981 Libuše Niklová

○ Accordian Animals for Fatra, 1963–65
  ⬢ Inflatable Animals for Fatra, 1969 (p. 172)

1934–2019 Emma Schweinberger

○ Giano Vano Side Table for Artemide, c. 1960s
  ○ Chi Table Lamp for Artemide, 1962
    ⬢ Dedalo Umbrella Stand, 1966 (p. 204)

1934–2017 Reiko Tanabe

⬢ Murai Stool, 1961 (p. 223)

1934–2016 Lella Vignelli

○ Stacking Dinnerware with Massimo Vignelli, 1964
⬡ Metafora Coffee Table #1 with Massimo
  Vignelli for Casigliani, 1979 (p. 232)
  ○ Handkerchief Chair with Massimo
    Vignelli for Knoll, 1985
    ○ Serenissimo Table with Massimo
      Vignelli for Acerbis, 1985

1936–2020 Nanda Vigo

⌂ Zero House, Milan (IT) 1959–62
⌂ Casa Sotto una Foglia with
  Giò Ponti, Vicenza (IT) 1964–68
  ○ Golden Gate Lamp for Arredoluce,
    1969–70
    ⌂ Casa Museo Remo Brindisi,
      Lido di Spina (IT), 1967–71
      ⬡ Due Più Chair for Conconi, 1971 (p. 233)
      ○ Light-Light Shelf for Glas Italia, 1999
        ○ H&S Table, 2019

1937–2011 Afra Scarpa

○ Pigreco Armchair with Tobia Scarpa, c. 1950s
⌂ Factory for Benetton with Tobia Scarpa,
  Treviso (IT), 1964
  ○ Coronado Sofa with Tobia Scarpa for
    B&B Italia, 1966
    ○ Ciprea Armchair with Tobia Scarpa
      for Cassina, 1967
      ○ Papillion Floor Lamp with Tobia
        Scarpa for Flos, 1973
        ⬡ Africa Chair with Tobia
          Scarpa for Maxalto,
          1975 (p. 200)

1938– Dorothee Becker

⬡ Uten.Silo, 1969 (p. 34)

1938– Susi Berger

⬡ Soft Chair with Ueli Berger, 1967 (p. 41)
  ○ Cloud Lamp with Ueli Berger for WB Engros, 1970
    ○ Boxing Glove Lounge Chair with Ueli Berger for de Sede, 1970
      ○ Fan Man Shelf with Ueli Berger for Röthlisberger, 1977
        ○ Stack of Drawers with Ueli Berger for Röthlisberger, 1982

1940– Antonia Astori

○ Cidonio Table for Driade, 1969
  ○ Oikos System for Driade, 1972
    ○ Kroma Dining Table for Driade, 1983
      ○ Aforismi Cabinets, 1984
        ⬡ Didymos Oval Table for Driade, 2014 (p. 27)

1942– Anne Krohn Graham

○ Silver Rattle, 1973
⬡ Traveling Flatware, 1978 (p. 106)
  ○ Picnic In Central Park Traveling
    Cutlery Set, 1992
    ○ Science Brooch, 1994

1942– Mira Nakashima

○ New Chair Rocker with Arms, 1991
  ○ Keisho Bryfogle Dining Table, 1998
    ⬡ Concordia Chair, 2003 (p. 166)
      ○ Conoid Desk, 2009
        ○ Value of the Void Side Table, 2020

1943– Jane Dillon

⬡ Moveable Chair, 1968 (p. 85)
  ○ Cometa Kite Light with Charles Dillon, 1972
    ○ Jobber Office Chair with Charles Dillon, 1975
      ○ Multipla Chair with Peter Wheeler for Kron, 1992

1943– Ingegerd Råman

⬡ Water Decanter, 1958 (p. 184)
  ○ Candlestick Holder and Vase, 1981
    ○ Drop Pitcher, 1981
      ○ Cognac Glass, 1996
        ○ Wishes Bowl, 2001
          ○ Important Plate for Ikea, 2016

1944– Lucia Bartolini

○ Safari Sofa with Archizoom Associati, 1967–68
  ○ San Remo Halogen Floor Lamp with Archizoom
    Associati, 1968
    ⬡ Mies Chair and Ottoman made with Archizoom
      Associati, 1969 (p. 32)

1945– Renate Müller

⬡ Therapeutic Toys, 1969 (p. 164)
  ○ Sculptural Boat Play Area with
    Sails with Bernd Rückert, 2013
    ○ Birds Carpet with Amini, 2016

1945– Hiroko Takeda

○ Light Switches with
  Andries van Onck for Habitat, c. 1979
  ○ Tokyo Door Handle with
    Andries van Onck for Olivari, c. 1980s
    ○ Condor Chair with Andries van Onck
      for Magis, c. 1980s
      ○ Eve Ashtray with Andries van Onck
        for Magis, c. 1980s
        ⬡ Lem Adjustable Table with Andries
          van Onck for Magis, 1984 (p. 222)
          ○ Tiramisù Folding Ladder with
            Andries Van Onck for Kartell, 1991

1949– Etel Carmona

○ Esteira Screen, 1998
  ○ Tanajura Bottle, 2002
    ○ Esquadro Desk, 2007
      ⬡ 22 Chair, 2008 (p. 61)
        ○ Capadócia Screen with Carlos Vergara, 2017
          ○ Callas Bench with Inês Schertel, 2020

1950–2016 Zaha Hadid

⌂ Vitra Fire Station, Weil am Rhein (DE), 1994
  ⌂ Serpentine Pavilion, London, England (UK), 2000
    ○ Tea and Coffee Piazza for Alessi, 2003
      ⬡ Mesa Table, 2007 (p. 113)
        ○ Moon System Sofa for B&B Italia, 2007
          ⌂ London Aquatic Centre, England (UK), 2012
            ⌂ Hydar Aliyev Center, Baku (AZ), 2013
              ○ Zephyr Sofa for Cassina, 2013

1950– Paola Navone

⬡ Ghost Armchair for Gervasoni, 2004 (p. 167)
  ○ Sellerina Aluminum Armchair for Baxter, 2008
    ○ Low Lita Lounge Chair, 2011
      ○ Edible Christmas Calendar for
        Häagen-Dazs, 2015
        ○ Drops Textile for Dominique Kieffer, 2016

1951– Hisako Watanabe

⬡ The Analogon Desk with Kenji Oki,
  1984 (p. 234)
  ○ Babel Lamp with Kenji Oki, 1986
    ○ Papillion Sofa with Kenji Oki, 1988
      ○ Cosmic-Plant Coat Hanger with
        Kenji Oki, 1989

1953– Karin Schou Andersen

⬡ Flatware, 1979 (p. 23)
  ○ Catering: Termotray and Plate for
    Bendt Brandt, 1984
    ○ Jello Bicyclestand with NATION for
      Out-sider, 2011
      ○ ROMA Bench with Grønlund, 2012

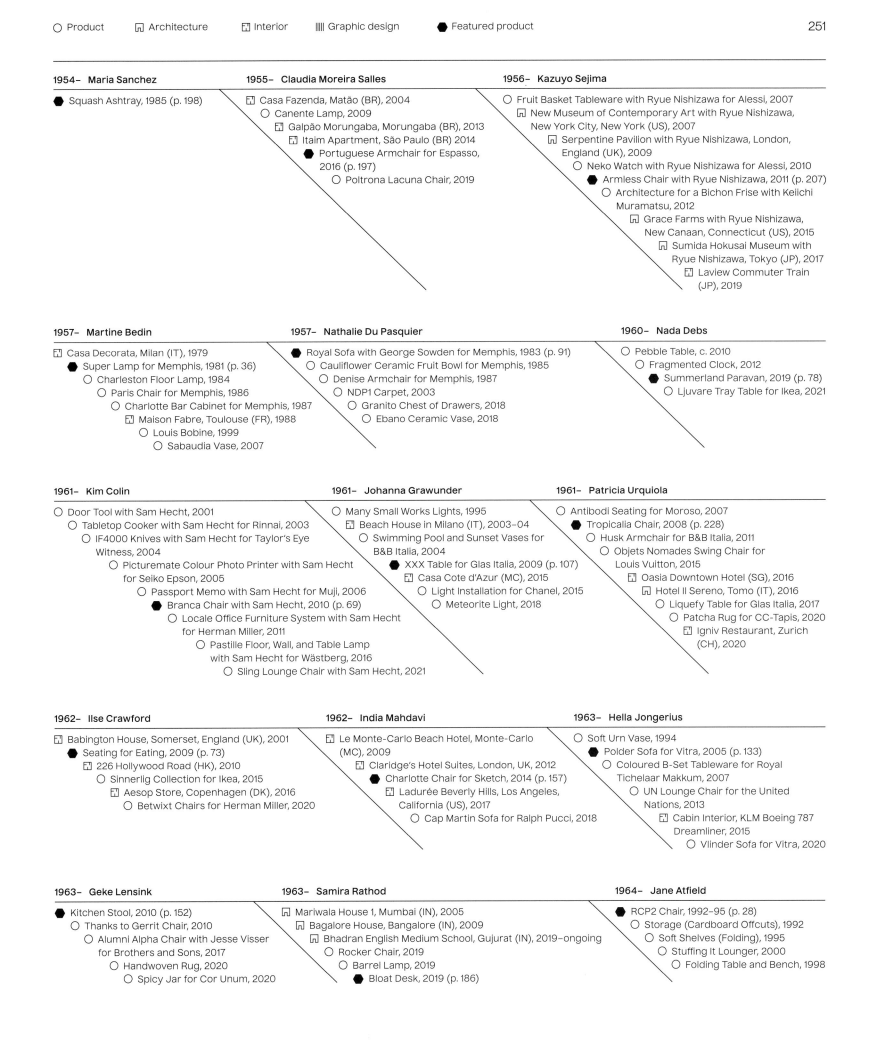

1954– Maria Sanchez

⬢ Squash Ashtray, 1985 (p. 198)

1955– Claudia Moreira Salles

⊡ Casa Fazenda, Matão (BR), 2004
○ Canente Lamp, 2009
⊡ Galpão Morungaba, Morungaba (BR), 2013
⊡ Itaim Apartment, São Paulo (BR) 2014
⬢ Portuguese Armchair for Espasso, 2016 (p. 197)
○ Poltrona Lacuna Chair, 2019

1956– Kazuyo Sejima

○ Fruit Basket Tableware with Ryue Nishizawa for Alessi, 2007
⌂ New Museum of Contemporary Art with Ryue Nishizawa, New York City, New York (US), 2007
⌂ Serpentine Pavilion with Ryue Nishizawa, London, England (UK), 2009
○ Neko Watch with Ryue Nishizawa for Alessi, 2010
⬢ Armless Chair with Ryue Nishizawa, 2011 (p. 207)
○ Architecture for a Bichon Frise with Keiichi Muramatsu, 2012
⌂ Grace Farms with Ryue Nishizawa, New Canaan, Connecticut (US), 2015
⌂ Sumida Hokusai Museum with Ryue Nishizawa, Tokyo (JP), 2017
⊡ Laview Commuter Train (JP), 2019

1957– Martine Bedin

⊡ Casa Decorata, Milan (IT), 1979
⬢ Super Lamp for Memphis, 1981 (p. 36)
○ Charleston Floor Lamp, 1984
○ Paris Chair for Memphis, 1986
○ Charlotte Bar Cabinet for Memphis, 1987
⊡ Maison Fabre, Toulouse (FR), 1988
○ Louis Bobine, 1999
○ Sabaudia Vase, 2007

1957– Nathalie Du Pasquier

⬢ Royal Sofa with George Sowden for Memphis, 1983 (p. 91)
○ Cauliflower Ceramic Fruit Bowl for Memphis, 1985
○ Denise Armchair for Memphis, 1987
○ NDP1 Carpet, 2003
○ Granito Chest of Drawers, 2018
○ Ebano Ceramic Vase, 2018

1960– Nada Debs

○ Pebble Table, c. 2010
○ Fragmented Clock, 2012
⬢ Summerland Paravan, 2019 (p. 78)
○ Ljuvare Tray Table for Ikea, 2021

1961– Kim Colin

○ Door Tool with Sam Hecht, 2001
○ Tabletop Cooker with Sam Hecht for Rinnai, 2003
○ IF4000 Knives with Sam Hecht for Taylor's Eye Witness, 2004
○ Picturemate Colour Photo Printer with Sam Hecht for Seiko Epson, 2005
○ Passport Memo with Sam Hecht for Muji, 2006
⬢ Branca Chair with Sam Hecht, 2010 (p. 69)
○ Locale Office Furniture System with Sam Hecht for Herman Miller, 2011
○ Pastille Floor, Wall, and Table Lamp with Sam Hecht for Wästberg, 2016
○ Sling Lounge Chair with Sam Hecht, 2021

1961– Johanna Grawunder

○ Many Small Works Lights, 1995
⊡ Beach House in Milano (IT), 2003–04
○ Swimming Pool and Sunset Vases for B&B Italia, 2004
⬢ XXX Table for Glas Italia, 2009 (p. 107)
⊡ Casa Cote d'Azur (MC), 2015
○ Light Installation for Chanel, 2015
○ Meteorite Light, 2018

1961– Patricia Urquiola

○ Antibodi Seating for Moroso, 2007
⬢ Tropicalia Chair, 2008 (p. 228)
○ Husk Armchair for B&B Italia, 2011
○ Objets Nomades Swing Chair for Louis Vuitton, 2015
⊡ Oasia Downtown Hotel (SG), 2016
⌂ Hotel Il Sereno, Tomo (IT), 2016
○ Liquefy Table for Glas Italia, 2017
○ Patcha Rug for CC-Tapis, 2020
⊡ Igniv Restaurant, Zurich (CH), 2020

1962– Ilse Crawford

⊡ Babington House, Somerset, England (UK), 2001
⬢ Seating for Eating, 2009 (p. 73)
⊡ 226 Hollywood Road (HK), 2010
○ Sinnerlig Collection for Ikea, 2015
⊡ Aesop Store, Copenhagen (DK), 2016
○ Betwixt Chairs for Herman Miller, 2020

1962– India Mahdavi

⊡ Le Monte-Carlo Beach Hotel, Monte-Carlo (MC), 2009
⊡ Claridge's Hotel Suites, London, UK, 2012
⬢ Charlotte Chair for Sketch, 2014 (p. 157)
⊡ Ladurée Beverly Hills, Los Angeles, California (US), 2017
○ Cap Martin Sofa for Ralph Pucci, 2018

1963– Hella Jongerius

○ Soft Urn Vase, 1994
⬢ Polder Sofa for Vitra, 2005 (p. 133)
○ Coloured B-Set Tableware for Royal Tichelaar Makkum, 2007
○ UN Lounge Chair for the United Nations, 2013
⊡ Cabin Interior, KLM Boeing 787 Dreamliner, 2015
○ Vlinder Sofa for Vitra, 2020

1963– Geke Lensink

⬢ Kitchen Stool, 2010 (p. 152)
○ Thanks to Gerrit Chair, 2010
○ Alumni Alpha Chair with Jesse Visser for Brothers and Sons, 2017
○ Handwoven Rug, 2020
○ Spicy Jar for Cor Unum, 2020

1963– Samira Rathod

⌂ Mariwala House 1, Mumbai (IN), 2005
⌂ Bagalore House, Bangalore (IN), 2009
⌂ Bhadran English Medium School, Gujurat (IN), 2019–ongoing
○ Rocker Chair, 2019
○ Barrel Lamp, 2019
⬢ Bloat Desk, 2019 (p. 186)

1964– Jane Atfield

⬢ RCP2 Chair, 1992–95 (p. 28)
○ Storage (Cardboard Offcuts), 1992
○ Soft Shelves (Folding), 1995
○ Stuffing It Lounger, 2000
○ Folding Table and Bench, 1998

1964– Ayse Birsel

○ Orchestra Desk Accessories and Storage
  Solutions with Bruce Hannah for Knoll, 1990
  ○ Bidet and Toilet for Toto, 1995
    ○ Red Rocket Desk for Herman Miller, 2000
      ○ Resolve Office System for Herman Miller, 2001
        ⬢ Toogou Armchair with Bibi Seck, 2009 (p. 46)
          ○ Overlay Moveable Walls for Herman Miller, c. 2019

1964– Rianne Makkink

○ Ear Chair for Interpolis with Jurgen Bey, 2002
  ○ Birdwatch Cabinet Boy with Jurgen Bey, 2003
    ○ Stubborn Chair with Jurgen Bey, 2010
      ○ Kade Chai with Jurgen Beyr, 2008
        ⬢ Pixelated Rug with Nai-Dan Chang for
          CSrugs, 2020 (p. 158)

1964– Hikaru Mori

○ Iota Desk Lamp for Cassina, c. 1994
  ○ Stones Like Water Bathroom System for
    Piba Marmi Spa, 2007
      ⬢ Carmencita Lamp, 2012 (p. 163)
        ⌂ Renovation of Venice Biennale Japan
          Pavillion with Toyo Ito, Venice (IT), 2014
          ⌂ Controne River Park, Controne
            (IT), 2015
              ○ Ombra Table Square, 2019

1965– Jeannette Altherr

○ Leaf Cushion for Arper, 2005
  ⬢ SAYA Chair with Alberto Lievore for
    Arper, 2011 (p. 22)
      ○ Wing Coathanger for Arper, 2013
        ○ Cila Chair for Arper, 2017
          ○ Paravan with Lievore + Altherr Désile
            Park for Arper, 2019

1965– Carina Seth Andersson

○ Daag Vase for Svenskt Tenn, 2009
  ○ Vases and Textiles for Marimekko, 2016
    ○ Royal Stemware for Skruf, 2016
      ⬢ Blue Pallo Vase for Poltrona Frau, 2017 (p. 25)
        ○ Clay Bowls and Plates for Arket, 2017

1965– Matali Crasset

○ Essentiel de Pâtisserie Utensils for Alessi, 2010
  ⬢ Foglie Lamp for Pallucco, 2010 (p. 71)
    ⌂ Dar Hi Hotel, Nefta (TN), 2011
      ○ Dynamic Life Sofa for Campeggi, c. 2011
        ○ PS Light for Ikea, 2016
          ⊡ Tonic Archipelago Furniture Stations
            for Université Paris-Saclay, Paris
            (FR), 2020

1966– Tomoko Azumi

○ Table=Chest, 1995
  ○ LEM Stool with Shin Azumi for
    Lapalma, 2000
      ○ Furniture for the Supreme Court
        of the United Kingdom, 2009
          ⬢ Flow Chair for Ercol, 2015 (p. 30)
            ○ 001./ One Dot Eyewear for
              Tanaka Optical, 2020

1966– Shinobu Ito

○ Horeta Ceiling Light with Setsu Ito, 1998
  ⬢ Au Seating with Setsu Ito for Edra, 2003 (p. 125)
    ○ Hakobune Bathtub and Washbasin, 2006
      ○ Su e Giù Bed for Aisin, 2009
        ○ Mutable Spirit Armchair for Grassi Pietre, 2012
          ○ Origami Mix Textile for Illulian, 2019

1966– Monica Förster

○ Tray Side Table for Offecct, 2004
  ⬢ Glide Lounge for Tacchini, 2006 (p. 101)
    ○ Antelope Dining Chair for Swedese, 2010
      ○ Tower Measuring Set for Alessi, 2013
        ○ Four Elements Tiles for Marrakech Design, 2018
          ○ Tunes Candleholder for Georg Jensen, 2020

1966– Ineke Hans

○ Azur Table for Habitat, 1995
  ○ Under Cover Chairs, 1997
    ○ Magic Chair (Black Project series), 2002
      ⬢ Long Bench for Shorefast Foundation,
        2013 (p. 115)
          ○ Fresh Berry Bowl for Royal VKB, 2013
            ○ Instant Desk for Opendesk, 2017
              ⊡ Pink Salon Meeting Room for
                CapitalC, Amsterdam (NL), 2020

1968– Lindsey Adelman

⬢ Branching Bubble Chandelier, 2006 (p. 17)
  ○ Agnes Chandelier, 2010
    ○ Catch Floor Light, 2013
      ○ Branching Disc Chandelier with
        Nymphenburg, 2016
          ○ Chandelier for Nike, 2016
            ○ Paradise City Lighting Installation, 2019
              ○ Catch Box Table Light, 2020

1968– Rossana Hu

○ ZiSha Tea Project with Lyndon Neri, 2006
  ○ Common Comrades Stools with Lyndon Neri for Moooi, 2012
    ⌂ Suzhou Chapel with Lyndon Neri, Suzhou (CN), 2016
      ⌂ Tsingpu Yangzhou Retreat with Lyndon Neri, Jiangsu
        (CN), 2017
          ○ Yanzi Light for Artemide with Lyndon Neri, 2017
            ⬢ LAN Sofa with Lyndon Neri for GAN, 2018
              (p. 123)

1968– Inga Sempé

○ Pleated Suspension Lamp for Cappellini, 2003
  ○ Sweet Whipped Cream Sofa for Edra, 2007
    ○ Lunatic Table for Ligne Roset, 2010
      ⬢ w153 île for Wästberg, 2015 (p. 208)
        ○ Collo-alto Cutlery Set for Alessi, 2015
          ○ Pandarine Sofa for HAY, 2020

1970– Louise Campbell

○ Retreat Funnel Chair, 1998
  ○ Prince Chair for HAY, 2001
    ○ Campbell Pendant for
      Louis Poulsen Lighting, 2004
        ○ Furnishings Flexible Storage Units, 2011
          ⬢ Cutlery for George Jensen, 2014 (p. 59)

1971– Marie Burgos

⊡ Chelsea Penthouse, New York City,
  New York (US), 2011
    ⊡ Tuscan Style Loft, New York City,
      New York (US), 2014
        ○ Cayenne Chair and Ottoman, 2018
          ⬢ Milo Chair, 2018 (p. 58)

1972– Felicia Ferrone

⬢ Revolution Wine and Water Glasses, 2001 (p. 98)
  ○ Shift Table, 2010
    ○ Index Mirror for Boffi, 2012
      ○ Lilium Carafe and Cup for OTHR, 2016
        ○ Albany Vase, 2018

1972– Marialaura Rossiello Irvine

○ Juno Eco Chair for Arper, 2020
  ○ Quilt Porcelain Tiles System for
    Mosaico+, 2020
      ⬢ Fusto Bookshelf for Forma & Cemento,
        2020 (p. 124)
          ○ S 5000 Retreat Seating System for
            Thonet, 2021

1972– Cecilie Manz

○ Hochacht Ladder, 1999
  ○ Caravaggio Lamp for Lightyears, 2005
    ○ Minuscule Chair for Fritz Hansen, 2012
      ○ A1 Speaker for Bang & Olufsen, 2016
        ○ Moku Chair, 2016
          ⬢ Plint Coffee Table, 2020 (p. 159)

1974– & 1978– Veronica Dagnert & Helena Jonasson

○ Cast Lights for the Ace Hotel, London, England (UK), 2015
○ Cone Pendant Light, 2015
○ Vessels Glass, 2018
● Inox Table, 2018 (p. 76)

1975– Carol Catalano

○ Mambo Chair, 1990s
● Capelli Stool for Herman Miller, 1999 (p. 64)
○ DuoGlide Arthritis Knife for Dexter, 2006–08
○ Induction Tea Kettle, 2009
○ HE1000 Headphones for HIFIMAN, 2013–15

1976– Maddalena Casadei

○ Bella Mirror for Marsotto edizioni, 2010
⊡ Private Villa, Tuscany (IT), 2017
○ Bellaria Armchair and Sofa for Paola Zani, 2019
● Verso Table for Fucina, 2019 (p. 62)
○ Into Each Other Ceramics, 2020

1976– Carol Gay

○ U Magazine Holder, 2000
● NoAr Lounge Chair, 2010 (p. 102)
○ Metro Centro Table, 2010
○ Card Game Chandelier, 2013
○ Amplifier and Lamp Tower, 2018
○ Spherical Vase, 2019

1976– Agata Kulik-Pomorska

○ Second Life View Ladder with Pawel Pomorski, 2010
○ Blow Sofa with Pawel Pomorski, 2012
● PAPER+ Armchair with Pawel Pomorski, 2012 (p. 143)

1976– & 1977– Sofia Lagerkvist & Anna Lindgren

○ Materialized Sketch Chair, 2005
○ Animal Things for Moooi, 2006
○ Blow Away Vase for Moooi, 2009
● Furia Rocking Horse, 2016 (p. 144)
○ Resting Animals for Vitra, 2018
○ Library Lamp for National Museum of Sweden, 2018

1977– Vivian Beer

● Current Chair, 2004 (p. 37)
○ Spine Chair, 2008
○ Anchored Candy Bench No.4, 2011
○ Low Rider Lounge, 2013
○ Anchored Candy No. 6 (Cleo) Lounge, 2014

1977– Faye Toogood

○ Element Table, 2010
● Roly-Poly Chair, 2014 (p. 226)
○ Hill Quilt for Once Milano, 2017
⊡ Ibiza House, Ibiza (ES), 2017
⊡ Walter Segal House, London, England (UK), 2018
○ Puffy Lounge for Hem, 2020
○ Dough Tableware, 2021

1977– Donna Wilson

● Creatures, 2003 (p. 236)
○ Mushroom Cushion, 2017
○ Mermaid Hot Water Bottle, 2018
○ Abstract Assembly Chair, 2019
○ Waves and Ovals Rug for SCP, 2019

1977– Sandrine Ebène de Zorzi

● Kiti Makasi Chair with Michel Vamba Tiwete, 2013

1978– Kiki van Eijk

○ Kiki Carpet, 2000
● Soft Table Lamp, 2010 (p. 94)
○ Floating Frames Clock, 2011
○ Civilised Primitives Daybed, 2016
○ Freeform Lighting, 2018–19
○ Botanica Teatowel for TextielMuseum, 2019–20
○ Matrice Crystal Vase for Saint-Louis, 2020

1978– Mette Hay

● HAY Accessories with others, 2002–ongoing (p. 118)

1978– Moyo Ogunseinde

● Oko Chair, 2017 (p. 175)
○ Mmiri Serving Bowls, 2017
○ Sibi Kekere Small Spoon, 2016
○ Ayo Board Game, 2017

1979– & 1986– Andrea Flores & Lucía Soto

○ Fernández Sofa, 2015
⊡ Casa Cima, Chihuahua (MX), 2016
● Lira Coffee Table, 2020 (p. 99)

1979– Ania Jaworska

⊡ Installation for the Graham Foundation for Advanced Studies in the Fine Arts, Illinois (US), 2013
● SET Furniture, 2016 (p. 129)
○ Seat Cushions for Kvadrat and Febrik, 2020

1979– Ionna Vautrin

○ Binic Table Lamp for Foscarini, 2010
○ Ô Vases for Moustache, 2011
○ Mezzo Radio for Lexon, 2013
● Lamp TGV, 2017 (p. 231)

1980– Bec Brittain

○ Shy 08.1 Lighting, 2011
○ Echo 1 Lighting, 2013
○ Vise Lighting, 2013
○ Seed Single Pendant, 2016
● Aries IV.I Lighting, 2017 (p. 53)

1980– Chen-Yen Wei

● Afteroom Chair with Hung-Ming Chen for MENU, 2013 (p. 235)
○ Teddy with Hung-Ming Chen for MENU Nepal Projects, 2015
○ Sideboard with Hung-Ming Chen for Reform, 2017
○ Story Shelving Unit with Hung-Ming Chen for DWR, 2021

1981– & 1981– Nata Janberidze & Keti Toloraia

○ Invisible Wood Table, 2014
● Spiral Floor Lamp, 2017 (p. 128)
○ Life on Earth Stool, 2018
○ Sacral Geometry Coffee Table with Shotiko Aptsiauri, 2021

1981– Tamara Pérez

○ Gudpaka Lamp with gt2P, 2011
⊡ Infodema Headquarters with gt2P, Las Condes (CL), 2012
○ Less CPP N2 Wall Lights with gt2P, 2014
○ Imaginary Geographies Coffee Table with gt2P, 2018
● Remolton Monolita Chair with gt2P, 2019 (p. 179)

1982– Monling Lee

○ Neotenic Lounge with Justin Donnelly, 2018
○ Squiggle Vessel with Justin Donnelly, 2020
● Sport Sofa with Justin Donnelly, 2020 (p. 150)

1982– Jay Sae Jung Oh

○ Wild Mirror, 2011
  ○ Savage Chair, 2011
    ● Savage Sofa, 2016 (p. 176)

1982– Jungyou Choi

○ Hemp Vase with Kyuhyung Cho, 2012
  |||| Geurim Font with Kyuhyung Cho, 2016
    ● Word Table Light with Kyuhyung Cho for Dims., 2019 (p. 65)
      ⊡ Breezm Store, Seoul (KR), 2019

1982– Rachel Griffin

● Face Value Modular Tables, 2013 (p. 110)
  ○ Fragment Tableware, 2014
    ○ Mill Table Lamp for Free to Edition, 2016
      ○ Post Lamp Family for Muuto, 2017
        ○ Kink Vase for Muuto, 2018

1982– & 1985– Molly Purnell & Rachel Bullock

○ Confetti Planter, 2018
  ⊡ Dandelion Chocolate, San Francisco,
    California (US), 2018
      ○ Bobbin Bench, 2019
        ● Ribbon Chair, 2020 (p. 57)

1982– Mpho Vackier

○ Thandeka Server, 2016
  ○ Thulani Loveseat, 2017
    ● Oromo Dining Chair, 2019 (p. 229)
      ○ Fulani Dining Chair, 2020

1983– & 1983– Laelie Berzon & Lisa Vincitorio

○ Mia Coffee Table, 2015
  ○ Finn Easy Chair, 2016
    ● Halo Chair, 2017 (p. 42)
      ○ Ari Curve Sofa, 2020

1983– Qiyun Deng

● Soft Pack Sofa, 2014 (p. 79)
  ○ Graft Bioplastic Tableware, 2013
    ○ Clamshell Case with Benwu Studio
      for BMW, 2016
        ⊡ Great Migration Store Design with
          Benwu Studio for Hermès, Shanghai
          (CH), 2016

1983– Lucie Koldová

○ Muffins Lamp for Brokis, 2011
  ○ Brush Rug for Chevallier édition, 2016
    ● Jack O'Lantern for Brokis, 2018 (p. 140)
      ○ Cocon Chair for Master & Master, 2019
        ○ Sfera Light for Brokis, 2020

1983– Francesca Lanzavecchia

○ No Country for Old Men (Elderly Furniture Aid Objects)
  with Hunn Wai, 2012
    ○ Taco Service Table with Hunn Wai for Cappellini, 2015
      ● Pebble Desk with Hunn Wai for Living Divani,
        2018 (p. 148)
          ○ Pinch Mirror with Hunn Wai for FIAM Italia, 2018

1983– Aljoud Lootah

○ Unfolding Unity Stool, 2013
  ● Oru Cabinet, 2015 (p. 155)
    ○ Takya Stool, 2018
      ○ Spathe Rug, 2019

1983–, 1984– & 1984 Hillary Petrie, Stephanie Beamer & Crystal Ellis

○ Samuel Side Table, 2012
  ○ Pete & Nora Floor Lamp, 2016
    ● Kenny Dining Table, 2018 (p. 33)
      ○ Hornbake Sofa, 2019

1983– & 1986– Jessie Young & Emiliana Gonzalez

● UNA Chair, 2016 (p. 105)
  ○ Segment Stool, 2018
    ○ Dome Handles, 2019
      ○ Bow Floor Lamp, 2020

1984– Maria Bruun

○ Objects of Use Vases as MBADV, 2015
  ○ Base Bench as MBADV, 2015
    ○ The Seating Chair as MBADV, 2016
      ● Bigfoot Furniture, 2019 (p. 56)

1984– Marie Dessuant

○ Étagère de Coin Corner Shelf for Ligne Roset, 2010
  ○ Another Ceramic Candlestick for Another Country, 2012
    ● Day Bed with Philip Bone, 2017 (p. 81)

1984– Anna Karlin

○ Plumb Sconce, 2016
  ○ Wooden Chess Armchair, 2017
    ○ Layered Planters, 2017
      ● Lady Lamp, 2019 (p. 136)
        ○ Puddle Table, 2019

1984– Ana Kraš

○ Noodle Side Table, 2000; for Et al., 2020
  ○ Bonbon Lamp, 2010–17; for HAY, 2019
    ● Slon Round Table for Matter Made, 2015 (p. 141)
      ○ Mara Furniture, 2017

1984– Saša Štucin

○ Lenticularis Mirror as Soft Baroque, 2013
  ○ Puffy Brick as Soft Baroque, 2018
    ● Hard Round Armchair as Soft Baroque,
      2019 (p. 220)
        ○ Soft Metal Hanger as Soft Baroque, 2019

1985– Stephanie Ng

○ Luna Lana Light, 2013
  ○ VAAS Light, 2014
    ● Scoop Desk Lamp, 2015 (p. 169)
      ○ XY Chandelier, 2015

1985– Sabine Marcelis

○ Candy Cubes, 2014
  ⊡ Repossi Flagship Store, Paris (FR), 2016
    ● Soap Table, 2018 (p. 161)
      ○ Hula Chandelier for Nilufar Gallery, 2019

1985– Coco Reynolds

● Art Pendant Light, 2010 (p. 191)
  ○ Bermuda Wall Light, 2019
    ○ Lune Pendant, 2020

1985– Latifa Saeed

○ Bedouin Box, 2013
  ● Braided Chair, 2013 (p. 195)
    ○ Kinetic Khoos for Tashkeel, 2015

1985– Claudia Suárez Ahedo

○ Bench with Side Table, 2017
  ○ S1 Wood Chair, 2018
    ● Ch'up Chair, 2018 (p. 221)
      ○ COU Side Table, 2020

1987– Merve Kahraman

○ Revitalizer Lamp, 2015
  ⊡ Upper East Side Residence, New York City, New York (US), 2018
    ○ Zaziko Mirror, 2020
      ● Cassini Floor Lamp, 2019 (p. 134)
        ○ UPTE Dining Table, 2021

1987– & 1987– Sophie Lou Jacobsen & Sarita Posada

● Lamp 01, 2018 (p. 126)
  ○ Chair 02, 2018
    ○ Bench 01, 2018

1987– Dina Nur Satti

⬣ Baobab Bowl, 2018 (p. 173)
○ Acacia 1 Vase, 2021
○ Zir Vessel, 2021

1988– Yeşim Eröktem

○ Bebek Wooden Container with Doğanberk Demir, 2014
○ Robe and Towel Set with Doğanberk Demir for *Wallpaper** Handamde, 2016
⬣ Volume Side Table with Doğanberk Demir, 2016 (p. 95)
○ Sedir Sofa System with Doğanberk Demir for Habitat, 2018

1989– Lani Adeoye

○ Lilo Chair, 2015
○ Sisi Eko Floor Lamp, 2017
⬣ Bata Stool, 2019 (p. 18)
○ Kini Chaise Lounger and Umbrella, 2019

1989– Ilaria Bianchi

○ Duo Shelf, 2015
○ CastAway Coffee Table, 2015
○ I Can't Believe This is Not Stone! Bench, 2015
⬣ Blueprint Table, 2017 (p. 45)
○ Colonna Carrara Candle Holder, 2018

1989– Rosie Li

○ Stella Triangle Light, 2013
○ Bubbly Table Lamp, 2015
○ Hesse Light Chandelier, 2017
⬣ Pebble Hanging Lamp, 2018 (p. 153)

1989– Ignacia Murtagh

○ Kal Textile, 2014
○ El Plomo Side Table, 2014
⬣ Lof Tableware, 2016 (p. 165)
○ Nuna Rug, 2018
○ Lapis Benches, 2020

1989– & 1990– Mentalla Said & Jumana Taha

○ Moza Chair, 2016
⬣ Hizz Rocking Chair, 2016 (p. 196)
○ Tala III Coffee Table, 2018

1989– Mary Ratcliffe

⬣ Lyndoe Low Seat, 2019 (p. 185)
○ Dawlish Dining Table, 2019
○ INA Side Table, 2018
○ VSSL Container, 2020

1989– Mia Senekal

⬣ Quarter Coffee Table, 2019 (p. 209)
○ New Moon Sofa, 2019
○ Waning Armchair, 2019

1989– Sohyun Yun

○ Wavy Trays for Pernille Lauridsen, 2020
○ Layer Chair, 2015
○ TONE Shelf, 2019
⬣ TONE Table, 2019 (p. 238)

1990– Estefanía de Ros

○ Eclipse Sol Screen, 2016
○ Apolonio Rug with Gustavo Quintana, 2016
○ Lana Chair with Gustavo Quintana, 2018
⬣ Altar Console with Gustavo Quintana, 2018 (p. 193)

1990– Rand Abdul Jabbar

⬣ Forma II Stool, 2015 (p. 15)
○ Sin Marble Work, 2018
○ Earthly Wonders, Celestial Beings Vase, 2019

1990– Kawther Alsaffar

○ Cherry Bowl and Disk, 2009
○ Erganomic Handheld Vacuum, 2010
○ Door Storage, 2011
⬣ Bungee Chair, 2011 (p. 21)

1990– Wendy Andreu

○ Ou bien Chair, 2011
○ Regen Textile, 2016
○ Wobbly Carpet, 2018
⬣ Dragon Chair and Ottoman, 2020 (p. 26)

1990– Nikita Bhate

⬣ Tankan Lounge Chair with Pascal Hien, 2017 (p. 43)
○ Barza (Balcony) Lounge Sofa with Pascal Hien, 2017
○ Hover Roti Box with Pascal Hien, 2021
○ Flawless Rolling Board & Pin with Pascal Hien, 2021

1990– Lisa Ertel

○ Louise Lamp, 2013
○ Windowshopper Rug, 2016
○ Little Finger Vase, 2015
○ Franklin Table, 2016
⊡ Cola Taxi Okay with Anne-Sophie Oberkrome, Karlsruhe (DE), 2016
⬣ Dune Furniture, 2017 (p. 97)
○ Neil Chair, 2018
○ Hi-Light, 2019

1992– Utharaa Zacharias

○ SW Fluffy Chair, 2018
○ Donut Coffee Table, 2019
○ Five-Tier Leaning Shelf, 2019
⬣ Elio Lamp, 2020 (p. 239)

1993– Garance Vallée

○ Candle Holder, 2020
⊡ Installation for Nike, 2020
○ Triangle Chair, 2020
⬣ Puddle Table, 2020 (p. 230)

1994– Mimi Shodeinde

⬣ Dip Lounger, 2016 (p. 210)
⌂ Private Residence, Lagos (NG), 2016
○ Omi Table, 2018
○ Okuta Tea Set, 2018
○ Ice Wall Sconce, 2019

1
Alison Smithson, "Beatrix Potter's Places," *Architectural Design*, no. 37 (1967): 573.

2
"Good Design" was a term popularized on both sides of the Atlantic after WWII. It was thought of as a way to speed up economic recovery by creating everyday, mainly domestic products that could both improve people's lives, but in doing so, establish a consumer market.

Juliet Kinchin and Andrew Gardner. "What do We Mean By Good Design?," MoMA Magazine, March 4, 2019, www.moma.org/magazine/articles/38.

3
Anon. "The Frankfurt Kitchen," Museum of Modern Art, www.moma.org/interactives/exhibitions/2010/counter_space/the_frankfurt_kitchen.

4
Anna Maga. "Maria Chomentowska: Calling Cards of the Industrial Design Institute," Culture.pl, December 17, 2012, www.culture.pl/en/article/maria-chomentowska-calling-cards-of-the-industrial-design-institute.

5
Anon. "History of Polish Design," Institute of Industrial Design, www.iwp.com.pl/polish_design_history.

6
Margarete Schütte-Lihotzky was sent to the Soviet Union as part of the building brigade, but was jailed for four years during World War II for her communist activities and anti-Nazi campaigning. Hungarian Eva Zeisel spent eighteen months imprisoned in the Soviet Union, accused of plotting against Stalin.

7
In her book *Invisible Women*, Carolina Criado-Perez describes in detail the gendered nature of the home, but also the actual design of products, often formed to male biology.

Caroline Criado-Perez. *Invisible Women: Exposing Data Bias in a World Designed for Men* (London: Chatto & Windus), 2020.

8
Franca Helg established a design office with Italian architect Franco Albini; Luisa Parisi had a successful career with her husband, Ico Parisi; and Emma Schweinberger was married to Ernesto Gismondi, cofounder of Artemide, the company for whom she created a number of commercially successful designs.

9
Cat Rossi, "Furniture, Feminism and the Feminine: Women Designers in Post-War Italy, 1945 to 1970," *Journal of Design History* 22, no. 3 (2009).

10
Ibid.

11
Cini Boeri stated that "I've also been called a marriage wrecker, as I always proposed two rooms."

12
Francesca Esposito. "Cini Boeri Independence and Responsibility," *Klat*, September 10, 2014, www.klat-magazine.com/en/architecture-en/cini-boeri/66072 .

13
Jane Dillon. Interview with Jane Hall. Personal interview. London, December 16, 2020.

14
Glenn Adamson. "Jane Dillon: Ahead of the Curve," *V&A Blog*, July 19, 2009, www.vam.ac.uk/blog/sketch-product/jane-dillon-ahead-curve.

15
Jane Dillon likens the contemporary design of the chair to a throne, a traditionally patriarchal symbol of power. Dillon, interview.

16
Dillon, interview.

17
Liz McQuiston. *Women in Design: A Contemporary View* (New York: Rizzoli, 1988).

18
A recent publication, *Bauhaus Women: A Global Perspective*, goes into greater detail about many women who studied at the Bauhaus, along with *Bauhausmädels: A Tribute to Pioneering Women Artists*, which while limited in biographical information contains exceptional archival photography.

Elizabeth Otto and Patrick Rössler. *Bauhaus Women: A Global Perspective* (London: Herbert Press, 2019).

Patrick Rössler. *Bauhausmädels: A Tribute to Pioneering Women Artists* (Cologne: Taschen, 2019).

19
Liz Elsby. "Coping Through Art: Freidl Dicker-Brandeis and the Children of Theresienstadt," *Yad Vashem: World Holocaust Remembrance Center*, June 6, 2016, www.yadvashem.org/articles/general/coping-through-art-brandeis-theresienstadt.

20
Anon. "Hedwig Bollhagen," Werkstätten Für Keramik, www.hedwig-bollhagen.com/company/history.

21
Juliet Kinchin. "Manufacturing Poetry: The Toys of Libuše Niklová," *Inside/Out: MoMA/MoMA PS1 Blog*, September 13, 2012, www.moma.org/explore/inside_out/2012/09/13/manufacturing-poetry-the-toys-of-libuse-niklova.

22
Tereza Bruthansova. *Libuše Niklová* (Czech Republic: Arbor Vitae, 2013).

23
At the prize-giving party, the Museum of Modern Art's president, Nelson Rockefeller, described the ambitions of the competition to unite "scientist and designer, museum and industry … that should make a real contribution to the improvement of standards of living."

Museum of Modern Art. 1950. "Awards Given in International Low-Cost Furniture Competition," [press release], www.moma.org/momaorg/shared/pdfs/docs/press_archives/1291/releases/MOMA_1949_0005_1949-01-13_490113-5.pdf?2010.

24
Michael Kimmelman, "Celebrating 'Good Design' at MoMA: The Nut Dish and Other Populist Gems," *New York Times*, June 6, 2019, www.nytimes.com/2019/06/06/arts/design/moma-good-design.

25
Museum of Modern Art. 1950. "Awards Given in International Low-Cost Furniture Competition," [press release], www.moma.org/momaorg/shared/pdfs/docs/press_archives/1291/releases/MOMA_1949_0005_1949-01-13_490113-5.pdf?2010.

26
Pat Kirkham. *Women Designers in the USA, 1900–2000* (New York, New Haven, and London: Yale University Press, 2001).

27
Ibid., 279.

28
Dora Vanette, "Design Icon: Greta Grossman," *Dwell*, April 3, 2014, www.dwell.com/article/greta-grossman-designs-58d7e4a6.

29
Anon. "New Lamps Presented by Woman Designer in Home Furnished with Modern Pieces," *New York Times*, December 13, 1949, www.nytimes.com/1949/12/13/archives/new-lamps-presented-by-woman-designer-in-home-furnished-with-modern.html.

30
"Pioneering Industrial Designers Celebrated on New Forever Stamps," United States Postal Service, June 29, 2011, about.usps.com/news/national-releases/2011/pr11_078.htm.

31
Anon. "Walter von Nessen," Nessen Lighting, www.nessenlighting.com/walter-von-nessen.

32
Design historians including Clementine and Charlotte Fiell, Pat Kirkham, Liz McQuiston, Alice Rawsthorn, Cat Rossi, Libby Sellers, and Penny Sparke have all provided histories from the late twentieth century onward about the role of women in design history.

33
Ahmed Ansari. "What a Decolonisation of Design Involves: Two Programmes for Emancipation," *Decolonizing Design*, April 12, 2018, www.decolonisingdesign.com/actions-and-interventions/publications/2018/what-a-decolonisation-of-design-involves-by-ahmed-ansari.

34
Chrissa Amuah: founder of Africa by Design, a platform that promotes designers from sub-Saharan Africa, and AMWA Designs. Interview with Jane Hall. Personal interview. London, December 4, 2020.

35
In 2020, the Museo Jumex in Mexico City held a far-reaching retrospective of Clara Porset's work, publishing an accompanying booklet by Ana Elena Mallet and Adraina Kuri Alamillo. Lina Bo Bardi's biographer Zeuler R.M. de A. Lima's book, *Lina Bo Bardi*, gives a comprehensive overview of her life and work.

Ana Elena Mallet and Adraina Kuri Alamillo. *Clara Porset: Design and Thinking* (Mexico City: Fundación Jumex Arte Contemporáneo, 2020). The publication is also generously made available for download: www.fundacionjumex.org/en/explora/publicaciones/107-clara-porset-diseno-y-pensamiento.

Zeuler R.M. de A. Lima, *Lina Bo Bardi* (London: Yale University Press, 2019).

36
Addie Topacio: son of Mercedes "Ched" Berenguer Topacio. Email correspondence with Jane Hall. Personal email. London, January 4, 2021.

37
Rachelle Median, "These 7 Women Are the Pioneers of Philippine Design," *ANCX*, May 9, 2019, https://news.abs-cbn.com/ancx/style/style-profile/03/29/19/these-7-women-are-the-pioneers-of-philippine-design.

38
Anon. "Noémi & Antonin Raymond," Raymond Farm Center for Living Arts & Design, www.raymondfarmcenter.org/theraymonds.

39
Kurt G.F. Helfrich and William Whitaker, *Crafting a Modern World: The Architecture and Design of Antonin and Noémi Raymond* (New York: Princeton Architectural Press, 2006), 14.

40
Many designers are in fact critical of these events for collapsing the cultural identities of many different countries into one, categorized by region.

41
In the UAE, architecture is considered the more prestigious career choice, and remains dominated by men, with design still seen as a discipline for women.

42
Rand Abdul Jabbar. Interview with Jane Hall. Personal interview. London, December 9, 2020.

43
Interestingly, this is a global phenomenon, with many young designers turning away from mass production with large manufacturers in favor of developing closer relationships with artisans and other craftspeople.

Page numbers in *italics* refer to illustrations

A

A. Lange & Söhne 161
Aalto, Aino, Pressed Glass 4644 14, *14*
Aalto, Alvar 14
Aarhus School of Architecture 23
Abdul Jabbar, Rand, Forma II 15, *15*
Abet Laminati 167
Académie de la Grande Chaumière 187
Academy of Arts, Architecture, and Design,
    Prague 140
Academy of Fine Arts, Gdańsk 143
Academy of Fine Arts, Warsaw 66, 142
Accademia di Belle Arti di Brera 74
Acerbi, Adelaide 27
Aczel, Alejandra 16
Aczel, Susi, Round Coffee Table 16, *16*
Adelman, Lindsey 153
    Branching Bubble Chandelier 17, *17*
Adeoye, Lani, Bata Stool 18, *18*
Adidas 136
Adler Schnee, Ruth, Construction Furnishing
    Fabric 19, *19*
Àga Concept 175
Agnes Studio 193
Air Design Studio 234
Aïssa Dione Tissus 86
Al Nahyan, Sheikh Mohammed Bin Zayed 155
Alsaffar, Kawther, Bungee Chair 21, *21*
Albers, Anni 138, 182
    Free-Hanging Room Divider 20, *20*
Albers, Josef 20, 182
Albini, Franco 63, 120, 200
Alessi 42, 215
Allaert Aluminium 80
Allgemeine Entwurfsanstalt 117
Alta Quota 178
Altherr, Jeannette, SAYA Chair 22, *22*
Amefa Apeldoornse Messenfabriek 23
American Designers Institute 139
American Institute of Architects 119, 194, 205
American Institute of Interior Designers 216
American Pediatric Clinic Foundation 142
American Union of Decorative Artists and
    Craftsmen 88
American University of Beirut 78, 106
Andersen, Karin Schou, Flatware 23, *23*
Anderson, Edgar 24
Anderson, Joyce, Chair 24, *24*
Andersson, Carina Seth, Blue Pallo Vase 25, *25*
Andreu, Wendy, Dragon Chair and Ottoman 26, *26*
Another Country 81
Arabia Company 154
Archigram 32
Architectural Association 53, 112, 137, 138, 156, 205
Architectural Design 214
Archizoom Associati 32, 167
Arcosanti 167
Arket 25
Arper 22, 49
Art Deco 88, 104, 231
Art Institute of Chicago 98, 119, 151, 213
Art Nouveau 29, 106
Art Students League 93, 149
Artek 14
Artemide 204
ArtEZ University of the Arts 152
Arts and Crafts movement 24
Arts Student League 147
Arup 137
Ascher, Zika 156
Associazione per il Disegno Industriale 75

Astori, Antonia, Didymos Oval Table 27, *27*
Astori, Enrico 27
AstoriDePontiAssociati 27
Atfield, Jane, RCP2 Chair 28, *28*
Athenaeum of Lausanne 27, 204
Augustine, Francis 58
Aulenti, Gae, Tavolo con Ruote 29, *29*
Austrian Museum of Applied Arts (MAK) 130
Ave Interruttori 222
Aver Amazônia 61
AZUMI 30
Azumi, Shin 30
Azumi, Tomoko, Flow Chair 30, *30*

B

B&B Italia 200
Badovici, Jean 109
Baldon, Cleo, Counter Stool 31, *31*
Barcelona International Exhibition (1929) 188
Bardi, Pietro Maria 49
Barker Bros 111
Barragán, Luis 182
Bartolini, Dario 32
Bartolini, Lucia, Mies Chair and Ottoman 32, *32*
Baughman, Milo 151
Bauhaus 20, 39, 52, 84, 103, 104, 121, 135, 152,
    188, 189, 201, 210, 215, 217, 218, 235
Bauhaus Archiv 215
Baumgarten, William 83
Baumritter 83
Bazaar Sabado 199
Beamer, Stephanie, Kenny Dining Table 33, *33*
Becker, Dorothee, Uten.Silo 34, *34*
Beckmann, Liisi, Karelia Easy Chair 35, *35*
Beckmans Designhögskola 101
Bedin, Martine, Super Lamp 36, *36*
Beer, Vivian, Current Chair 37, *37*
BEGA 227
Benetton 200
Benetton, Luciano 43, 80
Benwu 79
Berenguer-Topacio, Mercedes "Ched",
    Metal Klismos Chair 38, *38*
Berenguer-Topacio Design Corporation 38
Berger, Otti, Rug 39, *39*
Berger, Susi, Soft Chair 40, 41, *41*
Berger, Ueli 41
Bergman, Ingrid 111
Bertha Schaefer Gallery of Contemporary Art 201
Bertoia, Harry 16, 138
Berzon, Laelie, Halo Chair 42, *42*
Bey, Jurgen 158
Bezalel Academy of Arts and Design 202
Bhate, Nikita, Tankan Lounge Chair 43, *43*
BHC School of Design 209
Bianchi, Ilaria, Blueprint Table 44–5, 45
Big Piano 186
Bill, Max 49
Bio Design Lab 97
Birsel, Ayse, Toogou Armchair 46, *46*
Birsel+Seck 46
Black, Professor Misha 218
Black Artists and Designers Guild 58
Black Mountain College 20, 182
Bleiswijk, Joost van 94
Bo Bardi, Lina, Bowl Chair 48, 49, *49*, 54
Boal, Aída, Angela Chair 47, *47*
Boeri, Cini, Ghost Chair 50, *50*
Bollhagen, Hedwig 121
    766 Watering Can 51, *51*
Bonacina, Vittorio 120
Bone, Philip 80
Borsoi, Acácio Gil 70

Borsoi Arquitetura 70
Botta, Mario 126
Bottoni, Agustina 45
Bouroullec, Ronan and Erwan 231
Bradford Technical College 218
Brandt, Marianne 215
    Kettle 52, *52*
Brazilian Modernism 49
Brazilian Museum of Sculpture and
    Ecology (MuBE) 102
Breuer, Marcel 103, 116, 137, 138, 189
Bristol University 226
Brittain, Bec, Aries IV.I 53, *53*
Brokis 140
Bronzini, Gegia, Striped Fabric 54, *54*
Bronzini, Marisa and Michaela 54
Brothers and Sons 152
Brown, Barbara, Frequency 55, *55*
Bruun, Maria, Bigfoot Furniture 56, *56*
Building Research Institute 162
Bullock, Rachel, Ribbon Chair 57, *57*
Burgos, Marie, Milo Chair 58, *58*
Burlington Zephyr 89

C

Calder, Alexander 149
California Contemporary 68
California Institute of the Arts 151
Camberwell College of Arts 192
Campana, Fernando and Humberto 102
Campbell, Louise, Cutlery 59, *59*
Canterbury College of Art 55
Capellagården 184
Cappellini 118, 167
Caranica, Gloria, Rocking Beauty Hobby
    Horse 60, *60*
Carhartt 226
Carl XVI Gustaf, King 25
Carmona, Etel 197
    22 Chair 61, *61*
Casabella 29, 63
Casadei, Maddalena, Verso Table 62, *62*
Casigliani 232
Cassina 79, 178, 200, 228
Castelli, Giulio 63
Castelli Ferrieri, Anna, Componibili Modular
    Storage System 63, *63*
Castiglioni, Achille 63, 228
Catalano, Carol, Capelli Stool 64, *64*
Catalano Design 64
Catholic University of Chile 179
Center for the Investigation of Industrial
    Design (CIDI) 16
Central Saint Martins 44, 134, 136
Central School of Arts and Crafts 131, 227
Central School of Arts and Design 216
Central School of Industrial Art 219
Centre Pompidou 145
C.G. Hallberg 215
Chaudhary, Palaash 239
Chen, Hung-Ming 235
Cheti, Fede 54
Chicago Architectural Biennale 129
Chicago School of Architecture 129
Chicago Tribune 19
Cho, Kyuhyung 65
Choi, Jungyou, Word Table Light 65, *65*
Chomentowska, Maria, Chair Model 66, *66*
Chouinard Art Institute 151
C.I. Design 137
Clemmensen, Ebbe 67
Clemmensen, Karen, Safari Lounge Chair 67, *67*
Coconi 233

Coffee Table 201, *201*
Coleman, Muriel, Coatrack 68, *68*
Colen, Bruce David 116
Colin, Kim, Branca Chair 69, *69*
Collegiate School for Girls 39
Colombo, Joe 63, 85
Columbia University 15, 68, 187
Comité de Proyectos 99
Comme des Garçons 226
Congrès Internationale d'Architecture
    Moderne (CIAM) 63, 214
Conradsen, Karen Margrethe 127
Constructivism 121
Conti, Sergio 100
Cooper Hewitt Design Museum 17, 46, 104, 106, 145
Cooper Union 157
Costa, Janete, Borsoi Table 70, 70
Costa, Lucio 197
Council of Industrial Designers' Design 190
Cracow University of Technology 129
Cranbrook Academy of Art 19, 37, 93, 129, 138,
    176, 194, 219
Crasset, Matali, Foglie Lamp 71, *71*
Crawford, Ilse 65
    Seating for Eating 72–3, *72–3*
Creative Playthings 60
Crespi, Gabriella, Scultura Coffee Table 74, *74*
Crespi, Raffaella, Lounge Chair 75, *75*
Critical Mannerism 117
Crodel, Charles 51
CSrugs 158

D
Dagnert, Veronica, Inox Table 76, 77
Daily Mail 127
Dalisi, Riccardo 124
Danish Art Foundation 59, 159
Danish Design School 59, 127
Day, Lucienne 55
    Calyx Textile 77, *77*
Day, Robin 77, 190
DAY Studio 95
De La Espada 72
De Padova 228
de Ponti, Nicola 27
Debs, Nada, Summerland Paravan 78, *78*
Delft University of Technology 158
Demir, Doğanberk 95
Deng, Qiyun, Soft Pack Sofa 79, *79*
Design Academy Eindhoven (DAE) 26, 65,
    72, 94, 110, 133, 148, 158, 160
Design Days (2014) 195
Design Group 135
Design Indaba 209, 229
Design M 34
Design Museum, London 28
Design Republic 123
Design Road Professional 155
Design Within Reach 60
Designers' Plan 151
Designmuseum Denmark 23, 25
Dessuant, Marie, Day Bed 80–1, *80–1*
Dessuant Bone 81
Deutsche Werkstätten Textilgesellschaft 104
Deutscher Werkbund 188
Diamond, Freda, Shelving *82*, 83, *83*
Dicker-Brandeis, Friedl 210
    Chair 84, *84*
Dillon, Charles 85
Dillon, Jane, Moveable Chair 85, *85*
Dimore 45
Dims. 65
Dione, Aïssa, Kara Fabric 86, *86*

Dior 156
Ditzel, Jørgen 87, 137
Ditzel, Nanna, Hanging Egg Chair 87, *87*
Domus 49, 54, 85, 116, 178
Domus Academy 62, 125
Donnelly, Justin 150
Driade 27, 167
Dryden, Helen, Candlesphere Candleholder 88, *88*
Du Pasquier, Nathalie 36
    Royal Sofa 90–1, *90–1*
Duchamp, Marcel 201
Dulany, Helen Hughes 139
    Coffee Service 89, *89*
Dura Company 88

E
Eames, Charles 93, 118, 241
Eames, Ray 118, 219, 241
    Lounge Chair *92*, 93, *93*
East Bay Artists' Association 68
ÉbéneSand 241
École Boulle 26, 241
École Cantonale d'Art de Lausanne 65, 79, 95
École des Beaux-Arts 145, 157
École Nationale Supérieure d'Architecture
    de Paris-La Villette 230
École Nationale Supérieure de Création
    Industrielle 71
École Nationale Supérieure des Arts
    Décoratifs 145, 202
École Supérieure des Arts Décoratifs
    de Strasbourg 81
Edra 125
Egg Collective 33, 128
Eijk, Kiki van, Soft Table Lamp 94, *94*
Eisler, Alberto 16
Eisler, Martin 16
ELLE Decoration 73
Ellis, Crystal, Kenny Dining Table 33, *33*
Emeco 183
ENFI 234
Ercol 30
Eröktem, Yeşim, Volume Side Table 95, 95
Ertel, Lisa, Dune Furniture *96*, 97, *97*
Escala 70
Estudio Persona 105
Etage Projects 161, 220
ETEL 61, 197
ETH Zürich 117
European Space Agency 134
Evostyle 191

F
Fabrica 43, 80
Fan Collective 97
Fatra 172
Fausto Celatti 36
Federal University of Rio de Janeiro 47
Fendi 86, 136
Ferrone, Felicia, Revolution Wine
and Water Glasses 98, *98*
Festival of Britain (1951) 77, 218
FIAM 50
Fichot, Francis 71
Ficks Reed Company 194
Flores, Andrea, Lira Coffee Table 99, *99*
FLOS 200
Fogo Island Inn 115
FontanaArte 29
Fordham University 173
Forlani, Marisa, Handicraft Monofilo
    Armchair 100, *100*
Forma 16

Forma & Cemento 124
Förster, Monica, Glide Lounge 101, *101*
Foscarini 231
Frankfurt Trade Fair (1969) 34
French Art Deco 104
French modernism 183
Front 144
Fucina 62
Fuller, Richard Buckminster 19
Furniture Forum 122

G
Gainsbourg, Serge 145
Galeria Amparo 60 70
Galeria Anna Maria Niemeyer 171
Galerie Jean Désert 109
Galper-Baldon Associates 31
GAN 123
Garbo, Greta 111
Gardner, Nicholas 220
Gay, Carol, NoAr Lounge Chair 102, *102*
Geller, Abraham W. 103
Geller, Marion 202
    F-2-G Floor Lamp 103, *103*
General Electric 89
General Motors 219
Georg Jensen 59
Gervasoni 167
Gesamtkunstwerk 192, 212
Geyer-Raack, Ruth Hildegard, Adjustable
    Floor Lamp 104, *104*
Ghent University 158
Gilded Expressions 177
Glas Italia 107
Glasgow School of Art 136
Gonzalez, Emiliana, UNA Chair 105, *105*
Good Design 19, 32, 151
Graduate School of Design, Harvard 122
Graham, Anne Krohn, Traveling Flatware 106, *106*
Grange, Jacques 145
Graphische Lehr- und Versuchsanstalt 212
Grassi, Luciano 100
Grawunder, Johanna, XXX Table 107, *107*
Gray, Eileen 147, 183
    Bibendum Chair *108*, 109, *109*, 239
Gray's School of Art 236
Gregori, Bruno 167
Griffin, Rachel, Face Value Modular Tables 110, *110*
Gropius, Walter 52, 122, 138
Gross Wood & Co 237
Grossman, Greta, Gräshoppa Floor Lamp 111, *111*
Gruen, Victor 116
Gruppo Zero 233
gt2P 179
Guangzhou Academy of Fine Arts 79
Guerriero, Alessandro 167
Gustav Adolf, Crown Prince 215

H
Habitat 28, 85, 115, 167, 222
Habitat (magazine) 49
Hadid, Zaha 179
    Mesa Table 112, *112–13*
Haël-Werkstätten 121
Haeusler, Helene 164
Hahn, Peter 215
Hakel, Arnold 16
Hakel, Gabriel 16
Hamburg State Art School 189
Hamill, Virginia 83
    Dinette Tea Set 114, *114*
Hannah, Bruce 46
Hans, Ineke, Long Bench 115, *115*

Hara, Kenya 76
Haraszty, Eszter, Triad Textile 116, *116*
Harkort, Dr. Hermann 51
Harper's Bazaar 147
Hartwig, Josef 210
Haus der Frau 188
Häusler, Philipp 130
Haussmann, Robert 117
Haussmann, Trix, Lehrstück II 117, *117*
HAY 118, 141
Hay, Mette, HAY Accessories 118, *118*
Hay, Rolf 118
Heal's Fabrics 55, 77
Heath, Brian 119
Heath, Edith, Tea Pot 119, *119*
Heath Ceramics 119
Hecht, Sam 69
Heide, Kurt 87
Heifetz Lighting Company 103, 202
Hein, Pascal 43
Helen Hughes Dulany Studio 89
Helg, Franca 63
    Primavera Armchair 120, *120*
Helios 39, 218
Helsinki Design Museum 35
Helsinki School of Art and Design 35
Helsinki University 14
Henderson, Nigel 214
Hepburn, Audrey 74
Heriot-Watt University 209
Herman Miller 46, 64, 83, 85, 93
Hermès 65, 86, 226
Heymann-Löbenstein, Margarete 51
    Tea Service 121, *121*
Hille 190
Hoffmann, Josef 130, 192, 212
Hofmann, Hans 93
Hosken, Franziska, Bar Cart 122, *122*
Hosken, James 122
Hu, Rossana, LAN Sofa 123, *123*
Hull Traders 156
Hungarian Royal Academy of Fine Arts 240
Hürlimann, Heinz Otto 218

I
IBM 116
Iittala 14, 25, 65, 131, 174, 216
IKEA 28
Illuminating Engineering Society of Finland 131
Industrial Design College, Rio de Janeiro 197
Industrial Designers Society of
    America (IDSA) 46, 139
Industrial Facility 69
Industrial Woodworking Corporation 60
Inscape Design School 229
Institute of Industrial Arts 154
Institute of Industrial Design (IWP) 66
Interieur Forma 16
International Exposition of Art and
    Industry (1928) 114
International Interior Exhibition, Cologne (1931) 104
International Style 187
Invisible Group 149
Irvine, James 62, 124
Irvine, Marialaura Rossiello, Fusto Bookshelf 124, *124*
Isakov, Gregory Alan 65
Ishimaru 234
Israel Museum 23
Istanbul Technical University 95
Istituto Europeo di Design Madrid 43, 134, 163, 221
Istituto Universitario di Architettura di Venezia 200
Italia Nostra 75
Italian Design Association 222

Italian Rationalism 75, 120
Ito, Setsu 125
Ito, Shinobu, Au Seating 125, *125*
Ito, Toyo 206
Ittens, Johannes 84, 104, 217
ITU 238

J
Jacobsen, Sophie Lou, Lamp 01 126, *126*
Jalk, Grete, GJ Chair 127, *127*
James Bond 137
Jan van Eyck Academie 97
Janberidze, Nata, Spiral Floor Lamp 128, *128*
Japan Women's University 206
Jaworska, Ania, Unit 6 (Armchair) 129, *129*
Jeanneret, Pierre 32, 181
Jeppesen, Poul 127
Jesser-Schmid, Hilda 212
    Bowl 130, *130*
Johansson-Pape, Lisa, Pendant Lamp 131, *131*
Johnson, Philip (architect) 20
Johnson, Philip (art director) 60
Jonasson, Helena, Inox Table 76, 77
Jongerius, Hella, Polder Sofa 132–3, *132–3*
Jongeriuslab 133
Josef Böck 212
Joshibi University of Art and Design 223
Juan Carlos I, King 228
Juhl, Finn 137
JUMBO 150

K
Kahn, Louis 205
Kahraman, Merve, Cassini Floor Lamp 134, *134*
Kamla Raheja Vidyanidhi Institute 186
Karasz, Ilonka, Armchair 135, *135*
Karhula 14
Karlin, Anna, Lady Lamp 136, *136*
Kartell 29, 63, 204
Katajanagi, Tomu 50
Kenji Fujimori 223
Kenyon College 17
Kiddie Products 60
Kjær, Bodil, Office Desk 137, *137*
Klee, Paul 84
Klint, Kaare 67
KLM 133
Knoll 16, 20, 29, 46, 116, 200, 205
Knoll, Florence 219
    Sofa 1206 138, *138*
Knoll, Hans 116, 138
Knoll Planning Unit 138
Kogan, Belle 89
    Centerpiece 139, *139*
Koldová, Lucie, Jack O'Lantern 140, *140*
Konstfack 101
Kraš, Ana 118
    Sion Round Table 141, *141*
KRIKI 230
Kruszewska, Teresa, Scallop Chair 142, *142*
KSA Design 23
Kulik-Pomorska, Agata, PAPER+ Armchair 143, *143*
Kunstgewerbeschule 189, 192, 212, 217
Kunstwebeschule, Bern 41
Kurzatkowski, Jan 66, 142
Kyoto City University of Arts 30

L
La Rinascente Development Studio 35
La Ruota 178
Ład Artists' Cooperative 142
The Ladies' Room 45
Lagerkvist, Sofia, Furia Rocking Horse 144, *144*

Lagos Gymnastics Association 175
Lagos State Sports Trust Fund 175
Lalanne, Claude, Table Lotus et Singe
    Carrée 145, *145*
Lalanne, François-Xavier 145
Lange Production 127
Lanux, Elizabeth Eyre de, Dressing Table *146*, 147, *147*
Lanzavecchia, Francesca, Pebble Desk 148, *148*
Lanzavecchia + Wai 148
LAUN 57
Laverne, Erwine 149
Laverne, Estelle, Daffodil Chair 149, *149*
Le Corbusier 32, 109, 181
L'École de Design Nantes Atlantique 231
Lee, Monling, Sport Sofa 150, *150*
Lee, Olga, Olga Lee Lamp 151, *151*
Légion d'Honneur 29, 71
Leipzig Trade Fair 164
Lensink, Geke, Kitchen Stool 152, *152*
Leonardo da Vinci 185
Levy, Arik 140
Lhote, André 68
Li, Rosie, Pebble Hanging Lamp 153, *153*
Liaigre, Christian 157
Libbey 83
Liberty 156
Liceo artistico Ripetta 154
Lievore, Alberto 22
Lievore Altherr 22
Lievore + Altherr Désile Park 22
Life magazine 83
Lindgren, Anna, Furia Rocking Horse 144, *144*
Lindh, Francesca, Double Tea Pot 154, *154*
Lindh, Richard 154
Lisbon Architecture Triennale 129
London College of Furniture 59
London School of Printing and Graphic Arts 156
London Transport 218
London Underground 218
Lootah, Aljoud, Oru Cabinet 155, *155*
LOT-EK 230
Luglio, Astrid 45

M
M. Singer & Sons 201
Mackenzie Presbyterian University 102
McNish, Althea, Golden Harvest 156, *156*
Made of Waste 28
Magis 222
Magistretti, Vico 79, 228
Mahdavi, India, Charlotte Chair 157, *157*
Maine College of Art 37
Mairet, Ethel 218
Maison & Objet 159
Makkink, Rianne, Pixelated Rug 158, *158*
Makkink & Bey 158
Malafor 143
Malaysian International Furniture Fair 169
Malmsten, Carl 184
Manero Academy 16
Manz, Cecilie 62
    Plint Coffee Table 159, *159*
Marcelis, Sabine, SOAP Table 160, *160–1*, 161
Marcks, Gerhard 121
Mari, Enzo 222
Marimekko 25
Marithé + François Girbaud 27
Maruni Wood 206
Marx, Enid 218
Marz Designs 191
Matégot, Mathieu 126
Matisse, Henri 147
Matter Made 141

Mattiazzi 69
Maurer, Ingo 34
MBADV 56
Melchior, Ib 31
Memphis Group 36, 90, 198, 230
Menu 65, 235
Metal Museum 37
Mexico Design Week 221
Meyer, Grethe, Firepot Series 162, *162*
MHS Planners, Architects and Engineers 223
Miami University 98
Michael Graves & Associates 123
Middle East Technical University 46
Mies van der Rohe, Ludwig 32, 39, 138, 183, 188
Minimat 209
Minton Factory 121
MIT 232
Mobili Italiani Moderni 178
Mobilia 75
Mobilia (magazine) 127
Modernism 93, 104, 109, 121, 181, 183, 229
Moholy-Nagy, László 122
Monica Förster Design 101
Montessori, Maria 34
Morais, Frederico 224
Mori, Hikaru, Carmencita Lamp 163
Moroso 228
Mosaico+ 124
Moser, Koloman 212
Mostra dell'Artigianato (1954) 100
Motley 236
Movement 8 177
Muche, George 211
Muji 124
MUJU 196
Mulberry 226
Müller, Renate, Therapeutic Toys 164, *164*
Mund, Holger 67
murmur 209
Murtagh, Ignacia, Lof Tableware 165, *165*
Musashino Art University 234
Musée d'Orsay, Paris 29
Musée du Louvre 241
Museu de Arte de São Paulo 49
Museum für Gestaltung 220
Museum of Ethnography 67
Museum of Fine Arts, Boston 37
Museum of Modern Art 20, 23, 29, 46, 103, 111, 116,
    127, 129, 144, 151, 168, 174, 202, 213, 223, 224, 240
Museum of Popular Arts Janete Costa 70

N
Nada Debs Furniture & Design Beirut 78
Nakamura, Masao 67
Nakashima, George 166
Nakashima, Mira, Concordia Chair 166, *166*
Nakashima Studios 166
NASA 134
Natalini, Adolfo 36
National Gallery of Victoria 155
National Institute of Fashion Technology 239
National School of Glass 25
National Taipei College of Business 235
National University of Cuyo 198
National University of Misiones 198
Navone, Paola 30
    Ghost Armchair 167, *167*
Nazis 16, 19, 20, 51, 130, 188, 192, 217
Nelson, George 190
Nemo-Cassina 163
Neo-Liberty movement 29
Neri, Lyndon 123
Neri & Hu 123

Nessen, Greta von, Anywhere Lamp 168, *168*
Nessen, Walter von 168
Nessen Studios 168
New Hope Experiment 187
New Jersey Designer Craftsmen 24
New Objectivity 52
New York School of Interior Design 38
New York Times 24, 213
New York University 58
New Yorker 135, 147
Ng, Stephanie, Scoop Desk Lamp 169, *169*
Niemeyer, Anna Maria 61
    Rio Chaise Longue 170–1, *170–1*
Niemeyer, Oscar 61, 170–1
Nike 230
Niklová, Libuše, Inflatable Animals 172, *172*
Nilufar Gallery 17
Niterói Contemporary Art Museum 171
Noguchi, Isamu 183
Nur Ceramics 173
Nur Satti, Dina, Naama Vase 173, *173*
Nuutajärvi Glassworks 174
NYCxDESIGN 33, 128
Nyman, Gunnel, Munankuori Bowl 174, *174*

O
Oakland Museum of California 68
Offecct 124
Office for the Reconstruction of the Capital 66
Ogunseinde, Moyo, Oko Chair 175, *175*
Oh, Jay Sae Jung, Savage Sofa 176, *176*
Oki, Kenji 234
Olga Lee Design 151
Olivetti 29, 85
Onck, Andries van 222
Ontario College of Art & Design University 185
Ontos Weaving Workshops 217
Op Art 55, 153
Order of Architects 75
Oromo tribe 229
Orrefors and Skruf 184
Örsjö Belysning 184
Özyeğin University 95

P
Pacific Design Group 68
Pallucco 71
Pamintuan, Ann, Cocoon Lounge Chair 177, *177*
Pani, Mario 182
Paolozzi, Eduardo 156, 214
Pape, Lygia 224
Parada, Guillermo 179
Parametricism 112, 179
Parisi, Ico 54, 178
Parisi, Luisa 54
    Desk 178, *178*
Parsons School of Design 18, 53, 157, 201
Pasadena Art Museum 119
Paul, Bruno 104
Pérez, Tamara, Remolten Monolita Chair 179, *179*
Pergay, Maria, Wave Bench 180, *180*
Perriand, Charlotte 32
    Ombre Chair 181, *181*
Pesce, Gaetano 176
Peter Marino 86
Petrie, Hillary, Kenny Dining Table 33, *33*
Pevsner, Nikolaus 211
Philadelphia Museum of Art 46
Philippine Institute of Interior design 38
Picabia, Francis 147
Picasso, Pablo 147, 201
Politecnico di Milano 29, 50, 63, 74, 75, 120,
    124, 148, 178, 198, 228

Politecnico di Torino 44, 167
Pollock, Jackson 201
Poltrona Frau 25
Polytechnic of Central London 28
Polytechnic for Toy Design 164
Pomorksi, Pawel 143
Ponti, Gio 49, 50, 178, 233
Pontifical Catholic University of Chile 165
Porset, Clara 199
    Butaque Chair 182, *182*
Posada, Sarita, Lamp 01 126, *126*
Postmodernism 36, 90, 117, 205
Powolny, Michael 192
Pratt Institute 46, 60, 139, 240
pre-Columbian textiles 20
Pritzker Prize 112, 205
Pucci, Ralph 183
Purnell, Molly, Ribbon Chair 57, *57*
Putman, Andrée 38
    Crescent Moon Sofa 183, *183*

Q
Quaker Oats Company 60
Quaker Silver Co. 139
Queen Anne style 205
Quintana, Gustavo 193

R
Radical Architecture Movement 29, 36, 167
Ralph O. Smith 111, 151
Råman, Ingegerd, Water Decanter 184, *184*
Ratcliffe, Mary, Lyndoe Low Seat 185, *185*
Rathod, Samira, Bloat Desk 186, *186*
Rationalism 32
Ravensburger 211
Raymond, Antonin 187
Raymond, Noémi, Circles 187, *187*
Red Wing Pottery 139, 240
Reed & Barton 139
REFORM Design Biennial 56
Regent Street Polytechnic School
    of Architecture 190
Reich, Lilly 32, 39
    Brno Chair 188, *188*
Reichardt, Margaretha, Weaving Sample
    189, *189*
Reid, John 190
Reid, Sylvia, S-Range Sideboard 190, *190*
Revere 88
Reynolds, Coco, Art Pendant Light 191, *191*
R.H. Macy and Co 114
Rhode Island School of Design 17, 19, 21, 64,
    78, 142, 153
Ricciardi, Sara 45
Rie, Lucie, Footed Bowl 192, *192*
Riggs, Wendell 199
Riihimäki Glassworks 174, 216, 227
RIMA (Riunione Italiana per le Mostre
    di Arredamento) 54
Roach, Ruth S. 106
Rodrigues, Sergio 70
Rogers, Ernesto Nathan 29
Roll & Hill 153
Rooms 128
Ros, Estefanía de, Altar Console 193, *193*
Roscoe Award 38
Röthlisberger 41
Royal Academy of Arts and Artistic Crafts,
    Zagreb 39
Royal Academy of Fine Arts, Budapest 116
Royal Academy of Fine Arts, Stockholm 215
Royal College of Art, London 21, 28, 30, 55, 77, 85,
    115, 137, 156, 165, 218, 220, 236

Royal Copenhagen Porcelain Factory 162
Royal Crown Derby 165
Royal Danish Academy of Fine Arts
    56, 59, 67, 87, 159, 162, 165
Royal Melbourne Institute of Technology 42
Rudolph, Paul 137
Rural Industries Bureau 218
Russian Glass and Porcelain Trust 240

S
Saarinen, Eero 16, 19, 194
Saarinen, Eliel 19, 138, 194, 219
Saarinen, Loja 194
Saarinen-Swanson 194
Saarinen-Swanson, Pipsan, Sol-Air
    Lounge Chair 194, *194*
Saeed, Latifa, Braided Chair 195, *195*
Saffar 21
Said, Mentalla, Hizz Rocking Chair 196, *196*
Saint Laurent, Yves 145
Salles, Claudia Moreira, Portuguese
    Armchair 197, *197*
Salone de Mobile 63, 79, 177
Samira Rathod Design Atelier 186
SANAA 206
Sanchez, Maria, Squash Ashtray 198, *198*
São Paulo Art Biennial 49
SÃR 43
Sargent, Cynthia, Bartok Rug 199, *199*
Savannah College of Art and Design 239
Scarpa, Afra, Africa Chair 200, *200*
Scarpa, Tobia 200
Schaefer, Bertha, Coffee Table 201, *201*
Schatz, Bezalel 202
Schatz, Zahara 103
    Table Lamp 202, *202*
Schild, Heinrich 51
Schnee, Edward 19
School of Fine Arts of Pernambuco 70
Schulz Leuchten 104
Schütte-Lihotzky, Margarete, Frankfurt
    Kitchen 203, *203*
Schweinberger, Emma, Dedalo Umbrella
    Stand 204, *204*
Scott Brown, Denise, Queen Anne Side
    Chair 205, *205*
Seck, Bibi 46
Secondary School of Applied Arts 172
Sejima, Kazuyo, Armless Chair 206, *206–7*
Sempé, Inga 118
    w153 île 208, *208*
Senekal, Mia, Quarter Coffee Table 209, *209*
Seoul National University of Science and
    Technology 238
Serpa, Ivan 224
SESC Pompéia cultural center 49
Sharjah Biennial 195
Sharon, Arieh 217
Shaw Ness and Murphy 19
Shodeinde, Mimi, Dip Lounger 209, *209*
Siedhoff-Buscher, Alma, Bauhaus Bauspiel 210, *210*
Sika, Jutta 130
    Coffee Set 212, *212*
Sinatra, Frank 111
Singer, Franz 84
Sint-Lucas School of Architecture 158
Sitterle, Harold 213
Sitterle, Trudi, Pepper Mill, Salt Dish,
    and Spoon 213, *213*
Sitterle Ceramics 213
Sketch 157
Skidmore, Owings and Merrill (SOM) 232
Skruf 25

Slade School of Fine Art 109
Smithson, Alison, D38 Trundling Turk I
    Armchair 214, *214*
Smithson, Peter 214
Smithsonian Design Museum 17, 46, 104, 106, 145
Smithsonian National Air and Space Museum 37
Society of Modern Art 135
Soft Baroque 220
Soft Geometry 239
Soft Pack Sofa 79, *79*
Soft Table Lamp 94, *94*
Soho House 73
Something Beginning With 42
Soto, Lucía, Lira Coffee Table 99, *99*
Sottsass, Ettore 32, 36, 85, 90, 107, 198
Sowden, George 90
Stadler, Willy 217
Stag 190
Stalin, Joseph 240
Starck, Philippe 71
State College of Design Center for Art
    and Media 97
Stave, Sylvia, Cocktail Shaker 215, *215*
Stedelijk Museum 25
Stern Brothers 83
Still, Nanny 227
    Grapponia Vase 216, *216*
Stockholm Design Fair 235
Stockholm Exhibition 215
Stockholm School of Industrial Design 111
Stockmann-Orno 131
Stölzl, Gunta 20, 39, 189
    Curtain Fabric 217, *217*
Straub, Marianne 39
    Moquette Sample 218, *218*
Strengell, Marianne 93, 116
    Throw Blanket 219, *219*
Štucin, Saša, Hard Round Armchair 220, *220*
Studebaker 88
Studio Alchimia 167
Studio Dessuant Bone 80
Studio Earnest 110
Studio Irvine 124
Studio-Lani 18
Studio Sayso 126
Studio Vit 76
Studio Word 65
Studioilse 73
STURT 191
Suárez Ahedo, Claudia, Ch'up Chair 221, *221*
Sugawara, Seizo 109
Superstudio 36
SVA 238
Swedish Society of Industrial Design 111
Swinburne University of Technology 169
Swiss Federal Office of Culture 117
Synthèse des Arts (1955) 181

T
Tacchini 101
Taha, Jumana, Hizz Rocking Chair 196, *196*
Taito 174, 227
Takeda, Hiroko, Lem Adjustable Table 222, *222*
Talking Drum 18
Tama Art University 125
Tanabe, Reiko, Murai Stool 223, *223*
Tanabe Reiko Design 223
Tashkeel 196
Tbilisi Academy of Arts 128
Team 10 214
TECTA 214
Telakowska, Wanda 66
Tendo 181

Tendo Mokko 223
Terpins, Jacqueline, Console Table
    Cello 224, *224–5*
Terra 31
Terragni, Giuseppe 75, 233
Terragni Foundation 75
Textile Arts Center 165
Theobald, Jean George 114
TheUrbanative 229
Thonet 124, 181
Thonet, Michael 144
Tiwete, Michel Vamba 241
Tokyo Design Academy 222, 234
Tokyo University of the Arts 163
Toloraia, Keti, Spiral Floor Lamp 128, *128*
Toogood, Faye, Roly-Poly Chair 226, *226*
Toogou Armchair 46, *46*
Topacio, Hector 38
TOTO 46
Triennale di Milano 32, 45, 54, 100, 174, 189,
    202, 233
Tynell, Helena 216
    Sun Bottle 227, *227*
Tynell, Paavo 227

U
Ugine-Gueugnon 180
UK Design Council 156
UNESCO 101, 196
United Airlines 219
Università degli Studi di Milano 204
University of Applied Arts, Belgrade 141
University of Applied Arts, Vienna 198
University of Art and Design, Helsinki 159, 174
University of Art and Design Linz 158
University of Arts, Crafts, and
    Design, Stockholm 25, 144, 184
University College London 175
University of Delaware 106
University of Ferrara 62
University of Helsinki 194
University of Illinois 98, 129
University of Minnesota 106
University of Naples Federico II 124
University of Pennsylvania 205
University of Santo Tomas 38
University of Texas 57
University of Westminster 28
Universtität der Künste Berlin 188
Urquiola, Patricia, Tropicalia Chair 228, *228*
U.S. Postal Service 168

V
Vackier, Mpho, Oromo Dining Chair 229, *229*
Vallée, Garance, Puddle Table 230, *230*
Vautrin, Ionna, Lamp TGV 231, *231*
Velten-Vordamm 51
Venice Architecture Biennale 129
Venturi, Robert 205
Verkerk, Herman 158
Versace, Gianni 74
Vester, Anne Dorthe 56
Victoria & Albert Museum 28, 30, 45, 85, 151
Vienna School of Applied Arts 130, 203
Vignelli, Leila 138
    Metafora Coffee Table #1 232, *232*
Vignelli, Massimo 232
Vigo, Nanda, Due Più chair 233, *233*
Vincitorio, Lisa, Halo Chair 42, *42*
Visser, Jesse 152
Vitra 112, 132
Vitra Design Museum 30, 34, 144
Vogue 88

W

Wai, Hunn 148
Wallpaper* Design Awards 163
Warner & Sons 218
Waseda University 166
Washington University 33
Wästberg 208
Watanabe, Hisako, Analogon Desk 234, *234*
Watkins, Philip 153
Weeks, David 17
Wei, Chen-Yen, Afteroom Chair 235, *235*
Weiner Kunstgewerbeschule 130
Whitworth Gallery 55
Wiener Kunst im Hause 212
Wiener Werkstätte 130, 192, 212
Wilson, Donna, Creatures 236, *236*
Wingårdh, Gert 184
Woman's Day 213
Women's Architecture School 66
Women's Art School, Cooper Union 83
Wood, Esther, Tripod Ashtray 237, *237*
Wood, Gross 237
Woodbury University 31
World of Interiors 226
Wright, Frank Lloyd 24, 187, 233
Wyld, Evelyn 147

Y

Ya'ad 202
Yamasaki, Minoru 19
Yarinsky, Michael 153
Yasumoto, Jun 62
Yoruba culture 18, 175
Young, Jessie, UNA Chair 105, *105*
Yun, Sohyun, TONE Furniture 238, *238*
Yves Saint Laurent 156

Z

Zacharias, Utharaa, Elio Lamp 239, *239*
Zaha Hadid Design 112
Zalszupin, Jorge 61
Zanat 101
Zanotta 35
Zanuso, Marco 50
Zayed University 195
Zeisel, Eva, Resilient Chair 240, *240*
Zito, Maurizio 163
Zorzi, Sandrine Ébène de, Kiti Makasi
    Chair 241, *241*
Zürich Kunstgewerbeschule 218

Phaidon Press Limited
2 Cooperage Yard
London E15 2QR

Phaidon Press Inc.
65 Bleecker Street
New York, NY 10012

phaidon.com

First published 2021

ISBN 978 1 83866 285 1

A CIP catalog record for this book is available from
the British Library and the Library of Congress.

Commissioning Editor: Virginia McLeod
Project Editor: Belle Place
Production Controller: Sarah Kramer
Design: Ariane Spanier

Printed in Italy

The publisher would like to thank Jocelyn Miller for her
diligent copy-editing of the text and thoughtful advice.
We are indebted to the designers featured for their time
and attention to their entries. Additional thanks go to
the following for their contributions to the making of this
book: Vanessa Bird, Robert Davies, and Holly Pollard.

About Jane Hall

Dr. Jane Hall studied architecture at King's College, Cambridge, and the Royal College of Art, London, where she received her PhD in 2018. She was the inaugural recipient of the British Council Lina Bo Bardi Fellowship (2013) and is a founding member of London-based architecture collective, Assemble, who won the Turner Prize (2015) for their work created collaboratively with the residents of Granby Four Streets in Liverpool. She is the author of *Breaking Ground: Architecture by Women* published by Phaidon in 2019.

Acknowledgments

Many thanks go to everyone who contributed their suggestions of designers not to be missed and gave their time to describe their perspective on the topic: Seyi Adelekun, Emily Wickham, Zoy Anastassakis, Catharine Rossi, Catherine Ince, Alice Rawsthorn, Vicky Richardson, Adélia Borges, Ana Elena Mallet, Hannah Robinson, João Guarantani, Gwendoline Webber, Ikko Yokoyama, Chrissa Amuah, Tomoko Azumi, Rachel Griffin, Rand Abdul Jabbar, Kawther Alsaffar, Jane Dillon, Karin Shou Andersen, Dori Tunstall, Claude Maurer, Viviane Stappmanns, Dorie Millerson, Mindy Magyar, Farida Abu-Bakare (Black Architects + Interior Designers Association), Malene Barnett (Black Artists + Designers Guild), Mitzi Okou (Where are the Black Designers), Design Can, Cooper Hewitt, Smithsonian Design Museum archives, and TENDO, as well as all of the other designers featured who enthusiastically answered my questions.

This book is dedicated to designers Cini Boeri, Althea McNish, and Nanda Vigo, all of whom passed away in 2020 during the making of the book. All three designers were part of a generation of women who studied design in the postwar period and, unusually for the time, forged successful careers independently of their male peers. These recent losses highlight the urgency of projects such as *Woman Made* that attempt to recuperate and center the legacies of designers from this era.